THE RAMEN KING AND I

THE RAMEN KING AND I

HOW THE INVENTOR OF INSTANT NOODLES FIXED MY LOVE LIFE

A Memoir

ANDY RASKIN

GOTHAM
BOOKS

GOTHAM BOOKS
Published by Penguin Group (USA) Inc.
375 Hudson Street, New York, New York 10014, U.S.A.
Penguin Group (Canada), 90 Eglinton Avenue East, Suite 700, Toronto, Ontario M4P 2Y3, Canada
(a division of Pearson Penguin Canada Inc.) · Penguin Books Ltd, 80 Strand, London WC2R 0RL,
England · Penguin Ireland, 25 St Stephen's Green, Dublin 2, Ireland (a division of Penguin Books Ltd)
· Penguin Group (Australia), 250 Camberwell Road, Camberwell, Victoria 3124, Australia
(a division of Pearson Australia Group Pty Ltd) · Penguin Books India Pvt Ltd, 11 Community Centre,
Panchsheel Park, New Delhi-110 017, India · Penguin Group (NZ), 67 Apollo Drive, Rosedale,
North Shore 0632, New Zealand (a division of Pearson New Zealand Ltd) · Penguin Books
(South Africa) (Pty) Ltd, 24 Sturdee Avenue, Rosebank, Johannesburg 2196, South Africa

Penguin Books Ltd, Registered Offices: 80 Strand, London WC2R 0RL, England

Published by Gotham Books, a member of Penguin Group (USA) Inc.

First printing, May 2009
1   3   5   7   9   10   8   6   4   2

"Ramen in the Morning" (*Asa Kara Ramen no Uta*) and portions of "Afterword 1" (*Atogaki Sono 1*)
from *Spider Monkey in the Night* (*Yoru no Kumozaru—Murakami Asahido Cho Tampen Shosetsu*)
© 1995 Haruki Murakami. Reprinted with permission.

Gotham Books and the skyscraper logo are trademarks of Penguin Group (USA) Inc.

LIBRARY OF CONGRESS CATALOGING-IN-PUBLICATION DATA
Raskin, Andy.
The ramen king and I : how the inventor of instant noodles fixed my love life : a memoir /
by Andy Raskin.
p.   cm.
ISBN 978-1-592-40444-5 (hardcover)
1. Raskin, Andy.   2. Raskin, Andy—Relations with women.   3. Journalists—United States—
Biography.   4. Editors—United States—Biography.   5. Authors, American—21st century—
Biography.   6. Man-woman relationships—United States.   7. Ando, Momofuku, 1910–2007.
8. Noodles—Japan—Miscellanea.   9. Japan—Description and travel.   I. Title.
CT275.R2656A3 2009
973.931092—dc22
[B]   2008032423

Printed in the United States of America
Set in Bulmer MT • Designed by Elke Sigal

While the author has made every effort to provide accurate telephone numbers and Internet addresses
at the time of publication, neither the publisher nor the author assumes any responsibility for errors, or
for changes that occur after publication. Further, the publisher does not have any control over and does
not assume any responsibility for author or third-party Web sites or their content.

FOR MY FAMILY,
WITH THANKS TO CAROL WASSERMAN

CONTENTS

THE RAMEN KING AND I

"It is said that real human nature reveals itself under extreme conditions. As I starved in prison, I realized that eating was one of the highest forms of human activity. Perhaps I have to go back this far to trace the origins of the development of instant noodles, though I did not have the slightest idea for Chikin [*sic*] Ramen at the time."

—Momofuku Ando, *Magic Noodles:*
The Story of the Invention of Instant Ramen

*T*here used to be a Japanese TV show in which two young hosts—a male and a female—would scream, "I wanna ___!" They always filled in the blank with some crazy thing, like "sing a duet with Yasir Arafat!" Then they would go out into the world and try to do what they screamed about, with one catch. They had to go *apo nashi*—without an appointment.

Among the show's best-known episodes were "I wanna eat Akashi-style dumplings with United Nations representative Yasushi Akashi!"; "I wanna officially change my first name, in honor of the Barcelona Summer Olympics, to Barcelona!"; and "I wanna get treated to sushi by the wife of the manager of the Hanshin Tigers baseball team!" In their most famous adventure, the hosts screamed, "I wanna trim Prime Minister Murayama's eyebrows!" and Japan's then highest official—an aging member of the Socialist Party—let them do it.

I was thinking of that show as the train sped from Kansai International Airport toward downtown Osaka, birthplace of Nissin Food Products. I was certainly arriving *apo nashi*. It had been two months since Mr. Yamazaki, a low-level employee in Nissin's public relations department, stopped answering my e-mails. His silence suggested that there was very little chance I would get to meet Momofuku Ando, the ninety-four-year-old billionaire who, in 1958, invented instant ramen in his backyard.

As for why I wanted to meet Ando, I wasn't entirely sure. I suspected, though, that it had something to do with my love life.

PART I

LETTERS TO ANDO

I should be thinner. I should do yoga. I should be married like the people in the *New York Times* wedding announcements. I should be richer. I should be able to hit higher notes on the trombone, given that I have been playing the instrument for more than thirty years. I should be more discreet.

I should live closer to my parents so I can spend time with them, because one day they will die and I will feel more alone than I can imagine.

I should not be so concerned with my parents, given how old I am.

I should eliminate processed sugars from my diet. I should find great parking spots, the way my father always does. I should be less afraid. I should call my sister more. I should reestablish contact with my high school friends Dan and Dave and Sam, because if I ever do get married, I'll have few old friends at the wedding, but mostly because I miss them.

I should not write about the letters.

I should be in the moment. I should be taller. I should employ more adverbs and similes, and rely less on anaphora. I should own a big house on Belvedere Street and decorate it for Halloween. I should glide on the dance floor. I should have no cavities.

On Saturdays, when playing Ultimate Frisbee in the park, I should make smart throws and spectacular diving catches. I should not want attention or validation. I should give things another shot. I should be more organized.

When Grandpa Herman bought me the Partridge Family album for my tenth birthday, I should not have cried because it was not the album with "I Think I Love You" on it. I should be friendlier with the guys who run the body shop. I should keep things under wraps. I should not be suffering from what the inventor of instant ramen identified—just prior to inventing instant ramen—as the Fundamental Misunderstanding of Humanity.

Because then there wouldn't be so many shoulds.

But there you are.

I should start in Uji City, on January 2, 2007.

Blessed by a stunning mountain landscape and famous for its fragrant green tea, Uji City is situated midway between Japan's ancient capitals Kyoto and Nara. The region is home to Byodo-in, the 950-year-old Buddhist temple that decorates the back of the ten-yen coin, and to the tourist destinations known collectively as the Ten Spots, each in some way associated with one of the final ten chapters of *The Tale of Genji*.

On January 2, 2007, three days and two months shy of his ninety-seventh birthday, Momofuku Ando played a round of golf in Uji, at the Nissin Miyako Country Club. The inventor of instant ramen shot a 109—56 on the front nine, 53 on the back. He founded the club himself, he once said, "due to my earnest desire to pursue golf as my hobby and to enjoy the game to my heart's content." In fact, *Thus Spake Momofuku*, a published collection of Ando's famous utterances, contains no fewer than twelve sayings about golf, including:

> *"As far as I'm concerned, eighteen holes is the only happiness that money can buy."*

"Don't worry. If I'm playing, the rain will stop."
"To be on a golf course when I die—that is my true desire."

Two days later, Ando gave a speech at the Osaka headquarters of Nissin Food Products, the instant noodle empire he had launched nearly fifty years earlier. He addressed an assembly of Nissin employees for thirty minutes and enjoyed a serving of Chikin Ramen in the company cafeteria. Expressing his desire for peace in the world, he unveiled a slogan for the New Year. His practice of coining, brush drawing, and officially unveiling New Year slogans dates back to 1964. Because the slogans were often somewhat cryptic, Nissin's public relations department began issuing official explanations in 1986.

Ando's slogan for 2007 was *Kigyo Zainin, Seigyo Zaiten*.

According to the official explanation, it meant that a company can be built by humans, but its success will always depend on God.

The next day, Ando suffered an unusually high fever. He was rushed to a hospital, where his wife, Masako, and several Nissin executives stood at his bedside. He was not on a golf course when his heart stopped beating, but at least he had played very recently.

In the weeks that followed, newspapers and blogs hailed Ando as a food pioneer. Many obituaries cited the number eighty-six billion, which was how many servings of instant ramen had been consumed on Earth in 2005, the most recent year for which data on worldwide demand was then available. Some journalists did the math: nearly twelve bowls for every person on the planet. An airline pilot who blogged on Salon.com declared, "The aviation world was rocked" by the news, explaining that he carried five packages of instant ramen on every flight. Another blogger joked that mourners might pour boiling water into Ando's casket, turning down the lid for three minutes. *The Economist* ran a story on Ando's death. So did *Time* magazine. For three days the most e-mailed article on the *New York Times* Web site was an opinion piece by Lawrence Downes titled

"Appreciations: Mr. Noodle." It began, "The news last Friday of the death of the ramen noodle guy surprised those of us who never suspected that there was such an individual."

I laughed when I read the *Times* piece. I laughed because I was not a person who never suspected there was an inventor of instant ramen. Here are excerpts from e-mails I received in the wake of Ando's death:

> *"Saw this on a blog today and thought of you." (Carla)*
> *"Are you OK?" (Matt)*
> *"Saw the death of Mr. Noodle. Couldn't help thinking of you."*
> *(Josh)*
> *"Not sure if condolences are in order." (Ellen)*

My father sent me the *Times* clipping in the mail, along with an obituary that ran in the Long Island newspaper. He attached a note on his personal stationery. "It even made *Newsday*," he wrote.

Zen just typed a text message that said, "He is died."

Three weeks after Ando's death, I stuffed a cup mute and a plunger mute into a knapsack, carried my trombone out to my car, and drove to rehearsal. The group I played in was a full big band—five trumpets, four trombones, five saxes, and a rhythm section—and it rehearsed in a warehouse in San Francisco's South of Market district. Some of us called it the Monday Night Band, but there was no official name.

We never had gigs. We only rehearsed. We rehearsed on a cement floor surrounded by drills, saws, and workbenches. Many of the men in the band were more than twice my age. The lead alto saxophonist had just turned ninety-two. His tone sometimes wobbled, and he had trouble hearing instructions. The average age of the rhythm section hovered around eighty. By comparison, the trombone section was downright youthful. Aside from me, everyone was in their seventies. The band was led by the bassist, a thin man with a white beard who, when he wasn't plucking his upright bass, worked in the warehouse building props for photo shoots and conference booths. A human figure made out of cereal boxes stared down at us from an open loft, and a golf cart dressed up to look like a spaceship (in which a telecom executive once made his entrance at a trade show) was permanently parked next to the grand piano.

Setting my trombone case on one of the workbenches, I screwed together the bell and slide sections and slipped in a Bach 7 mouthpiece. I blew a few notes, mostly low B-flats, to loosen my lips. I was playing the third trombone part, so I took a seat between the first and fourth trombonists, because that's the traditional trombone section arrangement.

"One hundred twenty-two," the bassist called out.

The sheet music was numbered. I searched the folder on the music stand in front of me and found "122" stamped on a Sammy Nestico composition titled "This Is the Moment." The bassist counted off two measures in a laid-back swing feel. The band jumped into it. The third trombone part wasn't very exciting—mostly whole notes and background figures—but I enjoyed harmonizing with the other horn players and trying to match their phrasing so we all sounded like one instrument. That's the goal when you're playing a Sammy Nestico chart.

The bassist had just waved his hand to cut off the final chord when Gary, the first trombonist, leaned toward me.

"Son, how much would you pay for a thick, juicy slice of prime rib, a baked potato, and a side of vegetables?"

Gary played a silver King Liberty from the 1940s with intricate floral engraving on the bell and a sound that filled you up. It was the third time in as many Monday nights that he had asked me the question about the prime rib, the third time he was going to share with me the deal he had found in Millbrae. I'm still not sure whether his memory was failing, or if he was just really excited about the deal.

"I don't know," I said, feigning a guess. "Twenty-three dollars?"

There was a time not long before all this when I would have informed Gary that, first of all, I don't eat a lot of red meat, and second of all, he was about to share his tip for the third time. But one of the things I had come to realize was that I loved when Gary shared restaurant tips. That his sharing of them was the point, not the tips themselves.

"Well, son, what would you say if I told you there's a spot in Millbrae where you only had to pay sixteen ninety-five?"

As Gary repeated the name of the restaurant, the bassist called out, "Eight." It was the number for "Four Brothers," the up-tempo Woody Herman classic that showcases the saxophone section.

"By the way," Gary continued, pulling the music for "Four Brothers" from his folder, "I read the news."

At first I had no idea what he was talking about.

"About your ramen guy."

I had forgotten telling Gary about Ando.

"Oh."

Gary normally lifted his horn to his lips long before an entrance, but even as the bassist began counting down to the first bar of "Four Brothers," Gary's silver King Liberty remained perched on his knee.

"Tell me again," he said, "why did you go to meet the inventor of instant ramen?"

Before I could answer, we had to start playing.

The trombone parts on "Four Brothers" consist mainly of short hits punctuating the saxophone melodies, and there are long rests while the saxophonists take their improvised solos. What I'm saying is that I had plenty of time to ponder Gary's question. I had plenty of time to sum it all up. Yet as we approached the fermata at the bottom of the page, I still wasn't sure what to say.

Dear Momofuku,

Matt says I'm supposed to tell you everything. He says this is the only way. The problem is that I don't remember many details, especially about the first time it happened. Matt says I should start with that first time and tell you what I remember, even if it's not that much.

I don't know what else to do, so I am following his instructions.

So what I remember is that I was twenty-five years old and that I was living with my girlfriend in a garden apartment on a pretty street in Brooklyn. Her name was Maureen. I don't remember being unhappy at the time, though I don't remember being happy either. You would think I would remember more details, given that we lived together for two years, yet the sum total of my memories of those years comprises around five minutes. I remember a scene in which Maureen and I are cooking something in our kitchen—a soup maybe—from a recipe in a Gilroy Garlic Festival cookbook. There was a well-attended party we hosted. Once, we went for a hike in the woods with our friend Mike, who along the way began identifying trees just by smelling them. "Cedar," he said, sniffing. "Hemlock." I remember Maureen being impressed by this, and that I got jealous.

Maureen was five foot two and had a bob of blond hair, and I met her after college, when we both signed on for the Long Island Youth Orchestra's summer tour of Asia. I remember that when the group arrived in China, the banner that greeted us said, "WELCOME WRONG ISLAND YOUTH ORCHESTRA!" The first time I kissed her, in a hotel in Malaysia,

I imagined a future together in which we would get married and have beautiful, musical children. After that summer, I worked as a computer programmer in Chicago, and Maureen would tease me about the large number of condoms I always purchased in anticipation of her visits. When she was hired by an English-language magazine in Tokyo, I quit my job and enrolled in the intensive course at International Christian University, a popular place for foreigners studying Japanese. I did this partly to pursue my interest in the language (which I had taken briefly in college), but mainly to be with Maureen.

We didn't live together in Tokyo, but one night, when I was staying at her apartment, I peeked at her diary and discovered that she had slept with her ex-boyfriend. Technically, it had happened during one of our many breakups. I remember feeling that I should not be jealous or angry because during a breakup people can do whatever they want. When we returned from Japan, we moved in together in Brooklyn.

I just called Matt and told him that writing this letter is too painful and that I don't want to do it. He said it's natural to feel that way, and to keep jotting down what I remember. OK.

After six months of living together, I stopped having sex with Maureen. I'm not talking about a drop in frequency or the occasional lack of interest that my friends who were in couples experienced. I mean stopped, as in altogether. The disappearance of my desire was especially puzzling given how attracted I had been to Maureen previously. I began making up lies about being tired or sick. The truth was that, more and more, whenever Maureen touched me, even if it was just on my arm or my neck, I would experience a physical sensation that I can only describe as repulsion. It was as if her fingers suddenly began emitting a tiny electric shock from which my body needed to protect itself. Confused and frustrated by my disinterest, Maureen asked what was wrong. I didn't know what to tell her because I didn't understand it myself. I remember that she developed many theories. "Are you just not interested in sex?" she would ask. "Are you gay?"

The first time it happened I was visiting my parents.

They still live on Long Island, in the house I grew up in. I spent the afternoon with them, and then I heard about a party in a nearby town. I drove over, and when I saw the woman hosting the party, do you know what I wanted to do? I remember this part very well, Momofuku. I wanted to kiss her. My desire to kiss her was so strong that, as it swept over me, I didn't think about Maureen or how she had slept with her ex-boyfriend or anything else in the world. There were a dozen or so people at the party, most of them playing poker and drinking whiskey. In the middle of the poker game, the host excused herself to go to the bathroom, and a few minutes later I followed. When she opened the bathroom door, I walked up and kissed her. Just like that. She kissed me back, and together we drifted into the bathroom and closed the door. We fell to the tiled floor and began taking off each other's clothes. I didn't have a condom, so we put our clothes back on, walked past the people playing cards, and got into my car. We drove to a 7-Eleven, where we bought a package of Trojans. On the way back to her apartment I couldn't wait, so I parked the car near a pond where my ninth-grade science class once took a field trip to study erosion.

The host and I had sex on the grass in the dark. When we got back to her apartment, everyone was gone, so we had sex in her shower, and again on her bed. I remember that, on the drive home to Brooklyn, I did my best to wipe the entire incident from my consciousness. I was not, I believed, a man who could cheat on his girlfriend. But I returned to Long Island under the pretense of visiting my parents several times. After each episode there was a sickening feeling in my stomach, and I swore to myself that I would never see the woman again. Of course, I always broke the promise. Over time, I convinced myself that Maureen was simply the wrong woman, and that if only I could meet the right one, I wouldn't do what I did.

The next thing I remember was looking for an excuse to break up with Maureen, and applying to several out-of-state MBA programs.

Sincerely,
Andy

*O*ne sign that you are suffering from what Momofuku Ando called the Fundamental Misunderstanding of Humanity is that you betray people you love. A related symptom is that it's hard to remember details of your past. You can remember some details, but the ones you think you would remember you forget, and the ones you think you would forget you remember. You find it especially difficult to describe people who have played an important role in your life. You want to describe them, but it's difficult. They quickly turn into ghosts.

You feel that it shouldn't be this way, but it is this way.

Why did I go to meet the inventor of instant ramen?

While considering Gary's question, I naturally thought about the letters. Of course, they were only part of the story. There was another part, a series of adventures that began, of all places, in a sushi bar.

The letters cover a period that began roughly after I graduated from college and ended when I was thirty-eight years old. I found out about the sushi bar toward the end of that span, just a few years before Gary posed his question. I should do a better job of explaining how the letters and the events that began in the sushi bar came together. The weird thing is that, as I try to recall what happened in the sushi bar, I can't remember any of the women. Often I was there on dates, but I remember only me, the sushi chef, and his wife. Another consequence, I am certain, of the Fundamental Misunderstanding of Humanity.

I first learned about the sushi bar two years after moving to San Francisco. The turn-of-the-century dot-com boom had gone bust, and I was working as a staff writer at a nationally published business magazine. One day, I happened to read a positive write-up about the sushi bar's monkfish liver on the restaurant-review Web site Chowhound. I called for a reservation.

A woman answered the phone. *"Hai. Hamako desu."*

I didn't speak Japanese right off the bat.

"Hello. Do you have a table for seven o'clock?"

"Sorry," the woman grumbled. "We don't take reservations."

I got in my car and drove over. There was no sign in front, making the restaurant difficult to locate. The only clue to its existence was a row of tall, green sake bottles in the front window. That, and a business card wedged into the doorframe that said HAMAKO in Japanese. Entering, I was greeted by a middle-aged Asian woman whose silver-streaked hair had been tied back in a complicated bun. I recognized her voice from the phone, and she seemed annoyed.

"Can I help you?"

I looked around. Just six tables and a sushi counter. No other customers.

"May I sit at the counter?" I asked.

"No," the woman said. "You need a reservation to sit at the counter."

The only other person in the sushi bar was the sushi chef. Standing silently at his station, he reminded me a lot of Shota's master.

Shota is the fifteen-year-old main character in a Japanese comic book series called *Shota's Sushi*. In Book One, his father's sushi bar comes under attack by an evil sushi chain. Shota learns how to make sushi to help out, but as a novice he can only do so much. A visiting sushi master recognizes Shota's prodigious talent, however, and takes the boy on as an apprentice. Shota hones his skills, first as an entry-level helper in the master's Tokyo sushi bar, and then as a contestant in the All-Tokyo Rookie Sushi Chef Competition. There are fourteen books in the original series, and eight more in a sequel series (in which Shota competes in the All-Japan Rookie Sushi Chef Competition). Shota's dream is to become a full-fledged sushi chef so he can return home and save his father from the evil chain.

I had been reading *Shota's Sushi* in the months before my first visit to the sushi bar, so I guess that's why I made the connection. Like Shota's master, the sushi chef in front of me was stocky with short gray hair, and his wrist muscles bulged out, presumably from making so much sushi. He seemed upset about something, and I had the feeling that, like many of the sushi chefs in the comic book, he was often upset about something. A clean white apron hung from his waist and a blue bandanna circumscribed his head.

Still pondering the catch-22 around the restaurant's reservation policy, I was directed by the woman to a two-top.

"Would you like a beer?" she asked. "We have Sapporo and Asahi."

I ordered a Sapporo. Then the chef screamed at me.

"Mr. Customer! Which sushi bars have you been to in San Francisco?"

I recognized "Mr. Customer" as a direct translation of *okyakusan,* the Japanese word for addressing patrons. But the way he asked the question made me feel as if I were on a first date and had just been asked to list my previous sexual partners.

I decided to be up front with him.

"I like Saji and Okina," I said. "Every once in a while, for lunch, I go to Tenzan."

The chef shook his head disapprovingly.

"I play golf with Shiba," he said, referring to Tenzan's head chef. "Next time you eat there, tell him that my sushi is better than his. Don't worry, he knows it's true."

Zen used to advise me on how to behave at traditional sushi bars.

I should say more about Zen, but for now I'll just say that Zen is his real name, short for Zentaro, and that he once told me that when ordering *omakase*—leaving the selection up to the chef—you should carry a picture of what he called "your five starving children." Near the end of the meal, Zen instructed, you should reach for your wallet and let the picture drop out, causing the chef to take pity on you when he tabulates the bill. Zen also shared with me his foolproof method for starting a relationship with a traditional sushi chef. "Ask about the guy's knife," Zen had said. "Specifically, ask how many times a day he sharpens it."

I asked the chef standing behind the counter, "Is your knife from Japan?"

The chef lifted his knife. The blade was facing in my direction, but he didn't say anything. I was getting nowhere with him, so I switched to Japanese.

"Ichinichi daitai nankai toide irun desu ka?"

Roughly how many times a day do you sharpen it?

The waitress was in the middle of pulling a tall bottle of Sapporo Black Label from a refrigerator next to the counter when she turned around and answered my question before the chef could.

"Actually, that's just his demo knife," she said in Japanese. "His real knife is at home, and it's huge." She held her hands in the air, about sixteen inches apart. "Like a sword."

She brought the beer and a glass to my table, and took my sushi order. The *hamachi* in the glass case looked particularly good. I also ordered *saba, tai, mirugai, hirame, maguro, negi-toro* maki, and, of course, *ankimo*—the monkfish liver. As the woman relayed my requests to the chef, I looked around the restaurant. A decorative white sake barrel rested on a tree stump in the center of the space, and what little there was of a kitchen—just a sink and a single gas burner—was in plain view behind the counter. Crayoned illustrations of the chef and the waitress adorned the walls, along with photographs of famous people dining at Hamako. In one of them, a younger version of the chef stood proudly next to the baseball star Ichiro Suzuki. I recognized several classical musicians, including the violinist Isaac Stern, the flautist Jean-Pierre Rampal, and San Francisco Symphony conductor Michael Tilson Thomas. One photo showed Yo-Yo Ma playing cello—*in the restaurant*.

Twenty minutes later, the chef lifted a plate of sushi from his work area and set it down atop the refrigerated glass case in front of him. The woman picked up the tray and carried it to my table, where she recited the pedigree of each piece.

"*Tai* from New Zealand," she said. "*Hamachi* from Japan." And so on.

Then the chef screamed at me again.

"Mr. Customer, you will not find better sushi than this in the entire United States!"

With that, the chef burst out laughing. He appeared to be imagining that I had actually set out on an epic quest to find better sushi than his in the United States, and that I would one day return to concede defeat.

Dear Momofuku,

In my first year at the Wharton School, the thing my classmates talked about most was how they dreamed of landing summer jobs with investment banks. Investment banks offered the highest summer salaries and bonuses; you could pay off all your student loans if you got an internship. I didn't know what anyone did at an investment bank, but because all of my classmates dreamed of working at one, I felt that I should dream about that, too. My grades were good enough to get interviews with several of them. The interviewers always asked, "What are you passionate about?" and I would say, "I'm passionate about trading stocks," or "I'm passionate about doing mergers and acquisitions." They must have seen through me because none of the banks made me an offer. At the last minute, a foundation specializing in overseas internships for Americans helped me get a position in the Tokyo office of an American computer company.

My job there was to find Japanese software to bundle with the company's hardware, so I was often on the phone negotiating. But even when I was on the phone, I would grab peeks at one of the marketing managers. She was petite, but her cheeks were disproportionately puffy, which I found attractive. Her legs were stunning. One morning we were standing together in front of the coffee vending machine, so I introduced myself.

"I'm Andy."

"I'm Harue."

That was all, but something in her voice, some overtone maybe, wrapped around me like a blanket.

I don't remember how I learned that Harue loved lychees, but I learned, so I started buying them at a fruit stand. Her cubicle shared a partition with my boss's; while talking to my boss, I would secretly leave lychees on top of the partition. I asked her out for dinner, and that night, when the dessert came, I learned that she judged the quality of a crème brûlée by how quickly it made her cry. Our first kiss happened the afternoon we went to see the Clint Eastwood movie Unforgiven. *We stopped off on the way at Hope-ken, a ramen restaurant famous for the tubs of garlic that customers were supposed to spoon over their noodles, and I went for the kiss in the theater, right after the lights dimmed for the opening credits. "Ooo, garlicky," Harue said, and as she laughed, I imagined a future in which we would live in Japan and eat great Japanese food. We would have beautiful mixed-race children.*

Harue and I often bought bento-box lunches and ate them together in the courtyard of the Tokyo Metropolitan Gymnasium, which was right next to our office. One day while eating there, I called her Pumpkin, and Harue responded by calling me Dark Cherry, as if those had always been our pet nicknames. She loved dragonflies but was scared of butterflies. At night we would cook together in my tiny apartment and eat dinner on my kotatsu, *a coffee table with a heater underneath. We were both fans of* Ryori no Tetsujin, *the cooking-show-meets-gladiator-competition that I had been calling "Chefs of Steel." (It would later be released in the United States as* Iron Chef.*)*

The night after the second time it happened, Momofuku, Harue came over and prepared soboro gohan— *sweetened ground beef over rice. The rice was from her parents' farm in Iwate Prefecture; it was so fresh that, when steamed, it smelled like a flower. While savoring Harue's soboro gohan, we watched a challenger chef named Koji "Mad" Kobayashi take on Iron Chef Chinese Kenichi Chen in a battle over potatoes. The announcer explained that Kobayashi had gotten his "Mad" nickname because he had apprenticed for years in Italy but couldn't find an Italian restaurant in Tokyo that met his standards. Rather than cook in a subpar kitchen, he had opted to work as a truck driver. A video introduction showed Kobayashi scowling in the driver's seat of an eighteen-wheeler, angry about the state of Italian cooking in Japan.*

Harue and I laughed and laughed as Kobayashi handily defeated Chen. Then she told me there was another TV show I might like.

"It's called Go Forth! Air Wave Youth," *she said.*

In the episode that night, the female host screamed, "I wanna take ceramic dishes from the Picasso exhibit and spin them on a pole like at the circus!" Peppy and perpetually giggling, the female host first practiced outside a train station with ordinary dishes—which promptly fell to the ground and shattered. "OK, I'm ready!" she cried, thrusting her fist in the air. Then she traveled to a small museum that happened to be exhibiting a collection of Picasso's pottery. A security guard listened to her request and relayed it to his boss, but it was no surprise when, after a commercial, he returned to inform the host that his boss had said no. Yet watching the female host fail, I noticed something that did surprise me: She seemed to be having a great time! She made me wonder if voicing desires and acting on them—even if you failed—might be a great way to enjoy life.

It was such a ridiculous notion that I promptly forgot about it.

The show's closing credits were still flashing on the screen when Harue felt something unusual under the kotatsu.

"What's this?" she asked, holding it in the air.

It was a used condom. The truth involved a woman I had met at a party and had brought home the previous evening. I made up a story about how I had been "practicing" by myself, and Harue pretended to believe it. Momofuku, I don't know if you can help me, because this was just the beginning. I'll write more tomorrow.

Sincerely,
Andy

I reached first for the Hamako chef's *tai*, and as it rolled around in my mouth, it made me recall the first book I had ever read in Japanese.

When I was a student at International Christian University, I lived alone in a tiny Tokyo apartment and absorbed ten new kanji characters every night, writing them over and over until I had memorized their meanings, stroke orders, and multiple pronunciations. In my pocket I always carried a Canon Wordtank—a portable electronic kanji dictionary—so I could look up unfamiliar symbols on trains, billboards, and menus. I heard that a good way to learn Japanese was to watch TV, but as a student I couldn't afford a TV, so instead I bought a radio with a TV-band tuner that played the sound of TV shows. On Tuesday nights I would sit by the radio listening to dubbed episodes of *Star Trek*, and for a long time I was at a loss to explain the presence of a character named Mr. Kato, whom I didn't remember from the American version of the show. I finally figured out that he was Mr. Sulu, the USS *Enterprise*'s helmsman (played by the Japanese American actor George Takei), and that the dubbers had simply given him a real Japanese name. Mr. Spock was still Mr. Spock and Captain Kirk was Captain Kirk, but for some reason Mr. Scott had been renamed Mr. Charlie. I never found out why.

It took about six months to master enough kanji characters—around two thousand—to start reading newspapers. When I felt ready to take on something longer, I went to the Yaesu Book Center, near Tokyo Station, and bought *Kanda Tsuruhachi Sushi Stories*. The cover showed four pieces of *nigiri* on a wood counter, and it caught my eye. A memoir penned by Yukio Moro-oka (a famous sushi chef), the book contains the lessons Moro-oka learned from his mentors—not only his father but also several other chefs under whom he apprenticed. For instance, his elders taught Moro-oka that sushi should never be eaten with chopsticks. "Sushi is made with hands, so it should be eaten with hands," Moro-oka's father used to say. In an exhaustive chapter titled "The Ideal Size and Shape of Nigiri," Moro-oka explains that fish should be sliced so that, when viewed from the side, the cut resembles an unfurled paper fan. His take on size is more complex. If a customer cannot eat a piece of sushi in one bite, it's largely the chef's fault for not adjusting the dimensions to suit the patron's mouth. Still, there are limits. A chef should never make a piece so big or small that he upsets the delicate balance between the fish and the rice. Moro-oka says that the only information he cannot reveal in the book is the ratio of salt to vinegar in his rice marinade, because his father once told him that the secret ratio was what made his sushi more than just rice and fish. So, to summarize what takes Moro-oka more than three hundred pages to explain, the rice is important and the fish is important, but the most important thing is the relationship between the rice and the fish. I got through the book in three months with the help of the Canon Wordtank. But I don't think I ever really understood what Moro-oka was talking about until the *tai* began melding with the rice over my tongue at Hamako.

Even then, it was just an inkling. I told the sushi chef:

"I like your fish. I like your rice. But what I love is that I can taste the relationship between your fish and your rice."

The chef stopped what he was doing. Then he put down his knife and stared at me. He introduced himself.

"My name is Tetsuo," he said. Motioning to the waitress, he added, "This is my wife, Junko."

Junko smiled warmly now. "Nice to meet you."

When I told them my name, Tetsuo shared that he and Junko were originally from Kobe, and that they had opened Hamako in 1984.

"Those were the days," he lamented. "Japanese businessmen on expense accounts were always stopping by. A business card was all the sign we needed."

"Where did you learn Japanese?" Junko asked.

I told her about studying at International Christian University, and how, after business school, I worked as a management consultant for six months in Fukuoka Prefecture, on the southern island of Kyushu.

Tetsuo screamed again, but this time it was at Junko.

"Toroku shite ii yo!"

I wondered if I had misunderstood. Because the meaning of what I thought I heard was, "Go ahead and register him!"

I had not misunderstood, because right after that, Junko walked over to the telephone and pulled out a small notebook. She opened the book, waving a ballpoint pen in the air.

"What did you say your name was?" she asked.

I repeated it.

"Hmm," Junko said. "We already have a regular customer named Andy."

She thought for a moment.

"I know. We'll give you a nickname. We'll call you Hakata Andy."

Hakata is the city in Fukuoka Prefecture where I worked as a management consultant.

Junko closed the notebook and clasped her hands together.

"Hakata Andy," she said, "now you can make a reservation."

When I got home I logged on to Chowhound and wrote about the visit to Hamako. I noted agreement with the previous entry about the monkfish liver—not pasty like at other places—and heaped praise on a piece of *mirugai* that was still squirming as it slid down my throat. I bragged about getting the nickname and being able to make reservations.

The subtext of my post was, "I am totally in with Tetsuo and Junko."

Before my second visit, I called ahead and said it was Hakata Andy. I made a reservation at the counter, and when I arrived, table-bound patrons stared enviously as Junko ushered me toward Tetsuo's station.

"Hakata Andy!" he said.

I ordered *omakase*, even though I didn't have a picture of my five starving children. Over the course of an hour, Tetsuo threw sixteen pieces of sushi—including abalone, oyster, and squid with *shiso* leaf—onto the wood tray in front of me.

In *Shota's Sushi*, when a contestant in the All-Tokyo Rookie Sushi Chef Competition serves a truly great piece of *nigiri*, the next few frames in the comic depict the judges in various states of sushi bliss. Their eyes bulge and their mouths pucker. They look possessed. Then they're shown hovering over an ocean, as if the sushi has transported them there. Images of shrimps, lobsters, fish, or whatever else they've just eaten spin around their heads. While savoring a particularly fine piece of *uni*, one the comic's judges finds himself hurtling through outer space. "It's like I'm flying in a universe of amazing sea urchin flavor!" he exclaims.

It wasn't quite like that at Hamako, and shortly before I asked for the check, I found out one reason why.

"Hakata Andy," Tetsuo said, "I am about to give you the second-best piece of fatty tuna you will eat in your life."

With that, he reached his pudgy hand over the glass case and dropped a soft mound of pinkish flesh onto my tray. I pondered the tuna, chopsticks in hand, for some time before gathering enough courage to ask the obvious question.

"How come not first best?"

Tetsuo did not look up from his work.

"You're not ready yet," he said.

There are many people who would refuse to patronize a restaurant in which they're expected to earn the chef's highest-quality cuisine. What I learned on my first night at the Hamako counter was that I was not one of them. Rather, I committed to becoming Tetsuo's sushi disciple. I submitted to his will, devoting months to learning his rules. Still I couldn't help but wonder: What was it about me that made me want to be worthy of first-best fatty tuna?

The biggest challenge early on was appreciating the holy status of the counter. One day a former business school classmate called to say that he was in town from Tokyo and wanted to get together for dinner. He had to wake up early the next morning to catch a bus to Yosemite National Park, so I called Hamako and asked for a reservation at six thirty—right when the restaurant opened.

"I guess you'll be sitting at a table, then," Junko said.

"Can't we sit at the counter?"

"No. The sushi counter opens at seven o'clock."

It wasn't clear what she and Tetsuo had to do to "open" the sushi counter. I thought about it and wondered if the policy was Tetsuo's way of showing that he valued himself. It was as if he were telling customers, "If you want to spend time with me, make it prime time. Don't be scheduling me in."

There were rules about the sushi, of course. No "funky" rolls. Nothing spicy. Customers were expected to place orders up front—no follow-on requests. On several occasions, I heard patrons cheerily ask, "What's fresh tonight?" and then watched as they were ushered out of the restaurant after a scolding from Tetsuo. Junko once revealed to me that she arranged the soy sauce dishes at every place setting so that Tetsuo could see them from his station. When he spotted customers dragging his art through a wasabi mud bath, he cut them off from premium fish.

The most important thing I learned, though, was that sitting at the Hamako counter entailed certain responsibilities, and that chief among them was massaging Tetsuo's easily bruised ego. Often he would complain about a sushi bar around the corner that was regularly packed with young, beautiful people. "How can that be?" he would ask. "Their sushi chefs aren't Japanese, and they serve ridiculous rolls stuffed with multiple kinds of fish." Deep down he must have known that most Americans love ridiculous rolls stuffed with multiple kinds of fish and don't care about the nationality of their sushi chefs. But I guess he had a hard time accepting that, because he would always follow up with a self-deprecating comment about how his sushi was not what it used to be.

"My hands are getting weak," he would say. "I guess I should retire."

I always told him that his sushi was as great as ever, which it was.

There's one date at Hamako I remember.

The woman was Japanese, and she was a fit model for an international clothing chain. We were sitting at the Hamako counter when Tetsuo began doing his pity-party routine about the sushi bar around the corner. This time, when he got to the part about how his hands were getting weak and how he should retire, he went one step further.

"Junko and I have bought a home near Lake Tahoe," he said. "We're going to close Hamako in December and retire there."

I almost spit out a hand roll. He was speaking in Japanese, so I double-checked that I had heard him correctly.

"Did he just say that he's going to close the restaurant in December?" I asked my date. It was just four months away.

"Yes," she confirmed. "That's what he said."

That's why I remember her, because she confirmed it.

I looked up at Tetsuo.

"You're going to close Hamako?"

"In December," he repeated.

Part of me was sad. But another part was happy, because Tetsuo had apparently shared the news with me before telling anyone else. Was it a sign that he was beginning to see me as worthy of first-best fatty tuna? When I got home, I wrote another post on Chowhound. The title was "Hamako Closing?"

The next night, my cell phone rang. It was Junko, and she sounded upset.

"Hakata Andy, did you write something about us on the Internet?"

I wondered how she had gotten my phone number, but then I remembered her asking for it during the registration process. I also wondered how she knew about the post, given that I had written it under a pseudonym. There was no use denying it.

"Is there a problem?"

"Our phone has been ringing off the hook. People want reservations."

At any other restaurant, it would not have been a problem. Junko assured me that it was a problem at Hamako.

"The calls are disrupting Tetsuo's sushi making," she said. "He's angry, and he wants you to erase what you wrote from the Internet."

"Chowhound doesn't let you erase a post from their site," I said. It was the truth.

"I don't know what a post is," Junko replied, "and I don't know what a site is, but can you just erase it?"

"I can't. It's impossible."

Junko made a clicking noise with her tongue. "Then you'll have to apologize to Tetsuo."

I felt shame for telling the world that I was close to them. (Even though I posted using a pseudonym, people on Chowhound knew me from the annual Chowhound picnic in Golden Gate Park.) But I was unable to admit that to myself, let alone to Junko.

"Why should I apologize? I mean, Tetsuo never said the information was top secret."

Junko paused, and then she said the thing that, when I think about it, sometimes makes me cry.

"Hakata Andy, maybe you shouldn't come back."

I told myself that I would just go to other sushi restaurants, and for a long time I wandered from sushi bar to sushi bar. I numbed out on sake bombs and inside-out caterpillar rolls. I sat at the kinds of sushi counters where multiple non-Japanese sushi chefs work in assembly lines, and frat-boy customers toast them with an endless supply of drinks.

Dear Momofuku,

Harue visited me in Philadelphia the next fall. I showed her around the University of Pennsylvania, and she swooned over the Ivy League–ness of the place. She was excited to see firsthand the Gothic architecture and preppy outfits she knew from Japanese fashion magazines. I promised to remain faithful when she went back to Japan, but I broke the promise several weeks later.

A classmate named Nancy invited me to spend New Year's Eve with her and a group of her friends in Manhattan, and I met them for dinner at a Mexican restaurant in the East Village. It wasn't so much her friend Kim's long blond hair or athletic figure that I found irresistible, but the way that she bit her lower lip while talking to me. She said she was a staff writer for an entertainment magazine, and on the side she was composing lyrics to a musical. I asked why she wasn't eating anything, and Kim explained that she was planning to run the five-kilometer race in Central Park at midnight. My belly was full of beer and beans and it had been more than ten years since my days as a middling member of my high school's cross-country team, but I wanted so much to be near her that I proposed to the group that we all run the race. It was a bitterly cold night, but all seven of them were up for it. Kim went home to change into her running outfit while I borrowed sneakers and leggings from another of Nancy's friends. As we gathered again at the starting line, I recalled my high school coach's motivational advice, which was to imagine that the greatest thing in life was waiting for you at the finish line. In

eleven grade, I recorded my personal best for five kilome-
ters while imagining a bowl of Kraft Macaroni & Cheese
(with canned Cheez Whiz, not powdered) at the finish line,
but during the New Year's Eve race, right from when the
starting gun sounded, I imagined Kim there.

Kim ran in the park every day, but I somehow managed
to keep her in my sights. I pursued her down the East Side,
and on the last turn, the one near Tavern on the Green, I
pulled even. She saw me and smiled, biting her lower lip
again. We crossed the finish line together, and a moment
later I kissed her. In the future I imagined this time, Kim
would write articles and musicals, and I would wear a suit
and take a high-paying position in finance. We would run
together in the park and have athletic children.

"You move fast," she said.

Momofuku, as I write these letters to you, I am remem-
bering more details. For instance, I remember that when
Kim visited me on the weekends in Philadelphia, I would
turn off the ringer on my phone so it went straight to
voice mail in case Harue called from Tokyo. I remember
e-mailing Harue as if nothing had changed. Once, when I
was staying at Kim's apartment in New York, we went run-
ning together in Central Park.

"What's your favorite book?" Kim asked along the way.
Her blond hair was tied back in a ponytail to keep it from
flying in her face.

The best book I had ever read was a Japanese comic
book called Cooking Papa. *Actually, it's a series of comic*
books (later adapted as an animated TV show) about a cor-
porate executive who has to hide the fact that he's a better

cook than his wife. Kim was a professional writer, so I felt that my favorite book should not be a comic book.

"Don Quixote," I said instead. It was my favorite "book" book.

"What do you like about it?" she asked.

"Well, it's funny, first of all . . ." I was running, so I had to pause every once in a while to catch my breath. ". . . and there's a lot of, you know, meta-stuff . . . like characters in the second part of the book . . . who know about Don Quixote from . . . having read the first part. . . . What's your favorite book?"

Kim found it easier than I did to run and talk at the same time.

"I like anything by John Irving," she said, "especially Garp."

I hadn't read many "book" books except for the ones required in English courses, but I had seen the movie version of The World According to Garp. *Mostly what I remembered was the oral sex scene in a car. Still, part of me wanted to get closer to Kim—to really know her—and the talk about books gave me an idea.*

"How about . . . after this we hang out . . . and write together?"

Kim kept running. She didn't say anything for a while, but then she did.

"What do you want to write about?"

"Maybe we could . . . both start with the same sentence and . . . see what we come up with."

I figured I was the first person to ever propose such a thing, but Kim informed me otherwise.

"Writers call that a prompt," she said.

Her apartment was close to the park, so we showered there, grabbed pens and a couple of notebooks, and walked up Broadway to the Barnes & Noble at Eighty-first Street. I bought coffee drinks while Kim found a table in the café.

"OK, what do you want to use as the prompt?" she asked.

I opened my notebook, but I couldn't think of anything.

"Come on," she said. "Just write down the first thing that pops into your head."

I wrote down the first thing that popped into my head and showed it to Kim, who read my prompt aloud.

"'Fruit trees are rare in these parts,'" she said. "That's your prompt?"

"Is something wrong with it?"

"It's a little bleak."

Ashamed of my bleak prompt, I tried to defend it.

"It could be hopeful. Like, there are precious things in the world, and you have to appreciate them."

Kim disagreed. "Andy, you're saying good things are rare in your life."

I wasn't saying it. I was just using it as a prompt. Still, rather than discuss with Kim how embarrassed I felt, I made an effort to never be bleak around her again. I stayed as upbeat as possible, and not long after that I began looking for a way out. After receiving my MBA, I was hired by an American management consulting firm that had just opened an office in Japan, so when the opportunity arose for a six-month Tokyo posting, I jumped. Kim and I got together the weekend before I left, and we talked about how we *were still going to be a couple and how we would wait for each other. Once I got to Japan, though, Harue practically lived in my apartment.*

The firm assigned me to work with a department store in Fukuoka Prefecture, on the southern island of Kyushu, and part of my job was teaching executives at the department store about commitment. I gave speeches about how they had to commit to buying inventory, commit to getting to know their customers, commit to vendors, and commit to each other. Meanwhile, I was dating two people. My co-workers knew that I had a girlfriend back in New York, so I had to hide my relationship with Harue. (My boss lived across the street from my Tokyo apartment, so when Harue came over, I not only turned off the ringer but also drew the blinds.) The queasy feeling in my stomach was now present almost all the time, and I was often depressed. Amazingly, I never made the connection between those feelings and what I was doing. Perhaps on some level I knew because I would write in my journal, "OK, I'm going to end things with Kim." Then I would write, "OK, I'm going to end things with Harue." But I was powerless to do either. I had even convinced myself, Momofuku, that it was because I didn't want to hurt them.

Sincerely,
Andy

*N*ot too long ago, a woman I was dating found the notebook in which I had written the letters to Ando. She read them all. Then she left a message on my voice mail breaking up with me. "It's obvious from these letters that you have a problem," she said, "and that you will never be able to function in a committed relationship." I called her back, but I didn't argue. One reason was that I don't argue as much anymore. Another was that I used to think pretty much the same thing.

I should talk about what happened after I was banned from Hamako. Specifically, I should explain how I became involved in the world of ramen, which would come to play such an important role in my life. I should say "descended into" rather than "became involved with." Because if sushi occupies a position in Japan's food hierarchy akin to that of haute French in the West, then ramen's culinary status hovers somewhere around the prestige of a sloppy joe.

The status of instant ramen? Probably several notches below that.

The first thing that happened was that I finished the last book of the *Shota's Sushi* sequel series. In the final episode, after vanquishing his archenemy in the tiebreaker round of the All-Japan Rookie Sushi Chef Competition, Shota returns home to save his father's shop from the evil chain. Exploiting his knack for converting enemies into friends, Shota reforms the chain's evil owners, who hire him as a consultant to guide their expansion into South Korea.

Having lost one important sushi chef in my life, I found reaching the end of the *Shota* books especially difficult. To fill the void, I visited the bookstore in San Francisco's Japan Center, and asked the woman at the information desk to recommend another comic book.

"You want English translations?" she asked.

"No, Japanese is OK. I tend to like the food-related ones."

The woman led me to the comics section in the back of the store. She scanned the hundreds of titles on the shelves for ideas.

"How about this one?"

She was holding *Oishinbo*, a long-running series about two food reporters. I remembered that the reporters got their jobs in the first few episodes by winning a taste test in which they correctly distinguished between tap water, well water, and Tanzawa Mountain mineral water.

"Already read a bunch of the *Oishinbo* books. But yeah, something similar would be nice."

She pulled another book from the shelf. It was Book One of *Cooking Papa*.

"Read those, too."

"How about *Natsuko's Sake*?"

The daughter of a sake-brewing family, Natsuko dreams of making sake from a legendary strain of rice left behind by her deceased older brother. The rice can't be cultivated using pesticides, so she has to convince an entire farming village to adopt organic pest-control methods. The son of a rival brewery falls in love with her, as does her own head of production. I shook my head because I had read five of the *Natsuko's Sake* books.

"*Natsu's Brewery?*" the woman suggested.

A prequel series about Natsuko's grandmother, who battles and overcomes the traditional exclusion of women from sake making.

"Read it."

"*The Chef?*"

A traveling chef for hire, Mr. Ajisawa uses culinary knowledge to solve clients' problems, which at first glance seem unrelated to food.

"Sorry."

"*Train Station Bento-Box Single Traveler?*"

Dai and his wife, Yuko, run a bento-box lunch shop. For their tenth wedding anniversary, Yuko presents Dai with a special train ticket so he can travel around Japan indulging his passion for bento-box lunches sold at train stations. "It'll be a nice vacation from me!" says Yuko, who stays home to mind their shop.

"Read that, too."

"*Embassy Chef?*"

Mr. Osawa, a twenty-eight-year-old chef, gets a job at the Japanese embassy in Vietnam, where his deft kitchen skills help the ambassador overcome various diplomatic crises.

"I don't think so."

"*Third-Generation Tsukiji Fish Market Man?*"

A human resources manager at a troubled bank, Mr. Akagi is ordered to lay off one hundred employees. He feels guilty, so he lays off ninety-nine and then lays himself off. Later, he goes to work for his father-in-law at Tokyo's famous Tsukiji fish market, where he's ostracized because he lacks fish knowledge.

"Sorry again."

"*Best Chinese?*"

I had read only Book One, but I didn't get into the plot line, which was about a boy born in nineteenth-century Szechwan Province who turns out to be a cooking prodigy.

I was about to leave when the woman made one last suggestion.

"How about *Ramen Discovery Legend?*"

"What?"

The cover of Book One showed a photograph of a bowl of noodle soup topped with bamboo shoots, a slice of pork, and several squares of dried seaweed. Next to the photograph, an illustrated young man was holding out an illustrated bowl of ramen in his left hand. He was looking straight at me, and his right hand was clenched in a fist.

"Go ahead," he seemed to be saying. "Try it!"

I purchased *Ramen Discovery Legend* Book One and decided to search for a sushi bar in which to read it. I was driving along Clement Street when I noticed a small storefront with a Japanese sign. Was it a sushi bar? Yes, it was. Its name, Murasaki, was written vertically down the side of the door in hiragana. Hiragana symbols are like letters in the alphabet, except instead of standing for consonants and vowels, each once represents a whole syllable. (Technically, therefore, hiragana constitute a syllabary, not an alphabet. An example: む is pronounced "mu.") You can write all Japanese words in hiragana if you want to—and in kids' books, that's how it is. But in adult writing, some strings of hiragana are replaced with kanji, the ideographs inherited from the Chinese.

When to use kanji and when to use hiragana is a matter of convention and style, but sometimes the decision conveys meaning. For example, if *Murasaki* had been written in kanji, it would have been just one character, 紫 , which means "purple." But, like I said, it was spelled out in hiragana: むらさき. And since (like Roman letters) hiragana have no implicit meaning, they give rise to homonyms. So *Murasaki* could have meant "purple," but it also might have been a reference to the sushi chef's code language.

I learned about the sushi chef's code language translating a newspaper essay while I was a student at International Christian University. The essay described how sushi chefs developed the code so they could talk business in front of customers. For example, *agari* usually means "rise up," but in the sushi chef's code language it means "tea." *Menoji* usually means "the eye kanji," but in the sushi chef's code language it means "five." (The connection is that it takes five brush strokes to write the eye kanji, 目.) In the sushi chef's code language, *murasaki* means "soy sauce."

Something about Murasaki looked right, and it wasn't just that the name might have been a reference to soy sauce in the sushi chef's code language. Through the window I could tell that there were only a few tables and one chef.

When I walked inside, he welcomed me from behind the counter.

"Irasshaimase!"

He looked about Tetsuo's age, but he was thinner and smiled more. Behind him, a calligraphy painting of a single kanji character—嵐, *arashi*—hung on the wall.

Arashi means "storm."

The chef motioned me to sit at his counter, and after surveying the contents of his refrigerated case, I ordered *hirame, maguro, saba,* and *uni* to start.

When the chef put a plate of his sushi in front of me, I reached deliberately for the *hirame.* In *Kanda Tsuruhachi Sushi Stories,* the sushi chef's memoir, Moro-oka divides sushi into four types: white-flesh stuff (*hirame, tai*), red-flesh stuff (*maguro, katsuo*), shiny-skin stuff (*saba, kohada*—shiny-skin stuff is usually pickled), and other stuff (shellfish, etc.). He says customers are supposed to eat the white-flesh stuff first because if they eat red-flesh or shiny-skin or other stuff first, they'll overwhelm their palates with fat or vinegar, and they'll be unable to enjoy the white-flesh stuff's delicate flavors. I was hoping that by reaching for the white-flesh *hirame* I could convey to the chef—without even speaking Japanese—that I knew what I was doing, but he didn't seem to notice.

Whoa. Did I see what I thought I saw?

To my left at the counter, a few seats away, a Japanese man was eating sushi. And plopped in the corner of his wood tray was a green clump. Even from a distance of several place settings, I could make out its coarse, grainy texture—the telltale sign of freshly grated wasabi. The green clump on my sushi tray was smooth and featureless. Powder-based wasabi.

The chef must have seen me staring at the man's fresh wasabi.

"Kare wa joren da yo," the chef whispered.

He was saying that the man was a regular customer. Fresh wasabi was apparently the chef's version of a loyalty reward.

"How did you know I spoke Japanese?" I asked.

The chef laughed but didn't say anything. Maybe he *had* noticed me eating the white-flesh stuff first.

The Murasaki chef went about his business and didn't engage me in further conversation, so I pulled out Book One of *Ramen Discovery Legend* and began reading it at the counter. The story's main character was twenty-seven-year-old Kohei Fujimoto, an entry-level executive at Daiyu Trading Company. During the day, Fujimoto wears a suit and acts like an ordinary salaryman. But at night, even though it's against company policy to moonlight, he secretly runs a ramen stall in the park. Fujimoto's dream is to achieve *dassara*. The word is composed of the kanji character 脱, *datsu,* which means "to separate from," and *sara*, the beginning of the word *salaryman*. Fujimoto wants to leave salaried life so that he can open his own ramen restaurant, but first he has to have lots of ramen adventures. Often he is accompanied by Ms. Sakura, a secretary at Daiyu, who knows about his secret ramen life. In the first episode, Fujimoto is having lunch with his boss at a ramen restaurant near their office. Fujimoto declares the broth substandard and makes a derogatory comment, which the owner of the restaurant overhears.

"Who are you to criticize my broth?" the owner retorts. "I simmer my pig bones and chicken carcasses for ten hours, and I serve over six hundred bowls of broth a day. Shut up, unless you think you can do better!"

The episode ends with Fujimoto defeating the owner in a ramen duel. Fujimoto wins by concocting a broth from the freshest free-range Nagoya chickens and the highest-quality *kurobuta* pork. He simmers it for twenty-four hours, reminding the owner of an earlier time, a time when the owner, too, simmered his broth that long, when the owner slept in his kitchen and woke up every few hours to skim off fat. Fujimoto reminds the owner that his ramen is his life. The owner comes to understand that Fujimoto has criticized his broth out of love, and he pledges to do better.

I was in the middle of the next episode when I noticed that the Japanese man with the fresh wasabi was staring at my comic book. He was in his mid-thirties, maybe a year or two younger than me. From his suit and tie I deduced that he had come straight from work.

He leaned over and spoke to me. His English was very good.

"You like ramen?" he inquired.

I looked up from the page I was reading.

"Not really. I just bought this book."

The man resumed eating his sushi. But a few minutes later, he addressed me again.

"Sorry to bother you, but have you ever heard of Ramen Jiro?"

I sipped some green tea.

"Is that a comic book?"

He didn't answer the question.

"I'm Masa," he said instead.

"Andy."

We shook hands.

"So, what's Ramen Jiro?" I asked.

Masa looked down at the sushi tray in front of him. From the look on his face, I could tell that I had just asked his favorite question in the whole wide world.

Dear Momofuku,

So I was dating Harue and Kim at the same time, and gradually cutting myself off from other people. My isolation only got worse after the consulting firm transferred me back to the United States. I was assigned to the firm's New York branch, so I was back together with Kim, turning off the ringer when she stayed at my apartment in case Harue called. I only saw Kim on weekends, though. As the newest consultant in the New York office, I got last dibs on client assignments, which meant spending Monday through Thursday, every week, at Kmart headquarters.

On Monday mornings I would wake up at five thirty, kiss Kim good-bye, and catch a cab to LaGuardia Airport, where I would board a plane to Detroit. I always called ahead to reserve a subcompact at the Detroit Avis (I hated big, boatlike cars), but the Avis agents would invariably upgrade me to a midsize. I would complain, and the agents would stare at me like I was speaking another language. "Sir," they would say, "it's bigger." Then they would hand me the keys to a lime-green Chevrolet Cavalier or a maroon Buick Skylark, and I would drive north along Interstate 75 to the city of Troy.

Kmart had hired a team of consultants from our firm to fix what it called the cross-dock problem. A year earlier, Kmart's warehouses had begun installing "intelligent" conveyor belts to route merchandise from supplier trucks to store-bound ones. The belts were supposed to save tens of millions of dollars a year, but for some reason it wasn't happening. My job was to find out why. I would follow the signs on I-75 to Troy and take the exit at Big Beaver Road, the city's main thoroughfare. Kmart headquarters was down a ways, past the industrial parks; it was right across the street from the Somerset Collection, a mall that considered itself too upscale to be called a mall. (The Collection's tenants included Neiman Marcus, Barneys, and Saks Fifth Avenue.) As you drive along Big Beaver, Kmart's offices were on the right, housed in brick-faced, hexagonal buildings linked by tube-encased hallways. The campus resembled a giant Habitrail (the modular hamster cage that was popular when I was a kid). Weirder, though, was the giant metallic skull that loomed over the cul-de-sac near the entrance. It was one of the spookiest things I had ever seen: a two-story-high cranium forged from smooth, shiny bronze. There were holes in its sides, and through the holes you could see lots of little metallic skulls inside the big one. In the lobby, a plaque explained that the skull was the work of an English artist commissioned to express the idea "We are our people."

According to the plaque, the sculpture was titled the "Kmart Corporate Head."

I couldn't see the Head from the Cross-Dock Team office, but it was always in the back of my mind. I had to cut through the parking lot to get to the warehouse (where I would question Kmart staff about the conveyor belts) and on the way over I would feel the Head's icy gaze upon me. I slept at night in the Somerset Inn, a small hotel attached to the Somerset Collection, and once I had a nightmare in which the Head was chasing me and I was trying to move

*my legs but I couldn't run away. I would ask Kmart em-
ployees if they found the Head creepy, but no one seemed to
mind it. All they talked about was the cross-dock problem.
They talked about how the conveyor belts were supposed to
scan a bar code label on every box, and how sometimes the
suppliers put the label in the wrong spot. They talked about
how the suppliers often used the wrong data format when
transmitting computerized packing lists. The result was a
huge reject pile in the warehouse that was expensive to sort
through. I advised my boss, the head consultant on the project, that the key to solving the cross-dock problem was edu-
cating the suppliers on how to prepare their shipments, and
he agreed. "Why don't you write a manual?" he suggested.
Actually, it was more of an order. So my job became writing
a book for Kmart suppliers about where to place bar code
labels on their boxes and how to create electronic packing
lists using the correct data format.*

*As awful as that sounds, for a while this arrangement
actually worked for me. I felt like my life was going great
because I was working for a big company and I had Kim,
who was beautiful and athletic and intelligent. Never mind
that I was still talking to Harue on the phone as if she
were my girlfriend. The even stranger thing, Momofuku, is
that I barely knew Kim. I mean, Momofuku, I'm telling
you virtually nothing about her. Nothing about who she
was aside from her blond hair and a handful of things
she said. I've told you more about conveyor belts than about
a woman I dated for two years. That's partly because I
can't remember much. But, for the most part, I never knew
what she loved or what she cared about or what she was*

afraid of. Why is it that I never realized how sad that was until now?

My Kmart book had grown to a hundred pages—all created in Microsoft PowerPoint—when Kim and I took a vacation in Seattle. We rented a car and drove to the San Juan Islands, where we planned to go mountain biking and stay in bed-and-breakfasts. We were boarding a ferry when she mentioned an old friend in Seattle.

"Is it a guy?" I asked.

It was a guy.

"Did you guys date?"

"For like a second."

I imagined the guy to be much taller than me, and much more handsome. I imagined that when they dated they were very close, much closer than Kim and I were, and that he was never bleak. I imagined that they laughed all the time and sang songs together in the car. I was jealous, even though I still had another girlfriend on the other side of the world.

When we went mountain biking, I wondered if Kim went mountain biking with her old boyfriend, and if he was a better mountain biker than me. One night, in one of the bed-and-breakfasts, she asked me to pull her hair during sex, and I wondered if that was because she was thinking about how he used to do that. She never told me his name, and I was afraid to ask what it was.

The day we planned to head back to Seattle, fog settled over the ferry port. We were in the car again, waiting in a long line to board the ferry, when I was so overcome with jealousy about going back to Seattle (because Kim's ex-boyfriend lived there) that I said, "I love you." Kim didn't say anything back. Instead she got out of the car and went for a walk in the woods around the ferry terminal. When she returned, she still wasn't talking.

We drove off the ferry on the Seattle side. The road had only one lane in each direction, but there was so much traffic that we were barely moving. I glanced at Kim in the passenger seat and she was staring straight ahead. I was pretty sure she was planning to break up with me. I panicked, marking all of the "lasts" in my mind: the last time I stayed at her apartment; the last time we saw a movie together; the last time we ran in the park; the last time we had sex.

I thought maybe there was still something I could do, so I put my hand on Kim's shoulder. Then I reached under her shirt. At first she seemed indifferent, but what followed was a car sex scene like the one in her favorite book (except that my genitals survived intact). Now everything was going to be OK, I thought, because without saying anything, Kim had basically told me that she loved me.

I spotted a blueberry bush on the side of the road.

"Let's get out and pick some blueberries," I proposed.

I pulled over, but Kim didn't get out of the car. Picking blueberries by myself, I felt the panic return. How could a woman say no to picking blueberries by the side of the road with a man she loved? The only explanation I could think of was that she didn't love me after all, and that she was still planning to break up.

We flew together as far as Chicago; from there Kim returned to New York and I to Detroit. I complained to the Avis agents about being upgraded to a midsize and left De-

troit Metro Airport in the front seat of a purple Pontiac Grand Am. The next morning I was so obsessed with whether Kim was going to break up with me that I found it impossible to write about bar code labels. In the middle of the workday, I drove across the street to Saks, where I picked out a lacy white bra and matching white panties that made me hot just looking at them, and the thought of Kim wearing them drove me crazy.

That night, in my hotel room, the phone rang.

"We need to talk," Kim said.

I don't remember anything else she said, but she made it clear that she wasn't happy and that she wanted to be apart. After I hung up, I threw the phone receiver at the wall so hard that it made a hole. How's this for self-delusion, Momofuku? I convinced myself that I was the victim, and that Kim had betrayed me.

The next morning, I left the hotel and got into the purple Grand Am. It was almost Thanksgiving, so the air was cold and heavy; Big Beaver Road was veiled in a thin layer of snow. I drove across the street to Kmart headquarters and parked in a spot directly in front of the Kmart Corporate Head. The lingerie I had bought for Kim lay on the passenger seat, in the bag from Saks. I felt that I should get out of the car because people were expecting me in the Cross-Dock Team office, but I just sat there, staring at the Head. Then I began to cry. Snow was falling now, partially obscuring the view through the windshield, but I could still make out the Head hovering in front of me.

Just then, I thought of Go Forth, and in the front seat of the Grand Am, I tried screaming the line from the show.

"I wanna ___!"

I got the first two words out. But I couldn't think of anything—not a single thing—to fill in the blank. This put me in touch with something I can only describe as horror. It was a horror I must not have been ready to face, because I only let myself feel it for an instant.

Sincerely,
Andy

*A*fter being asked his favorite question in the world, Masa told me that Ramen Jiro was a small restaurant on a triangular plot near the edge of Keio University, the elite school in Tokyo where he had been an undergraduate. Ramen Jiro served ramen, Masa explained, and eating ramen was all anyone did there.

"Yet," he insisted, "Ramen Jiro is not about ramen."

I asked what it was about.

"Difficult to explain," Masa said. He seemed to struggle for the right words. "I guess it's something on another dimension."

I ordered more sushi. For the next thirty minutes, Masa related his experiences at Ramen Jiro.

The first time he went, he was a freshman at Keio University. A senior had invited him, explaining on the way to the restaurant what to do and what not to do.

"The first rule," Masa said, "is that no matter what, you can't talk to the owner. He's this serious-looking old man, and you can only talk to him if you're on the university judo team. That's because he sometimes works out with those guys. Anyway, I was on the tennis team, so no talking. The second rule is that you can't leave any noodles or soup in your bowl. That is difficult because regular *chashumen* [a bowl of ramen with roast pork slices on top] usually comes with very thin pork slices. But this guy gives you very thick pork. There is a humongous amount of noodles, and a half-inch-high layer of liquid lard on top."

"It sounds disgusting," I said.

"Actually, it is disgusting," Masa confirmed. "The first time you eat it, you get sick. But the same day, around midnight, you start to feel like, 'Oh, my God, I wanna eat that again.' So the next day you go back, and you eat it, and you go, 'What the heck was I thinking? This is crazy. I don't want to ever eat this again.' Then you just keep going in this cycle, until finally you are addicted."

I ordered cold sake for both of us—a *junmai* from Kochi Prefecture.

Masa explained that the moment of truth in any Jiro visit was when you gave your order. There were basically just two items on the Jiro menu: small and large. What Masa had been talking about so far was the small. As a rule, a first-timer was not supposed to even think about a large, but Masa said the decision was harder than it sounded.

"The wait is always at least forty minutes. Then you finally reach the entrance, and this gray-haired, big-bellied owner looks up from his vat of boiling pig carcasses and says '*Nani?*' Then you have to say either '*sho*' (small) or '*dai*' (large). And even if you've made up your mind that there's no way you could eat a large that day, after standing in line in front of this owner and watching him cook soup for, like, five or ten minutes, you'll start whispering to yourself, 'Maybe I can do it! Maybe I can do it!' And when you're in that mode, you're in trouble. Because when he all of a sudden comes at you with '*Nani?*' you'll just blurt out '*dai!*'—large. And then you'll think, 'What the hell did I do? I can't eat that much.'"

"It sounds like you don't really know what you're going to do until you come face-to-face with this guy."

"Exactly. You get in front of him, and you really can't think straight."

Masa took a sip of sake and his face turned serious.

"Once, after I finished, like, one-third of the noodles, I felt like I had to go to the bathroom."

"Is that a problem?"

"There's actually a bathroom there, but no one uses it."

"Why not?"

"Because it's too embarrassing! Think about it. Everybody's waiting forty minutes to get in, and if you make them wait more, the owner's going to get mad at you. You're always feeling this kind of pressure. Pressure. Pressure. I started slowing down because I couldn't finish it, and I thought, 'Oh, my God, how can I get out of this place?' So I put the pork underneath the noodles, trying to at least hide it, and then I put the bowl on the counter and screamed, 'Thank you very much—good-bye!' And I just ran away and couldn't go back there for three or four months because it was so embarrassing. I was so traumatized because I couldn't finish it. I was like, 'What if it happens again?'"

Masa said he suffered alone for much of the time he stayed away from Ramen Jiro. Eventually, though, he admitted his failure to friends. To his surprise, he learned that many of them had encountered similar problems, so they banded together to perfect their pre-Jiro conditioning.

"You can't have a big breakfast, obviously," Masa warned. "But an empty stomach is almost as bad. My friends tried a lot of different foods before going there. This one guy figured out that the best thing to have was fruit. And the best fruit was an Asian pear. The worst was a banana. Don't even think about eating a banana. Anyway, we would eat a pear before going there, and then be like, 'I think I'm ready. I think I'm ready.'"

That night, when I got home from Murasaki, I typed "Ramen Jiro" into Google's Japanese search page. I found not only the street address and a map but also a Web site that oriented Jiro newcomers. A section called "How to Jiro" was divided into advice for novices ("If you need something to drink, order the tea") and advice for Jiro old-timers ("Don't even think about ordering tea. Remember, this water goes into the Jiro broth and boils the Jiro noodles. It's too precious to be wasted on tea"). Referencing a schematic diagram of the counter—with locations labeled A, B, C, etc.—the Web site deconstructed the ordering ritual that Masa had described. I learned, for instance, that when the owner was ready to present your bowl, his younger assistant, Mr. Sakai, would stand at the location labeled G (near the cash register) and repeat your order back to you. In other words, he would say *"sho"* or *"dai,"* depending on which you had chosen. This, it turned out, was a cue meaning, "Your order is ready, what toppings would you like?"

The Web site outlined acceptable responses, which were a kind of Japanese code:

Karame: *Extra soy sauce flavoring*
Dokayasai: *Double-extra bean sprouts and cabbage*
Abura: *Extra-thick layer of lard*
Abu-abu: *Double-extra-thick layer of lard*
Nin-nin: *Double-extra minced garlic*

According to the Web site, if you didn't make your topping call quickly enough, Mr. Sakai would say, "Would you like garlic on that?" Hearing this line from Mr. Sakai was the ultimate Jiro disgrace, because it meant that you would be denied the pleasure of ordering extra vegetables, lard, and flavorings.

I settled on the codes for extra vegetables, extra soy sauce flavoring, and double-extra garlic, and practiced yelling them rapid-fire in my apartment.

"Yasai karame nin-nin! Yasai karame nin-nin!"

After a few weeks, when I felt ready, I proposed a story about Casio, the Japanese electronics firm, to Josh, the editor in chief of the business magazine where I worked. I had read an article about Casio in *Nikkei Business*—Japan's equivalent of *BusinessWeek*—that said the company was famous for shunning consumer input when designing products. The result was a history of strange gadgets that often turned out to be failures. Ill-fated Casio calculators of the 1970s and '80s, for example, included the QL-10, which doubled as a cigarette lighter; the PG-200, which doubled as a pachinko machine; and the QD-151, which, long before anyone knew what to do with one, doubled as a mobile stock-trading device. But once every decade or so, the company's "producer is king" approach led to huge hits, such as the first cheap portable calculator (the 1972 Casio Mini), G-Shock watches (which became popular with American skateboarders in 1991), and ultrathin Exilim digital cameras (promoted in 2002 as a fashion accessory).

I called Casio's press relations office and set up some interviews.

In Tokyo, I rode the Chuo Line to Casio's engineering center on the western outskirts of the city. There I interviewed Yukio Kashio, the youngest of the company's four founding brothers. In what was a highlight of the trip, Yukio showed me how to divide 1 by 3 on the Casio 14-B, a 1959 calculator the size of a desk. Cordoned off by ropes in the lobby and constructed from telephone relay switches (transistors were not available when it was designed), the machine clicked and clacked to produce the dividend.

After the interview, I returned to Tokyo proper and rode the subway to Mita Station. Exiting the turnstiles, I followed signs to Keio University. A light rain was falling, so I stopped at a supermarket to buy an umbrella. I also swung by the fruit aisle. Ten minutes later I was standing in line—pear in belly—at Ramen Jiro.

There were around twenty men—and no women at all—in front of me on line. The rain had gotten heavier, so everyone held umbrellas. Through a window in the side of the restaurant, I could see the owner. His thin gray hair was almost gone, and he wore a dirty white apron over a dirty white undershirt.

I rehearsed saying *"Sho!"* over and over in my head.

The wait was almost exactly forty minutes, just like Masa had said, and when I finally got near the front of the line, I saw the owner up close. His apron was smeared with dried pig and chicken blood, and the impressive belly protruding from his modest frame kept him from getting too close to the soup vats he was tending.

"Nani?" I heard him say.

I replied as decisively as possible, and with the best accent I could muster:

"Sho!"

The other men in line began giggling. The owner giggled, too. Taking pity on me, the man behind me explained what had happened.

"Actually, he didn't say *'Nani.'* He was just asking if anyone could make change of a one-thousand-yen note."

I had been so anxious about making the call that I wasn't listening very well. Now I had made a terrible mistake. My face flushed in embarrassment. I thought that maybe I should leave. Everyone in the restaurant was giggling.

Soon the owner really did yell *"Nani?"* and I guess I felt the need to compensate for my mistake.

"Dai!"

The giggling stopped.

I proceeded toward the counter. It was reddish orange and had two levels, one for eating, and another, above, for bowls in transit between patrons and the staff. Behind the counter stood the chef and a younger male helper, who I deduced was Mr. Sakai. Apparently willing to forgive my earlier gaffe, Mr. Sakai motioned me to the only open seat. It was on the left side of the counter.

Inside, Ramen Jiro was a cacophony of slurping. The middle-aged man next to me was sitting on his suit jacket and had removed his tie, presumably to keep it clean. Some kids, probably students from Keio, had slung white bath towels around their necks, which they occasionally used to wipe the mixture of sweat and splattered soup from their faces. A sign on the wall just above the counter said RAMEN JIRO CORPORATE PHILOSOPHY. Below the title, there were six points:

- *Live cleanly, rightly, beautifully. Take walks and read books, laugh and save money. On weekends, fish, golf, and transcribe Buddhist texts.*
- *Live for the world, for others, for society.*
- *Love & Peace & Togetherness*
- *Have the courage to say you're sorry.*
- *Unbalanced flavors lead to unbalanced hearts. Unbalanced hearts lead to unbalanced families. Unbalanced families lead to unbalanced societies. Unbalanced societies lead to unbalanced countries. Unbalanced countries lead to an unbalanced universe.*
- *Would you like garlic on that?*

When my bowl was filled with noodles and soup, Mr. Sakai brought it over.

"Would you like garlic on that?" he asked.

Maybe I wasn't fast enough or maybe he figured that because of my earlier mistake, I wouldn't know the secret calls. The ultimate Jiro disgrace. I had spent all that time studying the Web site and practicing the codes in my apartment for nothing.

I pretended not to hear Mr. Sakai and yelled, *"Yasai karame nin-nin!"*

Mr. Sakai looked at me and smiled as he ladled on the extra vegetables, extra soy sauce flavoring, and double-extra garlic. The Web site had said that Mr. Sakai was a nice guy and could be an important ally in difficult situations. Sure enough.

I examined the bowl in front of me. It was huge, yet looked doable. Of course, by now my judgment was unreliable. The noodles were thicker and darker than the average ramen noodle, and the broth—a combination of pork- and chicken-based stocks—was topped, as Masa had promised, with a half-inch layer of liquid lard. I picked up a pair of chopsticks in my right hand, and a soupspoon in my left.

I began slurping.

In contrast to *Shota's Sushi*, which depicts happy sushi competition judges hovering over an ocean, when Fujimoto tastes a great bowl of ramen in *Ramen Discovery Legend*, he's shown floating in a cloud of Nagoya chickens, dried anchovies, and the other ingredients he discerns on his tongue. And during my first five minutes of slurping at Ramen Jiro, that was how I felt. There was an explosion of pork and chicken flavor. In particular, the roast pork slices on top were richly marinated in soy sauce and nicely fatty.

Slowly, though, I began feeling full. Then my stomach started to hurt. I moaned.

"Uuuuuuuuu."

I was not the only one moaning. Some of the people around me were also in pain. Slurping and moaning, slurping and moaning. Occasionally, I paused to catch my breath. There was no way I could go back to Masa without finishing.

It took nearly an hour, but I finished. I was shaking from the pain, and sweat dripped down my back.

The owner saw my empty bowl.

"*Arigato*," he said.

When I got up to leave, I felt feverish. I remembered how Masa told me that I would be sick, so I went back to my hotel and lay down on the bed in my room. I couldn't sleep for long, though, because that afternoon I had to interview Casio's CEO, Kazuo Kashio, at Casio headquarters.

"Are you OK?" one of Casio's public relations officers asked. "You don't look well."

"Jet lag," I said, and somehow I made it through the interview. When I got back to San Francisco, I called Masa.

"Wait a second," he interrupted. "Tell me again what the owner said after you put your empty bowl on the counter."

I repeated it. *"Arigato."*

"Oh, my God!" Masa cried. "He never thanks first-timers."

Masa explained that in the world of Ramen Jiro, I was now like a god. Two weeks later, though, I woke up in the middle of the night. Some sushi I had eaten for dinner was making its way back up my throat. I felt like someone had stabbed me in the ribs. I threw on some clothes, hailed a cab, and told the driver to take me to the nearest emergency room. When I got there, the doctor on duty ran some tests.

"Have you eaten anything super-fatty recently?" he asked.

I described the bowl of ramen at Ramen Jiro.

"I can't be sure if there's a connection," the doctor said. "On the other hand, I can't be sure there isn't. What I can tell you is that your gallbladder is infected and has to be removed."

I called Masa from the emergency room telephone booth and shared the diagnosis.

"Oh, yeah," he said. "Same thing happened to my friend."

There was a window in my hospital room, but I was on such a high floor that I couldn't see anything except sky. Maybe it was because I had never had surgery before, or maybe it was the lack of a street-level view, but my hospital room felt separate from life. As if I had been taken out of the game and asked to reflect on my performance from the sidelines.

The night before the surgery, I caressed the smooth skin of my stomach, which would soon be cut open. (It was going to be a laparoscopic surgery, in which the gallbladder is removed through a small incision in the belly button, but still.) Strangely, or maybe not so strangely, I found myself thinking about Tetsuo and Junko and all the good times at Hamako. Here was Tetsuo surprising me with a whole crab for my birthday; Junko kicking out a customer for requesting a spider roll; Tetsuo lifting up a whole yellowtail tuna to show me the part he had cut for me.

A phone sat on the table next to my hospital bed, and I stared at it for a while. I still remembered the number. It was April. Had they really closed the restaurant back in December?

I picked up the phone and dialed. It rang twice before I heard Junko's voice.

"Hai, Hamako desu."

They hadn't closed after all. But I was too ashamed to say hello, so I quickly hung up the phone. I told myself it was because I didn't know how to say "gallbladder" in Japanese.

I woke up after the surgery with pain in my side and bandages around my stomach. An orderly wheeled me back to my room to recover, and later that afternoon, my friend Andy came to visit. Known by my family as "the other Andy," he's my oldest friend. We met in summer camp when we were fourteen years old, and now he was living in Petaluma, north of San Francisco, with his wife and children. On the way over, he had stopped at my apartment to pick up my mail.

I lay in bed while the other Andy went through the letters. Halfway through the stack, he held up a magazine.

"Dude, what's this?"

The other Andy was holding the February 23, 2004, issue of *Nikkei Business*. Its cover was a close-up, shot from above, of a container of Cup O' Noodles.

Dear Momofuku,

Harue sent me an online greeting card for my most recent birthday. This is the last vestige of our relationship—acknowledging each other's birthdays by e-mail. Usually I type out a brief note, but she sends online greeting cards. The card she sent this year showed a cartoon penguin singing a song that consisted of three notes. Sometimes I play the penguin song over and over, and each time the three notes end, I think about what I did.

I cried and cried in the Kmart headquarters parking lot, and since I couldn't stop crying, I called in sick and drove to the airport. I flew back to New York, where I cried in my apartment. I just kept on crying. The following Monday morning, I told my boss that I couldn't stomach the idea of flying to Detroit, and he said that if I couldn't do that, then I couldn't work for his management consulting firm. I quit the next day.

For weeks I walked around the Upper West Side, unemployed, like a zombie. I walked up Broadway and down Broadway. I didn't know what to do or where to go. One day, I noticed an advertisement for a class called "How to Write a Magazine Article" at the West Side YMCA. It always sounded like fun when Kim had talked about researching stories for her magazine, so I enrolled in the class. Of course, Kim lived around the corner from the YMCA, so I was also hoping that I would run into her and she would want to date me again.

Looking back now, Momofuku, I see that enrolling in the class was one of the few times in my adult life—aside from studying Japanese and some adventures around Japanese food—when I pursued a desire that was at least partially unrelated to women. The writing class would lead my romantic life to spiral even further out of control, but now I see that it also led me to you.

It didn't take long to find a new job. The head of a Japanese computer consulting firm with an office in New York plucked my résumé from a personnel agency and hired me to do what he broadly termed "Internet business." The job wasn't very demanding, so on company time I pitched story ideas to magazines. These were magazines that not many people had ever heard of, like Java Developer's Journal *(a publication devoted to the Java programming language)* and Bank Technology News. *Meanwhile, Harue applied to a college in Manhattan. It was her dream to study graphic design, and it was her dream to do it while living in Manhattan with me. She almost didn't get in. The admissions department accepted her on the basis of her portfolio, but they sent her acceptance letter to the wrong address; by the time she got it, the deadline for the deposit had passed. I was so sure that I could be faithful if we were together again that I called the head of the graphic design department and asked if there was anything he could do. He kept saying no, so I stayed on the phone with him for forty-five minutes. Finally, he said "maybe," and a week later, after receiving a second acceptance letter, Harue wired the deposit.*

I was afraid that what had happened with Maureen might happen with Harue—that living together would increase the chances I would cheat—so I arranged for Harue to rent a room in an apartment owned by a friend. Still, we did so many things together. We ate at nice restaurants. We went apple picking on Long Island. We sat in the stands at New York Yankees games, and we danced along with the grounds crew to the Village People's "Y.M.C.A." We watched Seinfeld. *I was afraid at first that Harue wouldn't understand the jokes, but one of the greatest pleasures in my life became listening to her descriptions of episodes I had missed. She could barely stop laughing long enough to relate the plots. Harue was my date at family events like Thanksgiving. Aunt Pat, who fashioned herself a Buddhist—her outgoing voice mail greeting asked, "If not now, when?"—took a liking to Harue, who soon began accompanying Pat and me on secret Nathan's-hot-dog runs before Passover seders. Pat could never figure out how to pronounce Harue's name, so Harue told her that it sort of rhymed with* caraway. *After that, Pat always called her Caraway Harue to make sure she got it right.*

In short, Harue was my girlfriend. I often thought that she was the "one" I was meant to be with. And she was beautiful. Men in Manhattan would turn around on the street to gawk at her. My friends would tell me they were jealous. I think I was in love with her. But none of that mattered.

My first story assignment for a magazine that most people had heard of came from Playboy, *although it was the Japanese edition. My friend's wife, Kumiko, worked as an overseas editor for the magazine and wrote reviews of Manhattan restaurants for Japanese businessmen. Kumiko paid me to translate the reviews so restaurant owners could hang them in their windows. She liked my translations, and one day she asked if I wanted to write a story under my own byline. The one she had in mind involved a dating service that catered to graduates of Ivy League and other top colleges. Kumiko said that, while Japan was lousy with matchmaking services, she had imagined that all Americans simply fell in love without third-party assistance. Japanese readers, she believed, would be fascinated to learn of an elite dating service in the States. I signed up for the service and ordered personal profiles for twenty-five women in the mail. (This was just before online dating caught on.) The profiles listed educational backgrounds, ages, and answers to questions such as "What is your idea of a perfect Sunday morning?" I told Harue what I was doing, and that I was only doing it for the byline. She wasn't happy, but she trusted me.*

A twenty-seven-year-old filmmaker's idea of a perfect Sunday morning was "coffee, sex, and Soho—not necessarily in that order." I called her on a Saturday night and we arranged to meet early the next day at a café on Spring Street. On the phone she had said, "You'll know me because I'm pale." Pale can be good, but over her pale skin she wore a white jump suit, white tights, and white go-go boots. At the café she told me her last name, and it was a name you hear at the end of public television programs when they announce the underwriters. She stressed that she produced her films with her own money because her side of the family had been cut off from the side that underwrote TV shows. We got to only two out of three items in her perfect Sunday, so my article for the Japanese edition of Playboy *wasn't very exciting.*

For the next few weeks, however, my mind kept going back to the twenty-four profiles that were still stacked in a corner on my desk. I called another woman from the stack, and we ate dinner at a French restaurant. A week later, we went out to dinner again, but this time she invited me back to her apartment. She told me that I was irresistible, and because she said it, I believed that I was. I called another woman from the stack, and when she came up to my apartment, I had to ignore the look from my doorman that said, "How could you do this to Harue?" When I got through the first stack, I ordered another.

It was around this time that I noticed a menu option on America Online titled "Member Directory." I clicked on the heading, and a box popped up with a search form. After I typed in the key words "Manhattan AND single AND female," a list of one hundred single women appeared. There was an icon next to the user names of people who were online, and a button to send an instant message.

"Hi," I wrote to the woman whose user name was NYCTeach212.

"Howdy," NYCTeach212 typed back.

I didn't think about Harue at all. I only thought about how exciting it was to be talking to a woman I had never met. I told NYCTeach212 that I had an MBA and that I spoke Japanese and that I played the trombone. I didn't mention that I had a girlfriend. She said she was a schoolteacher, which I guess was obvious from her user name.

"This might sound crazy," I typed. "But would you like to get together for a drink?"

NYCTeach212 and I met at a bar on the Upper East Side. Cute, petite, Jewish. A few hours later, we were making out on her sofa. She said, "What really turns me on about a man is his trapezius, and you have a nice one." Momofuku, after all these years, I can remember how good it felt to have a stranger compliment my trapezius, but I can't remember many words spoken by the women I was supposedly close to.

Soon I was spending hours a day on America Online, sending instant messages to women I had met through the member directory. I would arrange dates while "working" in my office, and all day I would look forward to them. If Harue called to make plans, I would say that I was hanging out with my friends Dan or Dave or Sam, or that I wasn't feeling well. And I wasn't only cheating with women I met online. I met people in coffee shops and in the gym, in restaurants and at parties. I met them at conferences and on business trips to Japan.

Occasionally, I would think about what I was doing—the most intense moments of clarity came just after sex with someone who was not Harue—and it was as if I had awoken from a dream in which I had been possessed by someone else, someone utterly indifferent to betraying someone he cared about. I would feel dirty and ashamed. Like with Maureen, I would promise myself over and over that I would never cheat again as long as I lived, and often I would remain faithful for several weeks or even months. I would convince myself that I was a good boyfriend, as if these loyalty periods wiped away what I had done. But without fail, and with increasing frequency, I found myself back in the dream, calling women from the dating service and typing keywords into the America Online member directory.

Remarkably, even though I was spending so much of my energy on romantic pursuits, I came up with an idea for an Internet start-up. I hatched it with a colleague at the Japanese consulting firm. His name was Zen, and the idea involved frequent flier miles and viral marketing. I wrote the business plan, and our boss gave us seed money. We pitched the plan to venture capitalists in San Francisco, and one of them offered to invest a million dollars, on two conditions: (1) The company had to relocate to Silicon Valley, and (2) I had to take over as CEO. We had made Zen the CEO, but the venture capitalists couldn't always understand his English.

At first I told Zen that there was no way I was moving to Silicon Valley. I had a girlfriend who was in school, so I couldn't leave New York. I told Harue the same thing, and she seemed happy that I was finally taking action to commit to her. But then I went for a run in Central Park, and on the jogging path I began thinking about other things. I thought about how that feeling of physical discomfort (which I had first experienced with Maureen) had returned when I was with Harue, and how in California, there would be no family to keep up appearances for. There would be no doormen to shoot accusatory glances. It was as if two people inside of me were battling. One was in love with Harue, and the other couldn't wait to be free of her.

The day I left New York, Harue stood next to me on the curb as I hailed a cab. I loaded my suitcase into the trunk, hugging her.

"Maybe you'll come join me when you finish school," I said.

"Maybe," she replied.

I got into the cab, and as the driver pulled away, I turned to wave good-bye. As you know, Japanese etiquette dictates that when you see someone off who leaves in a car, you're supposed to stand there until the car is completely out of sight. I was only a few blocks away, though, when Harue turned to walk home. Her figure got smaller and smaller through the back windshield, and I believe that as she disappeared, Momofuku, so did my soul.

Sincerely,
Andy

I had never been inordinately concerned with instant ramen. There were exceptions, of course:

- The day my mother brought home a bag of Oodles of Noodles. That was what Nissin called its instant ramen in 1972, when the company launched the product in the United States. I remember, if not many details of that day, an air of excitement in our kitchen as my mother brought the noodles to life in boiling water.

- The semester in college when the cafeteria workers' union went on strike. The university refunded each student $72.80 a week to buy food. My roommate and I made the most of the money by stealing a heating coil from the chemistry lab and "cooking" various flavors of Cup O' Noodles.

- The year I was a student at International Christian University. Back then, Japan's automated-teller machines were open only during regular bank hours—weekdays from nine to five. I would often forget to make pre-weekend withdrawals, but thanks to instant ramen, I survived many Saturdays and Sundays on just the few hundred yen in my pocket.

Aside from those times, I had never given instant ramen much thought. I can only assume, therefore, that if I had not been kicked out of Hamako and had not met Masa and had not finished the large-size bowl at Ramen Jiro, I would not have paid much attention when the other Andy held up the issue of *Nikkei Business* magazine with the Cup O'Noodles close-up on the cover.

After the other Andy left the hospital, I opened the magazine. The cover image turned out to be a teaser for a feature story about Nissin Food Products that began with a two-page spread. On the left side, a chart showed the meteoric rise of Nissin's sales, from near zero in 1958—when the company introduced the world's first package of instant ramen—to nearly $3 billion. On the right side of the spread, a bowl of noodle soup with an egg on top hovered above the face of an old Asian man. The hair that remained on the sides of the man's head was white, and his skin was peppered with age spots. He wore dark sunglasses, a black suit, and an expensive-looking gold tie. His mouth was open, as if he had been discussing something very exciting. A caption identified the man as Momofuku Ando, chairman of Nissin Food Products, and the inventor of instant ramen.

Until that moment, I had never heard of Ando, and I didn't know anything about Nissin except that, when I lived in Japan, I used to see Arnold Schwarzenegger in the company's commercials. In one of them, he wore a kimono and performed the traditional tea ceremony ritual, but instead of pouring hot water into a teacup, he ladled it into a container of Cup Noodles. (Nissin dropped the *O'* from the American product name in 1993; henceforth, so will I.) I was surprised, therefore, to learn that there was an inventor of instant ramen, and that he had not invented it until he was forty-eight years old.

There were many interesting facts about Ando in the article. Just prior to inventing instant ramen, for instance, he had been the head of an Osaka credit association that lent money to small businesses. After a spate of bad loans, the association went bankrupt, costing him nearly all of his personal assets. Then, for reasons not fully explained in the story, Ando built a wooden shack in his backyard, filled it with cooking equipment, and spent most of 1957 and part of 1958 in the shack. He repeatedly steamed noodles, dried them, and poured hot water over them, but he produced only failure after failure. "I thought and thought about how to do it right," the article quoted Ando saying. "I thought so hard that I began to piss blood." His eureka moment came while watching his wife prepare a batch of tempura in boiling hot oil. When he dipped his noodles into the same hot oil, Ando found that frying not only dried them but also left the noodles with small holes that made them highly absorbent. This was before flavor packets, so Ando sprayed chicken stock onto the noodles before frying. He settled on chicken as the soup flavoring because his youngest son, Koki, liked it. Either Ando didn't know how to spell *chicken* or he simply transliterated back the Japanese transliteration of the English word. When his invention went on sale on August 25, 1958, the package said CHIKIN RAMEN in Roman letters across the top.

The article also explained that Ando had invented the cup of Cup Noodles, which Nissin began selling in 1971, and that it was partly the result of a dream that he had one night in the late 1960s. In 1999, Nissin erected a museum dedicated to the invention of instant ramen across the street from Ando's house; the centerpiece was a full-scale replica of his backyard shack. A photograph on page 37 of *Nikkei Business*—showing a man boiling water over a campfire—turned out be a scene from an annual Nissin retreat. Every summer, newly promoted managers gathered on Futonjima, a deserted island in the Inland Sea of Japan, where they lived for three days and two nights and ate little more than Chikin Ramen. On Futonjima the managers made fires by rubbing sticks together, and they dug their own latrines. Ando's son Koki, who has been Nissin's CEO since 1985, explained in an interview that such measures taught employees to get in touch with their true desires and to express those through new ramen products (as his father had done), even if their ideas seemed outlandish at first. "Only weird people can create something new and interesting," Koki said in the story. "Right now Nissin's weirdo-to-normal-person ratio is about one in ten. I'm trying to up that to around two in ten. Any higher, it could become difficult to manage the company."

The story ended with a sidebar—under the heading "Your Enemy Is Within"—about how Nissin forced the managers of its various product lines to compete head-to-head for resources. The internal competition was credited with inspiring successes such as the now-famous "egg pocket." When the Chikin Ramen brand manager noticed old men cracking raw eggs on top of their noodles, he introduced a concave well in the noodle brick that kept the yolks from running. Sales skyrocketed.

Josh, my editor, had lived briefly in Tokyo as a child, so he was always up for sending me on reporting trips to Japan. He liked stories with counterintuitive management lessons, and Nissin seemed to offer them in spades. Still, a question lingered in my mind.

Why would a man who ran a credit association, after losing nearly everything, spend a year in a shack trying to invent instant noodles?

With the help of a nurse, I wheeled my IV to a cubicle outside my room, using one of the hospital's PCs to access the Nissin Web site. I found an e-mail address for the Nissin public relations department and downloaded a free kanji font so I could type in Japanese. While studying at International Christian University, I once spent a week memorizing the seasonal greetings that appear in the first lines of formal Japanese business letters. I chose one for early March.

Greetings.
Even in the black soil, one can sense the onset of spring.
I am a journalist working for a nationally published business magazine in the United States. Lately, I have been reading about Nissin's chairman

and founder, Momofuku Ando, and I would very much like to interview him for a story about the history of Nissin and instant ramen. Would it be possible to arrange an interview in June? I can travel to Japan anytime during that month.

Sincerely,

Andy Raskin

The hospital sent me home and I rested in bed for several days. When I finally got back to my office at the business magazine, an e-mail reply from Nissin was waiting.

Mr. Andy Raskin:

Thank you for your interest in Nissin. Can you please tell me, exactly what do you want?

Hisanori Yamazaki

Public Relations Department

Nissin Food Products Co., Ltd.

Had I not been clear enough in the previous e-mail? I sent another.

Dear Mr. Yamazaki:

These days, one can certainly smell the chrysanthemums.

Thank you for your reply.

I would very much like to write an article about Nissin for my business magazine, which is published nationally in the United States. Toward that end, I was hoping to interview Momofuku Ando about his invention of instant ramen and about the history of your company. If possible, I'd also like to speak with your current CEO, Koki Ando, and some other senior executives. (Can you recommend folks who have a good perspective on Nissin's current strategy?) Finally, I read the recent article about Nissin in *Nikkei Business*, and I was fascinated to learn about your management training retreat on the deserted island in the Inland Sea of Japan. Would it be possible for me to attend?

Sincerely,

Andy Raskin

After a few weeks, Yamazaki had not written back. He had included a phone number in his e-mail signature, so I called and left a message, but he never returned the call. Finally, I asked a Japanese researcher in my magazine's Tokyo bureau to contact him for me.

Not long after that, I got an e-mail from the researcher.

"He hasn't written back to me either," she wrote. "Honestly, I've never seen anything like this."

Dear Momofuku,

A year after I moved to San Francisco to become CEO of the start-up company, the venture capitalists asked me to resign. There were many reasons for this, including their desire to quickly earn a tenfold return on their investment, the end of the dot-com boom, and our agreement from the start that we would eventually hire someone with more Silicon Valley clout. But I can't help thinking that another reason was that I had been spending virtually all of my time on America Online, substituting "San Francisco" for "New York" in the member directory.

While drawing up budgets and financial plans, I would send messages to women I had met through the member directory. While making presentations to the board of directors or talking with customers or employees, I would be thinking about whether I had a date that night and wondering how it was going to go. I still approached women at parties and in coffee shops, and I began playing the trombone in a funk band, which became another way to meet people. Some of these encounters were one-night stands, but most were up-and-up dates that occasionally led to months-long relationships (during which I was always unfaithful). It's amazing that I functioned at work at all, not to mention as a chief executive officer.

When the venture capitalists asked me to step down, I hired my own replacement, and then quit with a six-month severance package. Arranging and going on dates began taking more of my time, and virtually everything else in my life fell away. I lost touch with most of my old friends, especially male friends, who were getting married and starting families. I barely spoke to my parents, and on the rare occasions when I visited them in Long Island, I would tell them I was going out at night with my high school friends Dave and Dan and Sam when really I was going out with women I had met online.

Shortly before leaving the company, I began seeing a therapist. She had an office on Divisadero Street, and I would see her during my lunch hour twice a week. I would sit on the edge of her couch and tell her how depressed I was. I would talk about how I was a failure and how I was not accomplishing anything in my life and how I was afraid I would never live up to my potential. Again, I did not connect these feelings to the lack of integrity in my relationships. In fact, if I spoke to the therapist about women at all, it was to let her know that I had fallen head over heels for somebody new, or that things hadn't worked out and I was moving on. She would say, "You talk about the end of your relationships as if they were minor inconveniences, as if you were describing something as meaningless as walking out the wrong door of a movie theater." For a long time, I told her nothing about the cheating or the fact that I was meeting a different woman practically every night through online dating sites. I was hiding it from myself, so I guess it was only natural that I hid it from her.

When the severance package ran out, I began selling freelance articles to several business magazines, and one of them offered me a full-time staff position. The editor in chief gave me a small office, where I spent hours trading e-mails with women I met online. I discovered Craigslist, a free Web site with an extensive area for online personal ads that made it even easier to meet women. I usually posted ads with the title "Grab Some Sushi Tonight?" I would take dates to an out-of-the-way sushi bar where I knew the owners, an elderly couple that had given me a special nickname to make reservations. I would probably still be doing that if not for what happened next. It began only three months ago, so I remember more of the details. I'll explain as best I can.

It started when I wrote an article about a record company in San Francisco. The company produced music CDs for chain stores—albums like Pottery Barn: Summer in the City *and* Eddie Bauer Legends of Soul. *The executive I profiled invited me to his annual Christmas party, and the night of the party, I drove to his office in my blue Volkswagen Beetle. This was less than two weeks after I had undergone surgery to remove my infected gallbladder, so my body still felt weak. I remember wearing jeans and a dark blue Emporio Armani shirt.*

The office's interior was a throwback to dot-com chic. The walls were exposed brick and had been decorated with old album covers. Three of the company's conference rooms had been outfitted with their own bars and appetizer tables, and a deejay was spinning records in the hall. Men wore Banana Republic dress shirts of a shade known around Silicon Valley as "biz-dev" blue. I meandered through the rooms, dividing my time at the various appetizer tables so as not to look like a pig. I chatted for a while with the executive I had profiled.

"Loved your article," he said.

We were still chatting when a woman with dark skin and long black hair walked into the party. She was pretty in a tomboyish way, and her head was cocked in a manner that suggested readiness to pick a fight. She began talking to a tall man with bushy sideburns. Did she know this sideburns man? Were they together? I tried to figure it out. From across the room I heard her laughing at the sideburns man's jokes. It was a nasal chuckle, but I found it endearing, maybe because I was listening to it while admiring the way her black T-shirt hugged her chest. What was her relationship to the sideburns man? No, I concluded, she was not with him, and sure enough he said good-bye to her in a just-friends way and left the party. I told the executive that I needed another drink, and when I returned I maneuvered myself to a position just a few feet from the woman. For ten minutes I stood next to her, nursing a plastic cup of chardonnay and trying to think of something to say. She spoke first.

"So you just stand near people you like?"

"Sorry?"

"You just get close enough so they get uncomfortable and have to talk to you?"

I pretended not to understand.

"The 'hover technique.' That's what you should call it."

"Maybe I was hovering a little."

Her name, she said, was Amanda.

"So," she asked, "which ones do you own?"

"Huh?"

"The records on the wall. Which ones do you own?"

"Oh—"

"No," she interrupted. "Lemme guess." She motioned with her chin toward the Rolling Stones' Sticky Fingers.

"I'm sorry," I said, imitating a TV game show announcer. "Don Pardo, tell her what she'll be taking home as a consolation prize."

The nasal chuckle again. "OK, so which ones?"

I pointed to Signed, Sealed & Delivered.

"Nice."

I admitted that I only had it on CD.

"I'll accept that," Amanda said, and from the way she said it, I decided to ask for her phone number. She gave it to me, and I handed her my business card.

"Senior Writer," she said, reading the title. "OK, Senior Writer. Call me."

Our first date was dinner at a tapas restaurant in the Mission District. I ordered paella and fried plantains. I remember not knowing what to do with my arms. I tried putting them on the table. I tried putting them in my lap. Back on the table. I learned that she worked in public relations for the National Football League, and that she was constantly traveling around the country for promotional events. Often she was accompanied by famous football players. I found this attractive, but also intimidating. "Jamal Lewis says I have a nice butt," she told me over dinner. It wasn't Jamal Lewis, but another football player whose name I can't remember. Sipping sangria, she listed her favorite activities, which included triathlons and long bicycle rides. "Basically, I'm looking for a guy who can keep up with me," she said, and right then I wanted very much to keep up with her. She said that whenever she felt depressed, *she would repeat her father's mantra, "Positive, positive, positive!" Her parents had moved to Fort Lauderdale, where her father, a former salesman, ran a stickball league for retirees. He sent out an e-mail newsletter every month with statistics about the league—team standings, runs batted in, earned run averages.*

"So, tell me more about you, Senior Writer."

I wondered if the fact that she already had a nickname for me meant that she needed shorthand to keep track of all the men who were trying to keep up with her.

I told her who I thought I was, which means that I told her about the company I had founded, and that I used to be a management consultant and that I had an MBA. I told her that I played the trombone in a funk band, and that I could speak Japanese.

"I hope this doesn't bother you," she said, "but of all the places I want to visit in the world, Japan is not very high on my list."

By this point, Momofuku, I had so little idea of who I was that I pretended the rank of Japan on her travel wish list wasn't an issue. I changed the subject, commenting on her accent.

"Are you from New York, Amanda?"

"Westchester. You?"

"Brooklyn. Then, when I was twelve, we moved to Long Island."

"My dad grew up in Brooklyn. Did you play stickball?"

In my part of Brooklyn (or maybe it was just in my generation), stickball was not as popular as stoopball and punchball. We played some stickball, but not that much.

"We played stickball all the time," I said.

She smiled.

"If things work out, Senior Writer, maybe you can pinch-hit one day in the league."

I kissed her later that night, and in the future that I imagined, we would do triathlons and go on long bike rides. She would introduce me to famous football players, and we would visit her parents in Florida. I would play stickball with her father, hitting mostly triples and home runs. The next thing I remember about Amanda is waking up in her bed. I think it was two weeks later.

"What's your favorite book, Senior Writer?"

Shota's Sushi *had usurped the top spot from* Cooking Papa, *and* Ramen Discovery Legend *was rising fast in my rankings.*

"Don Quixote."

"What's so great about it?"

I told her about how it was funny, and about the meta stuff.

"What's yours?"

She pointed to a title in her bookcase across the room. It was the chick-lit best seller Good in Bed.

"What's so great about that one?"

"It's just so much like my life. It feels really real."

I wanted very much to know about her life, and I thought that maybe I could read about it in the book.

"Can I borrow it?"

The next day, she flew to Las Vegas for an NFL event. I gave her twenty dollars and told her to bet it on red at the roulette table. At night, my phone rang.

"Sorry, Senior Writer. It landed on black."

She sounded slightly drunk.

"It's OK," I said.

Slot machines churned in the background.

"Did you read Good in Bed*?" she asked.*

"Just the first chapter."

"What did you think?"

I wasn't getting into it. But I felt that I should like a book that was like her life.

"I like it."

"You don't sound like you like it."

"I like it."

"Tell me, Senior Writer. Do you think you're good in bed?"

The question caught me totally off guard, and I realized there was no good way to answer it. If I said that I was good in bed, then I would sound conceited. If I said I was bad, then I would sound like I lacked confidence. Truth is, I had been having a problem in that area. After the gallbladder surgery, a kidney stone began wending its way through my ureter, and my urologist had prescribed Vicodin to dull the pain. Between the stone and the heavy doses of Vicodin, I wasn't functioning normally. An old friend who's a psychiatrist offered to send me some Viagra samples, and I had been taking them for a couple of weeks. I was too ashamed to tell Amanda.

"It's not whether I'm good," I said, "but whether we are. A couple is good or not good in bed, not an individual person."

"Well, I don't think I'm good in bed," she said.

Looking back, it was an opening, a moment when she had lowered her defenses and admitted that she was afraid of something. But I had no idea how to respond to such a thing. Or maybe I was afraid that if I did respond, she might return to her question about whether I was good in bed. So I didn't say anything about it, and made an excuse to get off the phone.

We had been dating for two months when she invited me to a ski house near Lake Tahoe that she rented with several friends. We made the four-hour drive in her Jetta on Saturday morning, and skied at Alpine Meadows in the afternoon. We bought groceries at a supermarket in Truckee, and in the kitchen I made tomato sauce and meatballs. The first night it was just the two of us, so after dinner we had sex on the brown, L-shaped sofa in the living room.

"Do you think anyone can see in?" she asked in the middle.

I looked behind me at the large, open window across the room.

"The houses are pretty far apart," I said, "and the snow is piled high next to that window. Would you feel better if we went into the bedroom?"

"No," she said. "I like this."

It was the one moment I remember feeling close to her.

The next morning, I awoke alone, and when I got out of bed, a large man walked up behind me. Fully clothed, he began thrusting his hips toward me. "Yo, Andy, welcome to the house!" he said. It was Amanda's friend Hadman, and he was mock buttfucking me.

Momofuku, mock buttfucking is what some straight guys do to show they like each other. It's so fake gay that you *aren't gay, but you still get to express your feelings for one another. I used to do it with my high school friends—Dan and Dave and Sam—when we got together during college vacations. Still, I wasn't into it with Hadman because it was one thing to do that with your high school friends but quite another to have it done to you at seven in the morning by a six-foot-three, overweight stranger who has just arrived in Lake Tahoe. Nevertheless, I tried to play along. Hadman was being friendly, and I wanted to show Amanda that I could be buddy-buddy with her guy friends the way I always saw guys being buddy-buddy with each other on re-ality TV shows like* The Real World.

"Hey, Hadman. How's it going?"

"Dude, you keepin' up with her?"

"Tryin'."

Hadman finally left the room. I got into the shower and tried to forget what happened. Where was Amanda? She must have been making breakfast in the kitchen. I got dressed and went out to the living room. Amanda and Had-man were sitting at a long dining table, eating eggs and bacon.

"See those two snowdrifts out there?" Hadman said. He was pointing with his fork at two white mounds outside the window. "We call those Sarah."

I poured some orange juice into a glass, joining them at the table. "Why Sarah?"

"She's a gal in the house," Amanda explained. "Really big boobs. Hadman thinks the snowdrifts are the exact shape of her chest. He wants to date her, but I keep telling him, 'Sorry, dude, not going to happen.'"

"We'll see," Hadman said. "We'll see."

Hadman had brought along his dog, a hulking Labrador mutt. I tried to pet him, but he drooled on my foot.

"Oh, man, we had so much fun last weekend," Hadman said to Amanda. "You were crazy!"

Crazy?

Amanda and Hadman began reminiscing about the weekend before. I felt so left out, but I also felt that I would not look like a guy who could keep up if I admitted feeling left out, so I didn't ask them to change the topic or include me. As Hadman related the story—it involved a dance club and booze and a band—he kept sprinkling in the word bitch. He pronounced it "beeyotch." Sometimes he would say it looking at Amanda.

"Beeyotch!"

And she would say it back to him.

"Beeyotch!"

Finally, he said it while looking at me.

"Beeyotch!"

He was expecting me to say it back to him, but I couldn't say it. I just sat there thinking about what a great time Amanda must have had the weekend before, and how what she really wanted was to be with a man who enjoyed saying "Beeyotch!" What was wrong with me that I couldn't be that kind of man? She wanted a guy who could get mock buttfucked by strangers and be OK with that. I pretended to laugh at Hadman's jokes. Amanda was howling. Her laugh seemed less charming now. I was mad at her, but I had no idea why. I thought that maybe it was the Vicodin. Or maybe I knew why, but I was too afraid to acknowledge it.

I had been silent for so long at breakfast that when we retreated to the bedroom to change into our ski clothes, Amanda knew I was upset.

"Are you mad at me?" she asked.

"No. I think it's the Vicodin."

"You are mad at me. You know, he's not even a close friend of mine. I'm just humoring him."

I denied again being mad, which made me even madder.

"Maybe we should skip skiing today and go home," I said.

She heaved her ski boot off of her leg and threw it on the floor. She didn't look at me.

"Fine."

We packed our bags and loaded them into her car. Hadman waved good-bye, and I was embarrassed because he must have known we had gotten into a fight over the fact that I couldn't handle him. It was a long ride. Amanda didn't make it any easier by playing a cassette tape of James Taylor singing "Fire and Rain." I thought about how she was always so confident and how tight her abs were and how I liked the shape of her breasts under her T-shirt and how I would never see them again. "We're going to be together in this car for four hours," she said. "Can we just pretend to like each other?" She had a great job and friends like Hadman, and she didn't need me. We didn't say anything else the whole way home.

After she dropped me off, I called my sister, who still lives in Long Island. I told her what had happened and that it looked like it was the end of things between Amanda and me.

"This doesn't sound like the end," my sister said. "It just doesn't."

Amanda talked to her friends, and they must have said something similar, because she wanted to give our relationship another shot. I did, too, because all I had been thinking about since she dropped me off was how I couldn't keep up with her and how I wished I could figure out what was wrong with me.

The next weekend she went to the ski house but didn't invite me, and that night I placed an ad on Craigslist. This was just a few weeks ago. The title of the ad was "Sushi Tonight?" and the woman who responded was Cathy, a petite twenty-four-year-old Chinese American with a beautiful body and an Ivy League degree. We met for dinner at Sushi Groove South, a sushi restaurant that has a deejay. Over dinner, I asked Cathy if she cared about the age difference between us.

"I'm not an ageist," she said. "Just as long ask you don't need Viagra."

As she laughed, I excused myself to swallow one in the restroom. Later, as I was taking my clothes off in Cathy's apartment, I remembered that Amanda had once said, "You can't eat off a broken plate." She meant that once one person in a couple cheated, the relationship was doomed. I tried not to think about that. I tried not to think about anything at all.

The next week, Amanda e-mailed me a video of a man playing the trombone while dancing in a sexy way. Above the link she had written, "Can you play trombone like he can?" I saw it as a chance to prove that I could keep up. Maybe I was just feeling guilty. I grabbed my trombone and a James Brown CD and drove to her apartment. I put the CD into her CD player and skipped to the song "Papa Don't

Take No Mess." It starts with a solo by Fred Wesley, James Brown's longtime trombonist.

Amanda sat on her couch, watching. "Show me what you got!"

I pulled my horn out of its case, screwed together the bell and slide sections, and slipped in the Bach 7 mouthpiece. Then I tried to do a striptease while trombone-synching along with Fred Wesley. I slid my trombone slide when Fred slid his, and tried to move my hips like the guy in the video. But I was too self-conscious, and not very sexy. I got my jeans partly off, but I was too embarrassed to go further. I went to the couch to kiss Amanda; she didn't seemed turned on. Mostly, she looked sorry for me. The next weekend, she left for Lake Tahoe again. I was researching a magazine story in my apartment when my doorbell rang.

"Buzz me up, Senior Writer."

She had come home early from the ski house. I thought it was because she missed me, but it was because she wanted to break up with me.

"I feel like you're not really there," Amanda said. "I think you have some things to work on before you can be in a relationship."

I pretended not to know what she was talking about, and asked her to reconsider. I sat down on the sofa in my living room. Amanda tried to hug me, but I pushed her away.

"You don't have to get violent," she said.

Soon after, Amanda walked out the door, and when she was gone, Momofuku, do you know what I thought about? I thought about how I would never get to play stickball with her father. And there was something so horrible about that, something that made me feel so alone in the world, that I posted an ad on Craigslist with the title "Drinks Tonight?" A serious woman who spoke fluent Italian and worked in human resources responded, and all we did was have a drink, but after the date, I still felt this unbearable loneliness. The next day, I posted another Craigslist ad, and it didn't help. The day after that, when I sat on the couch for my therapy session, I talked about feeling so incredibly alone, and then, for the first time, I talked about the Craigslist ads and the America Online member directory and how I had dated Harue and Kim at the same time, and how I always cheated in relationships. I talked about everything I've told you, Momofuku, though in even less detail because I had only fifty minutes.

"What is wrong with me?" I asked the therapist.

She talked for a while, and then she told me to copy down an address.

Sincerely,
Andy

I set my alarm for six thirty to make sure I had enough time. I left my apartment and smelled the San Francisco spring air. It reminded me of summer camp.

My sixth letter to the inventor of instant ramen ended with me scribbling down an address, so I'll fill in what happened after that. The address was on Dolores Street in the Mission District, and when I got there I was standing in front of a church. Except for its green spire, the church blended in neatly with the Victorian-style houses around it.

I parked my car and walked up three cement steps to a big white door. I turned around to see if anyone was watching. I felt self-conscious standing near a church, and by a weird coincidence this church was diagonally across the street from a bar in which Hadman was an investor. Amanda sometimes worked there as a guest bartender. It was early in the morning and therefore unlikely that anyone was in the bar, but I imagined that Amanda and Hadman were spying on me from inside it, laughing.

A sign to the left of the big white door said RING BELL over an arrow pointing to a button. I pressed the button, and a chime rang inside. I waited for what seemed like an eternity, but was probably five seconds. When the door opened, a woman's face peeked out. She was around fifty-five years old, with short white hair and rosy cheeks.

"Come on in," she said.

"Is this . . . ?"

"Yes."

One of the things I've thought about more than anything is whether I should say the name of the group that met at the church. I've thought about it for months, maybe years. I've thought about it so much because I want to be truthful. But I've decided that it might be best if I don't say the name, and I hope I can be forgiven for that. What I'll say is that there were twelve people sitting on sofas and chairs in what looked like the church's social room (a floor below the chapel), and that I sat on one of the sofas and listened. Some of the people spoke about an obsessive quality to their romantic lives. Some spoke about the guilt of cheating on their husbands, wives, girlfriends or boyfriends, yet how they were powerless to stop. All of them spoke about the horror not only of betraying people they cared about, but of having lost a sense of who they were.

They spoke for nearly an hour about things I had thought were unspeakable.

When it was over, the woman who greeted me at the door said, "That's all the time we have. Is anyone available to mentor newcomers?"

A man who looked in his early forties raised his hand.

"My name is Matt. If you're looking for a mentor, come talk to me."

People began rearranging the sofas into a neat square and stacking bridge chairs in the back of the room. I approached Matt, but I didn't know what to say.

"You looking for a mentor?" he asked.

"I don't know. I think so."

"OK," Matt said. "I'll tell you what. Put away some chairs."

Close up, Matt looked like a hardened version of Sean Penn, but his demeanor reminded me of Mr. Miyagi, the karate master played by Noriyuki "Pat" Morita in *The Karate Kid*. Put away chairs. *Wax on, wax off.* I put away some chairs and went back to Matt.

"What time do you have to be at work?" he asked.

It was Thursday, which meant I had to get to the magazine for Josh's weekly story meeting.

"I have about half an hour."

"Let's grab coffee."

I slung my laptop bag over my shoulder, and we left the church. Matt walked so quickly along Dolores Street that I had a hard time keeping up. There was a tightness about his face; his jaw muscles seemed perpetually engaged, even when he wasn't talking. He was under six feet, like me, and he wore a gray sweatshirt, dark jeans, and off-brand sneakers. He led me across the street to a café, where we each ordered a coffee drink. We sat down on a worn-out brown sofa by the front window. Next to us, a girl with tattooed shoulders was typing on a laptop. Matt must have sensed I was afraid she would overhear us.

"Don't worry about her," he said. "She's probably absorbed in her own problems."

"OK." I was still uncomfortable.

"So tell me why you're here."

I tried to summarize everything about Amanda and Kim and Maureen and Harue and how I felt so alone, but I didn't think I was making much sense.

"I can relate to that," Matt said.

"You can?"

"Listen, I was alone for most of my life. And I hurt a lot of people. I'm not proud of that."

"How did you change?"

"We're talking about you today. I'll be your mentor. But you'll have to do some things that I ask."

A few nights earlier, I had watched a movie called *Samurai Trilogy I: Musashi Miyamoto*. I had never watched a samurai movie in my life, and the only reason I watched this one was that it had popped up in the "Movies You'll ♥" list on my video rental store's Web site. The main character is a young man named Takezo, played by Toshiro Mifune. He's a fearsome but unruly warrior with little connection to those around him. His fellow villagers become convinced he's a menace, so they hunt him in the forest, rounding up his relatives so he'll turn himself in. But before the villagers find Takezo, a Buddhist priest builds a fire in the woods and cooks a hearty stew, luring Takezo with the aroma of a hot meal.

> *Priest: How's the food?*
> *Takezo: (devouring the stew) Why did you come?*
> *Priest: To capture you, of course. How about it? If you give yourself up to a priest, they'll probably treat you like a human being.*
> *Takezo: No way!*
> *Priest: Son, do you think you can win like this?*
> *Takezo: Of course!*
> *Priest: (chuckling) You're going to defeat everyone, even yourself. Is that it?*
> *Takezo: I'm not afraid to die! As long as I take some of them with me.*
> *Priest: What about your relatives? They're suffering because of you.*
> *Takezo: Let them die!*
> *Priest: What about the beautiful women?*
> *Takezo: I don't care!*
> *Priest: And their little children?*
> *Takezo: Shut up! I don't care! Let them die . . . (bawls)*
> *Priest: (whipping Takezo) You idiot! I beat you with the hand of your ancestors!*

The priest ties up Takezo with some rope. Then he walks Takezo back to his temple and throws the rope over a high tree branch, hoisting Takezo in the air so that he's dangling, bound around his chest, from the tree. Takezo hangs there, alive, for several days.

I asked Matt, "What kinds of things?"

"First," he said, "you'll have to stop dating for a while."

I wondered what he meant by "a while."

"No dates and no sex for ninety days."

I thought about Matt's request. In my adult life, barely a day had gone by in which I wasn't in—or in pursuit of—a romantic relationship. Three months seemed like an eternity. I could not imagine it.

"Are you kidding?"

"You can probably find another mentor who won't demand this of you," Matt said.

A beautiful woman named Otsu takes pity on Takezo, releasing him from the tree. She helps him escape, so the villagers capture her as bait. Thinking she's being held in a castle, Takezo scales the castle wall searching for her. The priest, spotting Takezo on the wall, offers to lead him to Otsu. But instead, the priest guides Takezo to a small room filled with books; as soon as Takezo enters, the priest slams and locks the door, making Takezo his prisoner.

> **Priest:** (*speaking from behind the door*) *Takezo, in this room, you will become a new man.*
> **Takezo:** *No! Get me out of here!*
> **Priest:** *Otsu will wait for as many years as it takes. In this room, there are many things for you to learn. When you have mastered them, we shall speak again. I leave you, wild fool!*

Three years later, Takezo emerges from the castle as a noble samurai warrior named Musashi Miyamoto.

"OK, I'll do it," I said.

Matt gave me his phone number.

"Call me at least once every day. Just check in, tell me how you're doing. Also, I'm going to give you a writing assignment."

"What kind of writing assignment?"

"Do you believe in God?"

As a kid I sometimes went to synagogue for holiday services. I had even gone to Hebrew school and had a Bar Mitzvah. But I didn't really believe in God. The only time I ever prayed was during the baseball play-offs, when the New York Yankees were losing and I asked Him to help them. Sometimes I would propose deals with God. My standard offer was a promise never to masturbate again, in exchange for a Yankee comeback. I would look at the Yankees in the batter's box, and if their helmets looked a little shinier, then that was God's signal that the deal was on. The Yankees pulled off miraculous victories, but I never held up my end of the bargain.

"Not really," I said.

"Listen, God for our purposes doesn't have to be the old man in the sky. He or She or It can be anyone. Or anything. Just as long as you can believe that this person or thing has your best interests at heart. Is there anyone who can be God for you?"

Just thinking about Matt's question embarrassed me. I glanced over at the girl typing on her laptop to make sure she wasn't listening.

"Come on," Matt urged. "Anyone."

"Momofuku Ando."

I just blurted it out, but somehow it seemed right.

Matt accepted the name without hesitation, even though he couldn't pronounce it. "Momojuku Condo. OK!"

"Momofuku," I corrected him. "Ando."

"Momofuku Ando. Right. So, you'll write letters to Momofuku Ando this week."

"Letters?"

"Write to him about your past relationships. Anything you think is relevant. Be sure to include everything you can remember, and write a letter every day."

The whole thing sounded ridiculous.

"I'm supposed to write letters to Momofuku Ando about my past relationships? And then what?"

"We'll meet on Saturday afternoon in Dolores Park, and you'll read me what you wrote."

"That's it? Just write letters and read them to you and I'm going to change?"

"No. The letters are just so you can see the scope of your behavior, so you can get it all down on paper. After that, we'll work on changing. OK?"

I didn't know what else to do.

"OK."

Matt got up to leave, but then he stopped.

"By the way, who is Momofuku Ando?"

"I read about him in a Japanese magazine. He invented instant ramen."

"You mean like Top Ramen?"

"Yes, that's one of his brands. He also invented the cup. You know, Cup Noodles."

Matt laughed all the way out of the coffee shop.

PART II

MOMOFUKU AND ME

A VERY BRIEF HISTORY OF MOMOFUKU ANDO, PART 1:
HALLEY'S COMET

To understand how the inventor of instant ramen helped me change, it would be useful to know something about his life. No better place to start than Halley's Comet.

You see, the baby who would grow up to invent instant ramen was born on March 5, 1910. That year, Halley's Comet made one of its near-Earth flybys. To most people, this was nothing more than a coincidence.

Nissin Food Products, however, has always made a big deal about the connection. For example, on the page devoted to Ando's birth in the catalog to the Instant Ramen Invention Museum, an illustration shows an icy white ball zooming past Earth. The entire planet is covered in clouds except for a small clearing, through which sparkling dust from the comet's tail gently settles over Japan.

There's no doubt about it. Nissin means to suggest that Ando— and maybe instant ramen itself—was sent from above.

*A*round the time I started to shave, I would stare at myself in the bathroom mirror and wonder what I was going to look like in the twenty-first century. In those days, my favorite TV show was a science fiction series about a permanent manned station on the moon. Everyone on the show carried laser weapons shaped like staple guns, and one of the characters was an alien woman who could morph into whatever animal she wanted. The show was called *Space: 1999*, which made the twenty-first century seem very far away.

In the version of my future I would see while staring in the mirror, I was always posing for a family portrait. My future wife was standing next to me, and in front of us our two children. My wife was of average height, thin, with dark hair, but I couldn't make out any features of her face. I couldn't see the children's faces very clearly either, but I could tell that one was male, one female. My future self's hair was shorter than mine in the mirror, and he wore glasses. He seemed dependable, honest, strong. Normal. The head of a family. Which is to say, when I imagined myself as an adult, I saw a man who was very much like my father. Of course, as it turned out, I was not much better than the writers of *Space: 1999* at predicting the future. Because in the early years of the twenty-first century, humans had not yet stepped foot again on the moon, and I was single, reading letters addressed to the inventor of instant ramen aloud in Dolores Park.

We sat near the top of the big sloping green. Matt listened from a few feet away, chewing on a blade of grass. He bobbed forward and back, as if to release energy that might build up and explode if he sat still. While I read the letters, he stared out over the Mission District rooftops toward the downtown skyscrapers. On a clearer day, he could have seen all the way across the bay to the loading docks in Oakland. Every once in a while, a white bulldog ran by, its jowls dripping, in pursuit of a just-launched tennis ball. Couples—some gay, some straight—lay on blankets around us. Like Dolores Street (at the bottom of the hill), Dolores Park was dotted with palm trees, the result of a post-1906-earthquake attempt to dress up the neighborhood. When I first moved to the city, I hated the palm trees because they seemed out of place. But now their out-of-placeness was exactly what made them beautiful.

"Read that part again," Matt said.

It was the part about cheating on Harue with women I had met through the America Online member directory. Matt closed his eyes, bowing his head while I reread the section. When I reached the end a second time, he opened his eyes.

"Put a star next to that passage," he said.

I drew an asterisk in the margin of my notebook. It felt good to have Matt not only listen but also give me this kind of mysterious instruction.

While reading the last letter, the one about Amanda, I began thinking about the differences between Matt and me. In particular, I felt ashamed that I was rich enough to afford a weekend at a Lake Tahoe ski house yet all I could do was complain about it. Was he thinking of me as a spoiled brat who made too much of my problems? Our daily phone calls were usually about me, but Matt had begun sharing glimpses of his life. He had been homeless for part of his adulthood, and he had battled an addiction to alcohol. He had gotten sober a few years before we met, and he was working as a counselor at a rehabilitation clinic. He rented an apartment, but it was above an all-night S&M club, so he rarely got much sleep. I had never interacted with anyone like him, let alone shared with such a person the intimate details of my life.

When I got to the part about the ski house, Matt asked me to put a star next to that section, too, and to reread it.

"I once met a guy like Hadman," he said when I was done. "Down in the Tenderloin." The Tenderloin is a San Francisco neighborhood with a tough reputation. "And this guy was about twice as big as me, and he said some nasty stuff. So I felt the way you felt, but in my case I used to carry a gun."

I was afraid to ask, but I asked.

"Did you shoot him?"

Matt pulled up another blade of grass, sticking it in his mouth with the first one.

"You don't want to know about that. I did a lot of bad things."

It struck me that the letters to Ando were not only the story of how things had gone very wrong in my romantic life, but also the story of how two seemingly very different men wound up sitting next to each other in Dolores Park.

After I read the last letter, we sat silently on the grass. The wind picked up, rustling the papers of my notebook.

Matt was the first to speak.

"How was that for you?"

I thought back over the previous week. Every night, after I came home from work, I had gone straight to a coffee shop and written a letter to Ando. When writing articles for the business magazine, I would agonize for days over the wording of single paragraphs. But these letters, once I got going, practically poured out of me.

How was it for me? If you had asked me before writing the letters if I was an honest man, I would have said yes. If you had asked me how I treated people—especially those I was close to—I would have said that I treated them very well. If you had asked me if I was living a full life, I would have said yes, and as evidence I would have proffered my career, my funny adventures at Japanese restaurants, and my

MBA. If you had asked me why I was still single, I would have said that I simply hadn't met the right person, and that as soon as I did, I would be so overwhelmed with desire that I would have no trouble remaining faithful to her.

Now I had to admit that the truth was very different. I had lied frequently to people I cared about, and had regularly betrayed them. I had promised myself over and over to stop, but I couldn't stop. My activities and career decisions—nearly every decision in my adult life—had been motivated primarily by the need to meet new women.

"Matt, I feel like maybe I'm a monster."

"You're not a monster, even though you might have done some monstrous things."

Somehow, because Matt said it, I was open to the possibility that it might be true.

"Will I ever be able to have a normal relationship?"

"Only Ando can answer that."

"What?"

"What you need to do now," Matt said, "is turn over your life to Ando."

"What does that mean?"

"Repeat after me," Matt instructed, closing his eyes. "O Momofuku."

In my mind I was already praying—that the couples on the lawn weren't close enough to hear us. I felt like an idiot, and I wondered if Matt was a religious zealot. In my America Online dating profile, in the space for a personal quote, I once wrote, "Control your destiny, or someone else will." I had heard the line in business school, attributed by one of my professors to the management guru Jack Welch. It reflected perfectly my belief that everything in one's life was under one's control. If you wanted badly enough to stop cheating on women, you simply stopped. If you committed not to date or have sex for a certain amount of time, even if it was difficult, you summoned the will to do that. I certainly didn't think that praying—let alone to an old man in Japan—was going to help. But Matt had been nice enough to sign on as my mentor, and I didn't want to upset him. Besides, I didn't know what else to do.

"O Momofuku," I repeated.

"Show me how to live so that I may better do your will."

Matt would later assure me getting kicked out of the sushi bar and getting sick at Ramen Jiro—along with everything that happened next—was all Ando's doing. I've come to believe that he might be right, though it's certainly open to interpretation. What is not, is that shortly after I began praying to Ando, ramen began showing up more and more in my life.

"Show me how to live so that I may better do your will."

*J*apanese bookstores are full of comic books about business. There's one about the life of Konosuke Matsushita, the founder of Panasonic, and another about Carlos Ghosn, the French executive from Renault who rescued Nissan Motor Co. There are comic books about Sony's Akio Morita, and about the origins of 7-Eleven, digital cameras, the bullet train, and the liquid crystal display.

There are several comic book versions of Ando's life story. My favorite, *The Challenges of Nissin Food Products,* begins with Ando's birth. In the opening frames, Ando's paternal grandfather lifts his newborn grandchild up to the night sky, and just then a white object streaks across the stars. Never mind that Halley's Comet wasn't visible to the naked eye until two months later. Edited under the auspices of Nissin, the comic contains other historical distortions. The nameplate on the house in which Ando was born says ANDO, for one, and the house appears to be in Japan.

In fact, Ando makes clear in his first autobiography, *Conception of a Fantastic Idea* (1983), that he was born in Taiwan while the island was under Japanese rule. (China ceded control of Taiwan in 1895 by signing the Treaty of Shimonoseki, ending the Sino-Japanese War.) Ando's family name started out as Wu, and the characters of his first name were pronounced "Bai-fu."

The comic book has not been the only attempt to downplay Ando's Taiwanese lineage. In 2001, *Nihon Keizai Shimbun*—Japan's

Wall Street Journal—made Ando the subject of "My Résumé," a serial column that relates the life stories of historic figures. The following year, the newspaper's publication arm compiled the columns and
released them as a book—*Magic Noodles: The Story of the Invention
of Instant Ramen*. In a preface, Ando states that he had been asked
for his consent to appear in "My Résumé" numerous times over the
years, but that he always refused out of modesty. In the spring of
2001, he was asked again.

> Needless to say, I turned down the offer—until I heard the
> following comment, conveyed to me by a member of my cor-
> porate communications staff:
>
> "Considering that instant ramen is widely seen as one of
> the foremost inventions of the twentieth century, it would
> seem strange if Mr. Ando did not appear in 'My Résumé.'
> People might think he's hiding something from the public."
> The comment was made, according to my staff, by the jour-
> nalist in charge of the "My Résumé" column.
>
> I have nothing to hide or be ashamed of in my life. I have
> done nothing that might make me an object of contempt or
> scorn. This is a fundamental belief that has sustained and
> supported me for ninety-two years.

Ando writes in *Magic Noodles*, "I spent my childhood" in Taiwan,
but all references to his Taiwanese parents are gone. No wonder,
then, that when *The New York Times* ran an obituary about Ando, the
newspaper initially stated that he had been born to Japanese parents
who happened to be living in Taiwan.

The *Times* later published a correction.

*M*att instructed me to keep a small notebook in my pocket at all times, and to write in it when I felt like breaking my commitment. Whenever I wanted to post a personal ad on Craigslist or ask out a woman at a party or in a coffee shop, I was supposed to write a memo to Momofuku Ando describing what else was happening or what I had been thinking about. For the first couple of weeks, I didn't write in the notebook at all. I went to morning meetings at the church nearly every day, but most of the time I was in a state of shock—there were also moments of euphoria—over confronting this part of my life. I couldn't believe that people in the meetings were talking openly about what they were talking about. I wondered what my colleagues at the magazine would have thought if they knew what I was doing before work.

Gradually, though, the cravings came back. It was difficult not to act on them, but I followed Matt's instructions and wrote in the notebook every time. In each entry, I marked the number of days that had passed in my abstinence period.

Momofuku: (17 days) Josh didn't like my story idea. Said it was "facile."

Momofuku: (19 days) I sucked today playing Ultimate Frisbee. Matt said I should try some new activities, especially new activities where women were not the central focus. So I showed up at an Ultimate Frisbee pickup game in Golden Gate Park. I dropped three passes, and one of the guys on my team said, "Maybe we should screen new guys before we let them play." Later I made a great pass that resulted in a score, but no one gave me any credit.

Momofuku: (22 days) I finally got Josh to let me run with my story idea and now I'm sitting here at my desk in my tiny office staring at the computer screen and I don't know what to write. I have no idea. Maybe it was facile.

Momofuku: (22 days) I am sitting around my apartment doing nothing. I have no friends. I'm bored.

Momofuku: (23 days) I just got bawled out by the managing editor. We were in the big story meeting and I was so afraid of being criticized that I said, "Would it be possible if I just said my idea and we moved on to the next person?" The managing editor called me into his office later and told me I was the most conceited person he had ever met and that he had worked with writers who had reason to be conceited but even they weren't as conceited as I was. I really, really want to go on a date tonight.

I noticed that, at least in these first few entries, almost every time I wanted to break my commitment, there had been some conflict. It did not escape me that the conflict usually involved men.

The next appearance of ramen in my life came several weeks later. I'll describe what led up to it, beginning with some entries in my notebook.

Momofuku: (31 days) I am in a coffee shop, and there is a woman at the next table I want to talk to. Just before coming here, my father called. Actually, he left a message on my answering machine. It started with, "Hi, And. It's Dad." He always calls me And, but I knew something was wrong because whenever my parents leave a message, it's always my mother who leaves it. My father spoke in his usual flat, unemotional tone, even though he was telling me that his mother was dead. "It's Grandma Sylvia," he said. "She succumbed to the cancer." I feel guilty because when I heard that Grandma Sylvia was dead, the first thing I thought about was her clam chowder. It was white, but loose, not starchy. The "secret" ingredient was dill, but she used so much of it that it was hardly a secret.

Momofuku: (33 days) Back in Long Island for Grandma Sylvia's funeral. It's two a.m. I am resisting the urge to go down to the den and log on to my mother's computer. Momofuku, if she only knew what I have been writing to you about. She picked me up at Kennedy Airport a couple of hours ago. She was waiting at the baggage claim even though my flight didn't get in until after midnight. The first thing she said was, "Are you hungry?" It was right out of a Woody Allen movie, so I said, "Ma, you sound like you're out of a Woody Allen movie." She said, "Just because I don't want you to starve, that makes me Woody Allen?" I didn't mean that she was Woody Allen, but that she reminded me of the mothers in Woody Allen movies. Whatever. I can't believe she's almost sixty-five. She's in great shape for her age. On the way to the short-term parking lot, she said she had eliminated processed sugars from her diet and that I should do the same. Basically, I think she was telling me to lose *weight. When we got to the parking lot, she led me to her new car. It's an SUV called a GMC Denali. I remarked that the car was huge, and she started rubbing her forehead, which she does when she feels guilty. She said the car was the president's fault, because he had pushed a law through Congress granting a tax break to anyone who purchased small trucks, and the Denali qualified. "It's going to be like $10,000 to buy this car when all is said and done taxwise," my mother told me. "We would have paid $30,000 for any other car we were looking at. So the president gave us no choice. I feel terrible. I want to put a bumper sticker on the back that says, 'The President Made Me Buy It.'" I'm staying in my old room. My parents have painted it blue and put frilly throw pillows on the bed so it looks like a guest room.*

In the morning, when I awoke, Grandpa Walter was standing in front of me. He had been sleeping in my sister's old room.

"Hey, buddy. How's it going?"

I rubbed my eyes. "Grandpa, I'm really sorry."

He seemed not to hear me, and I remembered that he had begun using a hearing aid. His once-broad physique—the product of years of working in machine shops and being on sailboats—had begun to slump.

"Listen, Andrew. Will you drive me to the cemetery?"

In her will, Grandma Sylvia had asked to be cremated and to have her ashes tossed over the Atlantic Ocean. That was because she and Grandpa Walter had spent nearly every summer of their lives sailing, usually off the coast of Brooklyn. When he was in his twenties, my grandfather found a small whaling boat beached in Sheepshead Bay. He took it to his father's metal shop, where he patched a hole in the hull, soldered on a mast, and made a sail out of canvas. He taught himself how to sail, then sold the whaling boat and bought another sailboat. My grandparents would sail north to New England, and as far south as the Caribbean. My father and his brothers grew up sailing, and so did I, though I never really took to it. Even though Grandma Sylvia had asked to be cremated, she had also requested a headstone bearing her name in the family's cemetery plot in Staten Island.

"Sure, Grandpa. I can drive you there."

My parents caught a ride with my uncle and left me the Denali. I backed the "car" out of the garage and onto the driveway, giving Grandpa Walter a hand getting in. As I drove toward the Long Island Expressway, we passed several split-level homes being torn down to make room for new construction. Grandpa Walter muttered a remark about surging real estate prices, and at the mention of money I made a note to write later in my notebook.

Momofuku: (34 days) I was thinking today, while driving Grandpa Walter to the funeral, that after the memorial service I wanted to call Jennifer, in Connecticut. What was I thinking about just before that moment? Grandpa mentioned real estate prices, and then I thought about how I don't own a home and how I'm the first entrepreneurial failure in four Raskin generations.

Max Raskin, Grandpa's father, emigrated from Russia, and with two of his brothers built a business converting horse-drawn carriages into motorized trucks. (To perform a conversion, Max bought a Model T Ford and scrapped everything but the chassis, which he soldered underneath the carriage.) According to the family history, the company, Standard Body Corporation, produced three-quarters of the trucks in metropolitan New York by 1931. When trucks from Ford and General Motors flooded the market, Max secured a niche, converting regular trucks into ice-cream trucks and other specialized vehicles. As a teenager, Grandpa Walter worked in Max's factory, helping

solder miles of copper tubing onto the insides of truck walls;
the interiors were cooled by pumping refrigerants such as
Freon gas through the pipes. Then Walter had a better idea.
He stamped a flow pattern in a metal plate the size of the
truck wall, soldered that to a flat metal sheet, and installed
the assembly in the side of a truck. He got a patent, and
with capital from his father, he founded a company called
Dean Products (named for its address on Brooklyn's Dean
Street), which sold heating and cooling surfaces to everyone
from Budweiser to NASA. My father worked for Dean until
he was forty years old, but he didn't always enjoy working
with his relatives, so he quit. His friend offered to teach my
father the home-building business in exchange for sailing
lessons. Later, my father formed his own, very successful,
real estate development company.

Driving along the expressway, I asked my grandfather a question
I had never asked him before.

"How are you feeling?"

"Whassat?"

The hearing aid. I repeated the question.

My grandfather tilted his head and opened his hand, which is
what he always did when he was sharing important information.

"You know, I went with a lot of girls before I met your grandmother."

This was unexpected and, needless to say, new territory for our
relationship.

"I thought you and Grandma got married when you were
nineteen."

They met on a beach, near Coney Island.

"Well, yeah, that's true. But there were some things before that."

Things?

"In any case," he continued, "when I met Sylvia, I knew that she
was special because it was going to be about more than just sex."

I tried, unsuccessfully, not to imagine my grandparents having intercourse.

"I knew that I could build something with her."

I didn't know what to say. "That's great" was the best I could muster. Ugh.

"It's very important to find that," he advised. "Very important."

We crossed the Verrazano Bridge. The sun was out, but fallen leaves were swirling in the wind. When we got to the cemetery, around twenty people were standing near Grandma Sylvia's headstone—mostly relatives and friends from my grandparents' sailing days. I helped Grandpa Walter out of the car and he joined the other mourners. He gave an unscripted eulogy, repeating the stuff about how he always knew he could build something with my grandmother, but this time he didn't explicitly mention sex. Later, we all had lunch at a nearby diner. I don't remember why, but instead of riding home with me, Grandpa Walter left with someone else, and my parents drove me back to their house in the Denali. On the way, my mother announced that she wanted to be cremated, too, but she didn't care to have her ashes spread anywhere. Rather, she hoped to be split into two urns that my sister and I would keep in our living rooms. I listened to my parents' conversation from the backseat.

"That's a little weird, Jude."

"What's weird?"

"It would be a little weird for them to have you in their living rooms."

"What's weird about that?"

"Where would they put you, on the mantel?"

"OK, they can bury the urns in their backyards."

"What if they move? You'll be buried in some stranger's backyard."

"They can dig me up and take me with them."

Shortly after the funeral, my grandfather moved to an assisted-living facility. To prepare his house for sale, my parents, along with my aunt and uncle, flew to Florida. They sent Polaroids to all our relatives of items my grandfather didn't want, and asked everyone to put in requests. I didn't have a big apartment, so I inquired about my grandmother's KitchenAid mixer. Everyone, it turned out, wanted the KitchenAid mixer. I settled instead for a framed photograph of my grandparents on their sailboat, a dictionary on a display stand, and Grandma Sylvia's recipe box. UPS delivered the package a few weeks later. I hung the sailing photograph in my living room, and set up the dictionary on its stand near my desk.

The recipe box was made of pressboard, its cover attached with a rusted hinge. Opening the box, I saw that it was stuffed with index cards. I wondered if Grandma Sylvia's clam chowder recipe was among them, so I reached in and pulled out a random card.

The title was "Cousin Jody's Asian Coleslaw," and the list of ingredients included "instant ramen, one-half cup (crushed)."

*T*he various accounts I have read of Ando's life agree on many points. For instance, they all state that his parents died in Taiwan when he was very young (although none explains how), and that, along with two older brothers and a younger sister, he was raised by his paternal grandfather, a textile distributor.

He calls his grandfather "a strict disciplinarian" and an excellent role model for life as an entrepreneur. Starting in elementary school, Ando was expected to do his own laundry and to cook for himself. He learned how to dress chickens, and made box lunches each morning for himself and his sister. He was surrounded by the vitality of commerce—steady streams of customers and suppliers, workers busily preparing shipments, and the sounds of looms operating in the neighborhood.

At age twenty-two, with an inheritance from his father, Ando started a company to import socks from Japan. He focused on synthetic fabrics that were just becoming available. Demand was so high that, to ensure supply, he left Taiwan and established a wholesale buying operation in Osaka. On the side, he took management classes at Kyoto's Ritsumeikan University. By the time he was twenty-eight, Ando had built a thriving business.

Four years later, during one of Ando's visits back to Taiwan, Japanese warplanes attacked Pearl Harbor. In *Conception of a Fantastic Idea*, Ando writes that, as he listened to radio reports of the bombing, he decided to return to Japan and never again set foot in his home-land. But in none of his autobiographies does he really explain why, and it's easy to draw the conclusion that he's not being entirely forthcoming.

Of the decision, he simply states (in *Magic Noodles*), "It is difficult to communicate exactly how I was feeling at the time, except to say that there was something cutting into my heart."

*T*he longer I was abstinent from dating and sex, the more ramen showed up unexpectedly in my life. Typically, it would appear just after I had written in my notebook.

> **Momofuku: (48 days)** *Josh just called me into his office. His office is on the side of the building with gorgeous views of the Bay Bridge and the Oakland Hills. He said he wants to do a story in the magazine about a new mobile phone that everyone's buying. The company that makes it is in Chicago, so I asked him if he wanted me to go there and do some interviews. He said that no, he wanted me to edit the story and hire a writer. So that means he's thinking about promoting me to an editor! I've never edited anything in my life, but I'm really excited to try it. I'm so excited that I wanna go online and meet someone. So it's not just when I'm down that I want to meet someone. It's also when I'm excited. Matt says excitement can be like money in your pocket, capital you think you can spend on getting someone to like you. What will I do with it if I don't spend it? My father once said, "Money burns a hole in your pocket." By "your" he meant my pocket, not pockets in general.*

I called a writer I knew in Chicago and left a voice mail message. He had just written a book about economic development in Asia, and I congratulated him on breaking into the *New York Times* best-seller list. The next day, he called back. I was at lunch, so he left a message:

"Cool, I'd be into doing the story. Give me a call back and we'll talk. And thanks for the kind words on the book. Hey, you used to live in Japan, right? Are you by any chance into instant ramen? Because I am getting totally into it. My favorite is an Indonesian brand called Indomie. Their Chicken Rendang has five—count 'em—five flavor packets. This is not instant ramen. This is theater!"

Momofuku: (58 days) I am so bored. I'm on vacation from work, but I didn't go anywhere, and I want more than anything to place an ad on Craigslist and meet someone. I thought maybe I would call Matt and ask him to reduce the ninety days to sixty, but I know what he'll say. I had two weeks of vacation time saved up, so it was, like, use it or lose it, but I couldn't think of anywhere I wanted to go, even though I still have some frequent flier miles left from my management-consulting days if I wanted to take a trip. I thought about going hiking in South America or scuba diving in the Caribbean, but the idea of going to those places by myself—without the chance to hook up with someone—seems lonely and boring. Two days ago, for the first day of my vacation, I went to a meeting at the church in the morning and then I spent the rest of the day cleaning my apartment. Yesterday I went to a meeting at the church, paid my bills, and watched TV. When I woke up this morning, I couldn't think of anything else to do, so I stayed in bed and read Spider Monkey in the Night, *a collection of Haruki Murakami short stories.*

I once met Murakami. It was while I was getting my MBA. I was taking a Japanese literature class at the University of Pennsylvania, and for my final project I translated one of his short stories. It took place in a hotel, and one of the main characters was a guest who was always smelling her hand. My professor happened to know Murakami's wife, who arranged for me to meet him at Princeton (where he was giving a lecture). I found him in a dark, Gothic hallway, and sitting on cement benches, we discussed the story I had translated. I asked Murakami what the smell on the woman's hand represented, but he wouldn't tell me. "What do you think it represents?" he kept asking back. I couldn't understand why a writer would write something like that and not tell a student what it represented.

Several stories in *Spider Monkey in the Night* had food-related titles, including "Croquettes," "Donut-ification," "Eel," "Beer," "Milk," and "Donuts Again." In the final chapter, Murakami had composed a song to the tune of "If I Had a Hammer." He called his version "Ramen in the Morning." "Honestly," Murakami wrote in an afterword, "I don't like ramen. I don't even like walking past ramen restaurants. But with this ramen song, it was as if I had been dragged by fate to write it. If you feel the urge, sing along."

Honestly, I had nothing better to do.

Delicious menma[1]
Roast pork in the morning
Ramen for breakfast, I am so glad
Broth is hot and good
Scallions so nice and green
Just that, there'd be love between my brothers and my sisters
I am satisfied

---

[1] A common ramen topping made from thinly sliced bamboo shoots. The similarity between this word and the Japanese pronunciation of *hammer* ("hanma") inspired Murakami to write the song.

Slurpin' it down
Bamboo shoots in the morning
Ramen for breakfast, I am so glad
Together you and me
Cheeks all nice and red
Just that, there'd be love between my brothers and my sisters
I am satisfied

Your loss if you don't eat it
Ramen in the morning
Today's another clear day outside, sun shining bright
I ate some seaweed
Drank some soup, too
Just eating that, there'd be love between my brothers and my
   sisters
I am satisfied

On the fourth day of my vacation, my friend Ellen called. It was Ellen who, a year earlier, turned me on to the record company that produced the CDs for Pottery Barn and Eddie Bauer. We had been driving to the beach in her car when I opened her glove compartment and discovered that it was filled with CDs branded by chain stores. She owned *Williams-Sonoma: Dinner Is Served, Pottery Barn: Sounds of Soul,* and *Swingin' Holiday,* a collection of big-band Christmas songs distributed by plus-size clothier Lane Bryant. "I don't know how I got that one," Ellen said at the time. "I'm a size four."

For a long time, Ellen and I enjoyed an ambiguous relationship that included a onetime hookup, but now I couldn't do that. She said she was house-sitting at her wealthy friend's home, and that there was a big pool. Her friend Carla would also be there, and Ellen invited me to join them. At first I thought it might be a bad idea, because the last thing I needed on Day Fifty-Nine was to be alone with two bikini-clad women, one of whom I had been involved with. But I was bored sitting at home, and Ellen and I wouldn't be alone.

Not that I thought it would do any good, but I found myself whispering Matt's prayer as I drove south on Highway 101.

O Momofuku, show me how to live so that I may better do your will.

The house was in Woodside, a Silicon Valley suburb famous for sprawling homes, wooded vistas, and dot-com millionaires. It took about an hour to reach it from San Francisco. Ellen's directions led to a curvy street and then a dirt road. I made my way up a long, steep driveway and parked in front of the house, one of the largest I had ever seen. The front door was open, so I walked in. The owners must have been art collectors; huge contemporary paintings hung on the walls. I spotted Ellen and Carla through the back window. They were sitting by the pool.

"Hey, you guys."

Ellen was overjoyed to learn that I had brought along *Jiffy Lube's Romantic Moments*, a CD I had purchased while getting an oil change.

"I cannot even believe this thing exists," Carla said.

Ellen wore an orange bikini and she was lying on a deck chair. Carla's bikini was turquoise, and her feet dangled over the pool's edge. Part of me was disappointed not to be alone with Ellen, but part of me was relieved.

"Hey, why aren't you at the magazine today?" Carla asked.

She and Ellen worked as freelance marketing consultants, but they were between contracts, and the downturn in the Silicon Valley economy was making it hard to find new jobs. I sat on the deck chair next to Ellen's.

"I'm off for a week. I had the vacation time."

"Use it or lose it," Ellen said.

"Right."

Carla wanted to know why I hadn't taken advantage of the opportunity to travel.

"I thought about it, but I couldn't come up with anywhere I wanted to go."

"Come on," Carla said. "There's no place you want to see?"

Carla slid into the pool and climbed onto an inflated blue raft. She paddled around with her hands.

"Mostly I've just been cleaning my apartment and reading," I said.

Carla didn't give up.

"You mean to tell me that there's nothing in the whole world that interests you?"

I thought about it.

"Well, there's this one thing," I admitted.

"Yeah?"

"You remember when I was in the hospital?"

Ellen remembered, sort of.

"For your spleen, right?"

"Gallbladder. Anyway, the day after the surgery, I read an article in a Japanese magazine about the inventor of instant ramen."

Carla sat up on her raft.

"The inventor of what?"

I repeated it.

"You mean, like Top Ramen?" Carla asked.

"That's one of his brands."

I told Carla and Ellen about how Ando spent a year in his backyard shack, and about the managerial training on the deserted island. I did not tell them that I had been writing letters to Ando about my love life. They were both laughing.

"He also invented the cup. You know, Cup Noodles. And he built a museum dedicated to instant ramen. It's supposedly across the street from his house."

"I can't explain why," Carla said, "but there's something inherently funny about instant ramen."

Ellen agreed. "I know a guy who writes songs about instant ramen and sings them at parties."

I told her about Murakami's ramen song, and sang a few bars.

"So, is this inventor of instant ramen still alive?" Ellen asked.

"Barely. He's ninety-four. According to the article, though, he sometimes comes to the museum and makes instant ramen with the visitors."

"What I would like to know," Carla mused, "is what makes a guy decide to spend a year in a shack trying to invent an instant noodle."

"Right?" I said. "I was wondering about that, too."

Carla lay back down on the raft, closing her eyes. "You know, you should interview him and write an article about his company."

"Tried that. Their PR department stopped returning my e-mails."

Ellen: "Where does he live?"

"In Japan. Osaka."

"You should just go there!" Carla yelled. "Just show up." She was still lying on the raft, but laughing now. "Maybe he'll make instant ramen with you."

With that, Carla began splashing water in the direction of my lounge chair. She prepared to defend herself, expecting me to lean over the edge of the pool and splash back. But she needn't have worried, because her suggestion had sent my mind elsewhere.

It had been ten years since my failure to fill in the blank while screaming the *Go Forth* line in front of the Kmart Corporate Head, and even longer since I had watched the TV show. Nevertheless, I began recalling the ramen-related things that had happened of late: the recipe from Grandma Sylvia's recipe box; the writer who had left an instant ramen recommendation on my voice mail; Murakami's song; Ellen's friend who wrote songs about instant ramen; and now Carla's suggestion. As I thought about these things, I heard a loud voice in my head telling me to ignore them. I had not yet learned to really listen to this voice, but it must have been saying something like this:

YOU SHOULD REALLY FORGET WHAT YOU ARE THINKING ABOUT DOING. YOU SHOULD REALIZE THAT THESE RAMEN-RELATED "THINGS," AS YOU SO ELEGANTLY CALL THEM, ARE JUST VERY MINOR CO-INCIDENCES THAT HAVE NOTHING TO DO WITH FATE, DESTINY, OR FIGURING OUT WHAT'S BEHIND YOUR PROBLEM. YOU SHOULD TAKE A VACATION TO SOMEWHERE NORMAL, LIKE A BEACH, AND GO SWIM-MING. YOU SHOULD FIND A WAY TO GET ALONE WITH ELLEN OR CARLA AND MAKE OUT WITH ONE OF THEM. MAYBE BOTH OF THEM. YOU SHOULD DO ANY-THING BUT WHAT YOU ARE THINKING ABOUT DO-ING, BECAUSE YOU WILL FAIL, AND THEN WHERE WILL YOU BE?

I was not able to hear these words yet, like I said. All I knew was that I felt like an idiot for wanting what I wanted. Maybe because Carla and Ellen were splashing water in my face, though, I stayed awake to my desire, and eventually I found the strength to stand up on one of the lounge chairs. My shorts and T-shirt were soaking wet, but I screamed the line so loud that all of Silicon Valley could have heard me.

"I wanna make instant ramen with Momofuku Ando!"

There wasn't much time left in my vacation, and I did not have an appointment.

*D*uring the war, Japan tightly regulated the manufacture and distribution of textiles, making it difficult for Ando to conduct business, so he expanded into other areas.

He launched a company to make slide projectors, which the government used to train unskilled workers at munitions factories. In nearby Hyogo Prefecture, he purchased a sixty-one-acre mountain and turned it into charcoal, which he sold as fuel. With a business partner, he manufactured prefabricated air-raid shelters.

The war made Ando rich. But as he writes in many of his books, the good times were about to end.

"I did not realize that an unimaginable misfortune was awaiting me around the corner."

When I got home from house-sitting with Ellen and Carla, I still wasn't sure that I was going to try to meet Ando without an appointment. But then I thought again about the recipe box and the voice mail from the writer in Chicago and Haruki Murakami's song, and I wondered if Momofuku Ando was indeed showing me how to live. It was a preposterous idea, but I enjoyed believing it, so I traded in my frequent flier miles for a round-trip ticket to Osaka. The next morning, I bought ten installments of *Ramen Discovery Legend* at the Japan Center bookstore, stuffing them into my suitcase. On the way to the airport, I called Matt and told him where I was going. He had never heard of anyone trying to meet the person they had chosen to stand in for God, but he wished me luck.

"May the noodles be with you," he said.

He was a big fan of *Star Wars*.

Momofuku: (60 days) A few hours into the flight to see you, I am having thoughts about trying to hook up with a woman in Osaka. No, I don't know anyone there, so I'm not talking about anyone specific. I mean, I'm having thoughts about trying to pick someone up. So what is happening right now? Everyone around me on the airplane seems riveted to the in-flight movie. It's a romantic comedy starring Ben Affleck and Liv Tyler. In one scene, Ben, as a single dad, visits a

video store and hits on the cashier, played by Liv. The mes-
sage is that all men and women should aspire to this—to
hitting on Liv Tyler and getting hit on by Ben Affleck. Men
and women except for me, that is, because I made a com-
mitment to Matt.

United Airlines offered a choice between an American-style meal
and a Japanese-style one. I chose Japanese-style, but the rice was cold
and dried out. I couldn't watch the movie without feeling bad, so I
pulled Book Two of *Ramen Discovery Legend* from my carry-on.

The episode I read was set at night, with Fujimoto cooking ramen at his stand in the park. There's a portable TV near his stove,
and he's watching an interview with a ramen "producer" named Mr.
Serizawa. An investor in several top-tier ramen shops (and a skilled
ramen chef in his own right), Serizawa asserts in the interview that
too many young men are being deluded by dreams of *dassara* and
betting their lives on ramen. "They study ramen on the Internet and
in ramen magazines," he says, "and some of them eventually learn
how to make good ramen. But 'good' won't cut it in this world."

Was I deluding myself that I could change?

Among the periodicals in the seat pocket, I found an issue of
President, a Japanese men's magazine. The cover headline said,
"Sanju-dai no kachikata." "How to Win in Your Thirties." Even
without opening the magazine, I was pretty sure that reading ramen
comic books and trying to meet the inventor of instant ramen without an appointment would not be among the recommended activities. I thought about all of the times I had traveled to Japan, and I
realized that I had never flown into Osaka.

I didn't know much about the area except for stereotypes.
Osakans are supposed to be friendlier and more outwardly emotional
than Tokyoites, and the city is famous for the street smarts of its mer-
chants. (A traditional local greeting literally translates as "You makin'
money?") A disproportionate number of Japanese comedians speak

the brash, guttural Osaka dialect. The only time I had ever lived in the Kansai area—the region on the western side of Honshu centered around Kyoto and Osaka—was when my Japanese teacher in graduate school sent me and four classmates to Kyoto to improve our Japanese. We stayed in a college dorm, and every day, we toured the city with an expert in a different field. An architect led us through a centuries-old *nagaya*—a long, narrow dwelling—and an archaeologist gave us a tour of several *kofun*—burial mounds the length of football fields that began appearing in Japan in the third century. Other expert guides included a doll artist, a woodworker, and a tofu maker. On the last day, as a surprise, our teacher put us on a bus to Enryakuji, a Zen temple atop Mount Hiei, where my classmates and I were forced to endure twenty-four hours of *zazen kunren* (Zen sitting training) with monks of the Tendai sect. Along with the five of us, seventy-five teenage boys—new employees of a gas station chain— participated in the training as a corporate initiation ritual. The monks showed us how to clasp our hands together in the *gassho* pose and to sit on our heels with our shins under our thighs—what the Japanese call *seiza*-style. I found it incredibly painful, and my classmate Barry, an amateur bodybuilder with oversized thigh muscles, moaned in agony. While enduring the pain, we had to chant along with the monks.

"En-Don-Sha-Shou-En-Ji-Sou-Zou-Kyou-Soku . . ."

The head monk explained the chant's meaning (which is also summarized on the Enryakuji Web site): "It is the darkness of your heart that leads to enlightenment." We had to sit *seiza*-style while he lectured us, and we were forbidden to speak during meals. At night we slept alongside the young gas station attendants on thin futons spread out on a tatami-covered floor. The monks made it clear that we were not supposed to talk after lights-out, but once it was dark, some of the gas station attendants crawled over to where my friends and I were sleeping and asked what we were doing in a Zen temple. We told them that we were forced to be there by our teacher. They said that they were forced to be there by their gas station company, and having bonded in this way, three of the boys asked to arm wrestle Barry. He beat them all—at the same time.

It was difficult not to question myself. I was on a plane to Osaka so that I could try to meet the inventor of instant ramen—to whom I had been praying because I was cheating in relationships and obsessively dating—without an appointment. I had brought a map showing the location of Nissin headquarters, but what would I say when I got there? I had no idea. Normally I prepared long lists of questions before interviewing an executive. I had nothing.

To calm myself, I rummaged through my carry-on bag for the *Nikkei Business* article and reread a section about Ando that I found comforting. It described a famous, long-ago incident in which an executive at Mitsubishi, Nissin's first big distributor, boasted that Mitsubishi could source everything "from ramen to missiles." Upon hearing that, Ando reportedly complained that the Mitsubishi executive should have said "from missiles to ramen," because ramen was the more important of the two.

As the plane made its final approach into Kansai International Airport, I looked out the window and saw whitecaps breaking over the Pacific Ocean. Would it be odd to say that they reminded me of drops of lard on top of a bowl of soy-sauce ramen? Well, they sort of did.

This is the story of how Ando was arrested by the Japanese military police.

During World War II, one of his companies produced engine parts as a subcontractor for Kawanishi Kokuki, a maker of combat seaplanes. Because the parts were for military use, the government supplied raw materials and performed a thorough inventory check every month.

One day (on this point, all of Ando's autobiographies concur), an employee in the company's accounting department informed Ando of a problem.

"The numbers don't look right," the man said. "It seems that someone is selling the inventory illegally."

Perhaps Ando is exaggerating when he states in *Conception of a Fantastic Idea* that the climate of World War II Japan was such that a man could be put to death if found guilty of misappropriating government property. In any case, he quickly reported the matter to the Osaka Police Department, where he was told to discuss it with the military police. At a military police station in Otemae, not far from Osaka Castle, Ando was greeted by a man he refers to in his autobiographies as Corporal K.

"Please wait," Corporal K said.

Ando waited, uneasily, in the military police station for what seemed like hours. "At the time," he writes, "a military police station was a place where even the devil feared to tread."

When Corporal K returned, he led Ando into a small room and began interrogating him.

"You're really something," Corporal K said. "You commit a crime and try to blame it on someone else. It's you who's been selling the parts on the black market, isn't it?"

*K*ansai International Airport was only ten years old and everything was clean and new. The terminal was one big, shiny electronic gadget.

I found my suitcase on the carousel and passed through customs. I hadn't slept on the plane, but I wasn't tired. On the contrary, I was excited. I was excited to see advertisements in Japanese and newspapers in Japanese. I was excited to read signs in Japanese. I was excited to be surrounded by Japanese people speaking and sending text messages in Japanese on sleek Japanese cell phones.

Momofuku: (61 days) I am excited by being surrounded by a lot of very attractive Japanese women.

I followed signs to the Japan Railways ticket office, where I reserved a seat on the Haruka Express Line to downtown Osaka. The man who sold me the ticket complimented my Japanese. *"Iya, hotondo wasureta kedo,"* I said, waving my hand in front of my face. When someone compliments your Japanese, it's polite to wave your hand in front of your face and say that, no, you have forgotten nearly everything. The truth was that I had forgotten many things, but hardly everything.

To reach the train platform, I had to first step outside the airport terminal. As I approached the exit, two glass doors parted automatically, and the rush of hot air made me sweat on impact. Osaka was like an oven. Making my way down an escalator, I cursed myself for trying to meet the inventor of instant ramen in July.

On the Haruka Express Line platform, I bought a bottle of C.C. Lemon from a vending machine, recalling how Harue and I used to sing the C.C. Lemon jingle, which was just the thirst quencher's name repeated over and over by a female singer who affected a Katharine Hepburn–like voice tremor. I held the bottle to my forehead to cool off. When the train doors opened for boarding, I rushed onto my assigned, air-conditioned car, and sat in my assigned seat.

The train was another shiny new gadget. Like all trains in Japan, it rode silently, with no shakes or jolts. This one ran on an elevated track, its tinted windows framing the Osaka skyline, which was not unlike the Tokyo skyline. There were apartment buildings and office towers as far as I could see, which was not that far because of the smog. Billboards on the tops of buildings advertised consumer loans and "capsule hotels"—the ultralow-budget hospitality option in which guests spend the night in stacked fiberglass tubes. (Think coffin, with a television at your feet.) Text of the day's news stories scrolled along an LED display over the train's bathroom. "Sumo's Asashoryu Apologizes for Drunken Rampage." "Hiroshima Officials Receive Suspended Sentences for Embezzlement." "Ichiro Extends U.S. Hitting Streak to Eighteen Games." A young woman in a beige uniform wheeled a snack cart through the aisle. "Cold oolong tea," she said in the high-pitched voice of Japanese women who sell things. "Rice balls. Mandarin oranges." Finding no takers, she pushed the cart to the end of the car and turned around, bowing to me and my fellow passengers. It struck me that only in a country where snack vendors must bow before leaving a train car will you find a television show about two hosts who scream, "I wanna ___!" (The converse, I surmised, might also be true.) Out the window, I noticed a grassy park with a baseball diamond. The train was moving so fast that I barely saw it, but before the park whizzed by, I watched a man throw a ball for his dog to fetch in left field. The scene was so familiar, so un-foreign. I imagined that the man knew I was on my way to meet the inventor of instant ramen without an appointment, and that he was telepathically telling me it was a waste of time.

When the doors opened at New Osaka Station, I wheeled my suitcase onto the platform and began to sweat again. From there I rode an escalator down to a sprawling underground mall. I was surrounded by restaurants and clothing boutiques and bakeries and travel agencies, but most of all, sweaty people on their way home from work. The evening rush hour was just beginning.

It was too late to visit Nissin, so my first order of business was finding a place to stay for the night. I walked toward one of the travel agencies, and as I passed through a narrow corridor, I felt a stream of cool air hit my sweaty head. Looking up, I saw an air-conditioning vent, and for about ten minutes I stood in that spot. An old man flashed me a look as if to accuse me of hogging all the cold air, and I felt weak and embarrassed.

Sleeping in a capsule was one option, but the travel office helped me find a room at a reasonably priced hotel. It was what the Japanese call a "business" hotel, which I knew from experience meant that, even though I was only five foot ten, I would hit my head on the bathroom ceiling. It would have private rooms and air-conditioning, and according to the listing, it was a twelve-minute walk from the station. Exiting the travel office, I noticed an outlet of Beard Papa's, the Japanese cream puff chain that had recently opened stores in New York and California. I bought a pumpkin-flavored one.

Momofuku: (61 days) I'm on my way to a business hotel not far from your Osaka headquarters. I keep passing attractive women walking in the opposite direction on the sidewalk. As I approach each one, I find myself staring into her eyes, hoping she'll return the gaze. It's as if I'm searching in the eyes of these women for answers, yet I don't know the question.

I didn't time exactly how long it took to walk to the hotel, but my guess is that it took exactly twelve minutes. (If something in Japan takes longer than it's supposed to, your watch is probably wrong.) I checked in at the front desk and rode the elevator to my room on the third floor. The room had a twin bed and a desk, on top of which sat a small TV and a phone. I hit my head on the bathroom ceiling.

I wanted to see if I had any e-mail, so I called the front desk and the receptionist directed me to an Internet café around the corner. In my in-box, there was a note from the researcher in my magazine's Tokyo office. She and the other office staff often took me out for dinner during my reporting trips, so she knew of my interest in Japanese food. "While you're in Osaka," she wrote, "why don't you visit the Gyoza Stadium?" The stadium, she had written, was a food court devoted exclusively to gyoza—Japanese pot stickers. I had heard of the Yokohama Ramen Museum, but I didn't know there was a gyoza version.

Momofuku: (61 days) I had the idea to search the America Online member directory for "Osaka AND gyoza lover." For a moment I took pleasure in the fact that a day was subtracted from my no-dating period when I crossed the international dateline, but then I realized it would get added back on the way home.

The clerk at the Internet café was no older than sixteen. I paid him for the fifteen minutes I had used the computer, and he complimented my Japanese. I told him that, no, I had forgotten everything. Then I asked what he thought of a ramen place I had noticed across the street.

"Mmm," he said.

In Japan, *mmm* does not mean "yummy." It means that there might be a problem.

"How did you hear about that place?"

"I saw the sign," I said. "It looked high-end."

The name of the restaurant had been carved in a shellacked tree stump.

The clerk shook his head.

"Mr. Customer, I'm going to be frank with you. The ramen there is not very good. It might be the worst ramen in this neighborhood."

He recommended instead a restaurant a few blocks away called Shisen Ramen.

"Mr. Customer, with ramen it's not always a good idea to be swayed by the sign."

It took me half an hour to find Shisen Ramen because it barely had a sign. The menu at Shisen forced me to choose between "original flavor" broth and "new flavor" broth, and with nothing to go on, I closed my eyes.

O Momofuku. Show me how to live so that I may better do your will.

I didn't hear an answer, so I chose "new flavor" on the premise that if the original was so great, why would they have had to make a new one? The soup was a rich, deep brown, and its surface was dotted with orange drops of chili oil. The toppings included chunks of blackened pork, scallions, and a clump of bok choy. I asked the waitress what made the broth so dark and tasty. She relayed my question to the chef, but he was not in the mood to share his recipe. "There's sesame in it," he barked. "And chicken."

Without a gallbladder, it's sometimes hard to digest fat. Halfway through, I was feeling queasy, so I took a break and skimmed another episode of *Ramen Discovery Legend*. Serizawa, the ramen producer, had been cast as the story's archvillain; he constantly challenged Fujimoto to ramen duels and belittled him as nothing more than a ramen-obsessed fool. But in the episode I read at Shisen Ramen, it was becoming apparent that Serizawa also had a good side, and that his harsh approach might have been a way of helping Fujimoto not only achieve *dassara*, but also find a ramen recipe that was true to himself.

"Compared to other traditional Japanese foods," Serizawa tells Fujimoto, "ramen has no past. There's no manual, no established theory. That's why you can express yourself through it. That's why it can help you understand yourself."

*T*o help modern readers appreciate the brutality of Japan's wartime military police department, Ando cites the case of a socialist writer whom the military police allegedly tortured to death in 1933. According to reports quoted by Ando, when the writer's remains were returned to his family, "his thighs were swollen to twice their normal size as a result of internal bleeding, bruises covered his penis and testicles, and there were 15 or 16 places where needles and spikes had been driven into his skin."

"The violence brought upon me," Ando writes in *Conception of a Fantastic Idea*, "was no less impressive."

In the military prison, Ando was beaten daily with a club and kicked in the stomach. He was forced to sit *seiza*-style with a bamboo pole inserted between his thighs and calves. This resulted in an agony that he describes as "not of this world." His cell was so crowded that there was no room to lie on the floor and sleep.

He was convinced that he would soon be dead.

*T*he first night in the business hotel, I dreamed about Harue. In the dream, she had gotten divorced and was living in Boston, but she was coming to visit me in San Francisco so we could get married. In reality, she was still married to a Japanese man she had met in Manhattan, and they were living in Tokyo with their two-year-old daughter. I woke up sweating, even though the air conditioner was on full blast.

It was nine thirty in the morning, but because of the jet lag, I was still exhausted. Sunlight streamed in through the curtains, making it impossible to go back to sleep, so I got out of bed and dragged myself into the shower. I bent my head, not only so that it didn't hit the ceiling, but also to get my hair under the nozzle, which was fixed at the height of my chest. As the water hit my belly, I thought about my "visiting Nissin" outfit.

The *Go Forth* hosts rarely got dressed up, but I had planned the outfit before leaving San Francisco. Gray slacks, blue Banana Republic dress shirt, black shoes, belt. No tie or jacket. The last part was due to Zen's influence. He had left our company a few months after I did, and under the tutelage of a management coach (a man we had hired at our company), Zen started his own management-coaching business in Japan. He believed that the nonconformity of not wearing ties or jackets projected power, and he called his look "Silicon Valley style." I was arriving without an appointment, so a little Silicon Valley style couldn't hurt.

At a 7-Eleven near my hotel, I bought a bottle of iced tea and two nori-encased rice balls stuffed with *umeboshi* (pickled plum). While in the store, I spotted packages of GooTa, a premium Nissin line that boasts high-quality, vacuum-packed toppings and goes for three dollars a serving. There were other ramen brands, but the Nissin products seemed to stand out, as if the packaging were screaming, "I am a great bowl of instant ramen!" Near the 7-Eleven, I spotted a small park, where I sat down on a bench to eat my breakfast and thought again about what I would say when I got to Nissin.

On *Go Forth*, the hosts usually just screamed what they wanted upon arriving at their destinations, but they traveled with a film crew that could provide at least a modicum of protection. The male host once screamed, "I wanna see for myself the strength of Chinese martial arts movie star Yuan Biao!" and when he spotted Biao about to enter a building, he ran toward him, waving a large paper fan. The male host is overweight and has no formal martial arts training, so it was easy for Biao and his two friends to subdue the host and secure him in a headlock. They repeatedly punched the host in the stomach until the *Go Forth* director came out from behind the camera and explained what was going on. I imagined screaming, "I wanna meet Momofuku Ando so I can figure out why I've never been able to sustain a long-term, committed relationship!" But I was a journalist who wrote stories about Japan, so my livelihood depended on getting in and out of the country. I didn't want to do anything that could compromise my ability to obtain a visa.

The *Nikkei Business* article quoted Ando saying that he played golf every week on Tuesday and Wednesday mornings. It was a Wednesday, so I had to find something to do before lunchtime. I boarded a subway train bound for Osaka's Naniwa district and followed the signs. I arrived at eleven o'clock, just as the doors were opening.

It was officially called Namco Gyoza Stadium, Namco being the name of a large Japanese video game company (known best as the developer of Pac-Man). The stadium was housed inside Namco City, a multistory video game arcade. Ascending a series of escalators to

Namco City's third floor, I entered what looked like the central square of a traditional Japanese village. It was a village, however, in which all of the storefronts were outlets of gyoza restaurants. Outside each shop, employees screamed the praises of their gyoza, doing their best to entice customers. "Get your juicy, garlicky gyoza right here!" A bulletin board in the middle of the square, next to a fake wooden footbridge, encouraged patrons to vote for their favorite gyoza; it also showed the previous day's voting results, broken down into male favorites and female favorites. I bought a three-piece set from Pao, the top male favorite, and ate it on a picnic table in the middle of the stadium. Pao's employees were screaming that their dumplings were made from beef, not pork, and that they packed extra beef jus. Sure enough, when I took a bite, some jus squirted onto my pants. An exhibit on the wall outlined the history of gyoza, which, like ramen, originated in China and became popular in Japan after World War II. A chart listed the ratios of soy sauce to vinegar commonly found in gyoza dipping sauces in different regions of Japan:

Tokyo	*7:3*
Kyushu	*1:1*
Shizuoka	*3:2*
Utsunomiya	*9:1*

People often ask me what fascinates me about Japan, and for a long time I never knew how to explain it. Here it is, though, in a nutshell:

There's a Gyoza Stadium on the third floor of a video game arcade called Namco City, and a chart on the wall lists the ratios of soy sauce to vinegar found in gyoza dipping sauces in different regions of the country.

I dabbed the jus stain with a wet napkin and rode the subway back to New Osaka Station. From there it was a short, sweaty walk to Nissin's Osaka headquarters.

*A*lthough he had endured physical torture, Ando always maintained that the most difficult thing about military prison was the food. Meals consisted of little more than boiled barley and pickles, and the dishes were covered in a layer of filth. A self-described clean freak of more than average means, he refused to eat.

Soon, however, he noticed how the other inmates' eyes sparkled at the sight of his untouched food. This, he wrote, affected him deeply.

> I felt that I had glimpsed the true nature of humanity at a very deep level. I didn't feel sorry for these people, or that they should be ashamed.
>
> This is difficult to explain, but when I began thinking that way, something changed in my soul. I became able to eat prison food that until then I was unable to eat. I drank stale-looking water from dirty glasses with no hesitation.
>
> Humans fill their minds with silly notions, so we often blind ourselves to reality. Had I not been conditioned to think otherwise, I would have seen the prison food and said, "It's covered in flies and maggots, but so what? Food is food." And I would have eaten it without thinking twice. In order to survive, humans must be able to change their thinking. Anyone who cannot do so has simply never suffered the truly

awful things in this world. To me, this was an unexpected revelation. Why is it that such discoveries await when we face our horrors? Why is it that humans perform above their normal abilities in such situations? Perhaps it is because we are forced to abandon every idea that is no longer serving us.

*T*he building was around fifteen stories high, its exterior covered in smooth olive-green tiles. It was probably constructed in the 1970s. Apart from the kanji characters for "Nissin Food Products" and Nissin's bowl-shaped logo near the top, the structure could just as easily have housed an insurance company. At street level, a gray slate walkway led to two red marble steps.

As I walked up the steps, the glass doors in front of me parted automatically.

The lobby stretched the full dimensions of the building, its floor comprised of the same red marble as the steps. The wall opposite the entrance was all glass; through it, I could see a rock garden and small koi pond. In the center of the lobby, two Greek-style sculptures, chiseled from what appeared to be white marble, stood on three-foot-high pedestals. I approached the sculptures and, for a minute or so, lingered between them. The one on my left depicted a naked man (Dionysus?) with his arms around two naked women whose joyful expressions hinted at the planning of, or winding down from, a ménage à trois. The sculpture on my right showed two men. One was curled up in agony, while the other hovered above, twisting the first man's arm.

It's hard to believe this now, but I stood between the sculptures completely oblivious to the symbolism.

"Can I help you?"

The voice belonged to an old man sitting behind a reception

desk. He wore an armband with the kanji for *security guard*, which made me think again of *Go Forth*. Security personnel were always foiling the hosts' plans. During the taping of "I wanna be a street vendor and serve yakitori to the mayor of Tokyo!" a member of the production crew was taken into police custody outside City Hall.

"I would like to meet Momofuku Ando," I said calmly.

The security guard picked up a telephone and dialed a number. There was a long pause.

"There's a foreigner at the front desk who says he wants to meet the chairman."

Another pause.

"Hai hai."

The security guard hung up the phone.

"Please proceed to the twelfth floor."

I couldn't believe it had gone so smoothly! Maybe people showed up all the time wanting to meet Momofuku Ando, and it was someone's job to greet them. The security guard even wrote out a name tag with my name in katakana—the second Japanese syllabary. Katakana symbols are like hiragana ones, except that they're used mostly for spelling onomatopoeia expressions and transliterating foreign words.

I affixed the name tag to my shirt and walked past the guard's desk. When I got to the bank of elevators, there was another sculpture, this one a bronze of Ando himself. It depicted the noodle inventor in a graduation-style cap and gown that, according to a plaque, commemorated an honorary PhD that he had received, in 1996, from Ritsumeikan University. Entering an open elevator, I pressed the button for the twelfth floor. The elevator doors closed, and when they opened again, a young woman was standing in front of me. She wore a gray skirt and a white blouse.

"Welcome to Nissin Food Products," she said, bowing.

I bowed back, and the woman led me from the elevator into a small room. Ah, the small room near the elevator.

When interviewing executives for magazine articles in the United States, I would often be led through mazes of cubicles on the way to spacious corner offices where the interviews took place. These walkthroughs offered valuable clues about what was going on in a company. Were people hard at work? Did they seem happy? At a troubled investment bank, for instance, I once spied a manager whaling away on a punching bag that hung by his desk. In Japan, though, executives almost always came out to meet me in small rooms near the elevators. It was the physical manifestation of keeping outsiders on the outside.

The small room near the elevator at Nissin was furnished with an expensive sofa and two comfortable-looking chairs. A photograph on the wall of Ando in a red gown and black mortarboard was presumably taken the day he received the honorary doctorate from Ritsumeikan University. Surveying the layout of the sofa and chairs, I knew that I was supposed to sit on the sofa. That's because it was the farthest piece of furniture from the door. Japanese business etiquette dictates that when you visit a company, you take the seat farthest from the door because the person nearest the door controls the exit, and therefore holds the power. I was showing up without an appointment, without a jacket, and without a tie. I thought about flaunting the seating protocol as well, but I didn't have the guts.

I sat down on the sofa.

"Would you like some coffee or tea?" the young woman asked.

Sweat had stained an area on my button-down shirt near my solar plexus.

"How about iced tea?" I said.

The woman bowed again, and told me to wait. Five minutes later, a tall, thin man entered the room. He looked around twenty-eight years old and wore a crisp white shirt and a plain green tie. I stood up and he bowed, holding out his business card. He spoke in Japanese.

"I am Yamazaki. Welcome to Nissin."

This was the man who had stopped returning my e-mails.

"Thank you," I said. "I am Raskin."

I thought about apologizing for showing up without an appointment, but decided not to mention it. I did apologize, however, for not having business cards. It was proper that I hadn't brought any because I was on vacation, but in Japan, it was always good to start by apologizing about something.

Yamazaki apologized in return.

"Osaka is very hot and humid now. I'm sorry you have to endure that."

The young woman returned with a glass of iced oolong tea, placing it deliberately on the table in front of me. She bowed and left the room again.

"It really is hot," I agreed. "Yesterday I stood for, like, ten minutes under an air-conditioning vent in New Osaka Station."

I wasn't sure if I should have said that.

Yamazaki motioned for me to sit down. He sat, too, in the chair closest to the door.

"So what brings you to Osaka?"

If he only knew. I wondered if he remembered me from our brief e-mail correspondence. When speaking to him, I copied how the security guard referred to Ando just by his title, but I prefaced it with "your company's" to make it sound more honorific.

"I'm the journalist who contacted you by e-mail a while ago, when I was trying to write a story about your company's chairman."

Yamazaki nodded.

"I know."

He didn't seem surprised to see me.

"I guess you weren't able to cooperate on the story," I said.

"It's very difficult to arrange interviews with the chairman. He just turned ninety-four."

"Of course." I wanted to appear understanding. "I was wondering, though. How did *Nikkei Business* arrange to interview him?"

Yamazaki chuckled through his nose.

"It took some time to set that up."

"Some time?"

"That reporter applied for an interview when the chairman was eighty-four."

I tried not to flinch. "I happened to be in Osaka on vacation, so I was thinking that maybe since I was here, it might be possible to visit the Instant Ramen Invention Museum."

"You can visit the museum anytime," Yamazaki said. "In fact, I'd be happy to meet you there and show you around."

I reached for the iced tea and took a sip, gathering my courage.

"I was also wondering if your company's chairman might be available to make instant ramen with me."

Yamazaki smiled again, but this time he began sucking air through his teeth.

"That might be difficult," he said.

In Japan, the sound of air being sucked through teeth means that you are not about to get what you have just asked for. Still, I asked why it might be difficult.

"Because, well, it might be difficult. He's ninety-four, you know."

During the six-year run of their show, the *Go Forth* hosts wanted to get treated to meals by wealthy people no fewer than thirteen times. In one episode, the male host traveled several hours by express train to the corporate offices of an entrepreneur said to be one of the richest men in Japan. In addition to wanting the entrepreneur to treat him to lunch, the male host brought along receipts for train fare and asked to be reimbursed for travel expenses. The executive turned out to be away on business, so the male host was greeted by an assistant. "Will you at least consider relaying my requests?" the male host pleaded. The assistant said no, and the male host was forced to hitchhike back to Tokyo.

Still, I thought it was worth a try.

"Would you at least consider relaying my request to your company's chairman?" I asked Yamazaki.

The sound of more air being sucked through teeth.

"I'll talk to my superiors," he said, "and we'll consider it."

He offered again to meet me the next day at the museum, and I figured I would take him up on it. A museum visit under Yamazaki's guidance could be the beginning of a friendship with him, a way to win his trust so that he would introduce me to Ando. On my way out, I apologized again.

"I'm really sorry for showing up without an appointment."

While apologizing, I bowed and backed onto the elevator, because in Japan you're not supposed to break eye contact with the person you're visiting until the elevator doors close.

"Don't worry about it," Yamazaki said. "And have fun in Osaka. See you tomorrow."

It was still early afternoon, so I walked back to the Internet café, where I e-mailed Zen. "You're in Osaka?" he replied. "I'll take a bullet train down to meet you tonight. It will be fun just to see your face." Jet lag overtook me, and when I got back to the hotel, I fell onto the bed. I slept for four hours.

*I*n protest of his treatment in prison, Ando embarked on a hunger strike. He became emaciated and suffered diarrhea.

"I decided that I would rather get sick than remain 'healthy' and suffer more torture," he wrote. "I think I contracted typhoid."

A fellow prisoner who was about to be released took pity on Ando, asking if there was anything he could do to help. Ando told the man to contact Yasumasa Inoue, a former army lieutenant and a longtime friend.

Inoue arrived the next day and had Ando set free. The prison ordeal had lasted forty-five days, and Ando was so weak that he needed assistance to walk. For two months, he recuperated at Osaka's Central Hospital. Upon his release, with Allied bombing of the Japanese mainland intensifying, he fled to nearby Hyogo Prefecture.

According to *Magic Noodles*, Lieutenant Inoue also introduced Ando to his wife. Ando never states when the introduction took place, except to note that it happened "during the war" and that it was "love at first sight." Born in Fukushima Prefecture, Masako "had a strong sense of duty." A picture, taken on their wedding day, appears in *Magic Noodles*. The kimono-clad young Masako is seated, while Ando, in a dark three-piece suit, stands next to her. A caption reads "Marriage with Masako (Kyoto)."

On March 13, 1945, five months before Japan's surrender, 329 Allied B-29s firebombed Osaka. According to an American prisoner of war who was held in the city, the raids went on nearly all night, leaving behind a twenty-five-square-mile "smoldering desert." The Allies bombed Osaka twice more in June, shutting down practically all economic activity. In August—the day after Emperor Hirohito accepted the Potsdam Declaration and ended the war—Ando traveled to Osaka to assess the damage.

Burned corpses still littered the streets. Ando's aircraft parts factory had been destroyed, as were his offices. While thinking about what to do next, he noticed that black markets for food had begun sprouting up around the city. Months later, at a black market behind Umeda Station, he came face-to-face with his destiny.

> One evening in winter, I happened to pass this area and saw a line twenty or thirty meters long in front of a dimly lit stall. Clouds of steam billowed from inside. I asked a person who was with me what all the fuss was about, and I was told that the stall sold bowls of ramen noodle soup. The people in line were dressed in shabby clothes and shivered in the cold as they waited their turn. I thought, "People are willing to go through this much suffering for a bowl of ramen?" For the first time, I paid deep attention to this food item.

Later, colleagues at Nissin said that whenever Ando saw a long line, he would stop what he was doing and investigate. "In a line," he has written, "you can see the desires of the world." Still, it would be more than ten years before Ando acted on his observation.

I didn't mention this in my letters to Ando because I was writing to him about women, but from the very first time I met Zen, he seemed obsessed with the fact that I am Jewish.

One of his favorite books, he would tell me, was *Business Methods of the Jews* by Den Fujita, the Japanese executive who founded Mc-Donald's Japan. (Fujita, who died shortly before my trip to meet Ando, was sometimes called "Jew of the Ginza.") Zen was always threatening to sign up for JDate, insisting that as a Japanese man he was "J" enough. Once, when we both still worked for the Internet company, I attended a Passover seder at a San Francisco synagogue, and Zen asked to tag along. He wore a yarmulke and asked the four questions, and he smacked his lips after his first taste of matzo ball soup. As the female cantor led the congregation in *"Dayenu,"* a traditional Passover song, he tried to follow along in Hebrew. When the song ended, the cantor translated the lyrics. "If God had led us out of Egypt," she said, "and had not executed judgment upon the Egyptians, *dayenu.* It would have been enough. If He had parted the Red Sea for us, and had not let us through it onto dry land, *dayenu.* It would have been enough." Later, in my car, Zen said, "Now I see why Jews are so successful. It's because you're so demanding." I didn't know what he meant by that, so I asked him. It turned out that he had misheard the cantor and thought *dayenu* meant "it would *not* have been enough." If God had only parted the Red Sea, not enough! I set Zen straight, but he was skeptical. "Do you really think anything short of the Promised Land would have been enough for you guys?"

When he called out to me in New Osaka Station, Zen was wearing a maroon Banana Republic dress shirt that, he later told me, had been selected by his image consultant. It struck me that he resembled Ernie from Sesame Street. My hair was thinning in front, and I was starting to look like Bert.

"Hey, Zen."

We shook hands. Zen rarely bowed.

"Hey, man," he said. "This is for you."

Zen presented me with a small shopping bag, and opening it, I found that it contained a copy of his new book. Titled *Wow Method*, it embodied the philosophy of his management coaching practice. Like most new books in Japan, Zen's came sheathed in a marketing banner. This one said, "You can't change your life just by reading a book!"

Which was clearly meant to imply that you could.

"So, Andy. What are you doing in Japan?"

I was hungry. "Let's get something to eat and I'll tell you about it."

I had visited Zen in Japan once before, in Tokyo, and we had spent two hours trying to find a restaurant. He would suggest places, but I kept nixing them, hoping for something better. We searched until we got so hungry that we had to settle for the nearest yakitori bar. After a mediocre meal of skewered grilled meats, I said, "I guess there's a cost in not choosing quickly." To which Zen replied, "You just figured that out?"

This time I was better prepared. On the way to the station, I had stopped by the Internet café and scanned Chowhound's international message board. An American exchange student had posted about an Osaka liquor store with a trapdoor that led to an exclusive sake-tasting cellar. The store's Web site listed rules governing the behavior of tasting patrons, such as "Conversation should center around sake. Work-related conversation is prohibited."

I told Zen about the place, and he said, "Wow."

We hailed a cab and when we arrived, it looked like any other liquor store, until the young male owner opened a hatch in the floor. We shinnied down to the basement, where the owner led us through a network of white catacomb-like tunnels lined with sakes from all over Japan. We chose several bottles, carrying them out to a round table, where the owner poured samples into small ceramic cups. Our conversation was borderline work-related, but we spoke in English, so the owner didn't give us any trouble.

"What are you doing here?" Zen asked again. "Magazine story?"

"Not a magazine story. Do you know about Momofuku Ando?"

Ando wasn't exactly the Bill Gates of Japan, but he was generally known as a famous entrepreneur.

"The guy who invented the noodles?"

"Yeah."

"What about him?"

"I'm here to meet him."

"What for?"

Zen was one of the closest people in my life. Still, I wasn't ready to tell him about Matt and the letters to Ando. My answer was truthful nonetheless.

"I'm not sure."

"Wow. When is your appointment?"

"I don't have an appointment."

"Wow."

The first bottle we tasted was an Urakasumi *junmai*, from Miyagi Prefecture. In my journal I wrote, "textbook green apple flavor." I related to Zen what had happened so far, and told him about Ando's shack and the museum.

"Just hearing about that shack makes me want to build one in my own backyard and spend a year in it inventing something," Zen said. "It's really giving me a hard-on."

The "hard-on" comment was an inside joke. When the venture

capitalists politely asked me to replace myself as CEO, Zen and I interviewed several candidates. One was a middle-aged woman who shared her vision for the company over a sushi lunch. Zen and I were excited by her ideas, and near the end of the meal, Zen told her so. "You know, talking to you is really giving me a hard-on," he declared. The woman nearly choked on a bite of tuna, and later, I asked Zen what he was thinking. He told me that he was under the impression that *hard-on* could be used to express excitement of any kind, and in polite conversation. He had apparently gotten that idea from a movie. "You know, like in *Top Gun*," he said, and he described a scene in which a U.S. Air Force gunner utters the phrase while firing on a target. I've never seen *Top Gun*, so I don't know if it's true. Needless to say, the woman didn't take the job.

The cellar rules prohibited the consumption of any food except *umeboshi* and Kinzanji miso—a chunky fermented bean paste from Wakayama Prefecture. We ordered an appetizer-size portion of both.

"Do you think he's going to meet you?" Zen asked.

"It's not looking good. His PR flak is not exactly giving me a warm-and-fuzzy."

Zen scratched his forehead.

"Andy, how fast did you put on your underwear this morning?"

"Huh?"

"Gimme the book."

It took a second to realize that Zen was talking about his book. I handed *Wow Method* back to him, and he opened it to page 29.

"Read this," he said.

In big, bold characters, the writing on page 29 said, "From one to ten, how would you rate the speed at which you put on your underwear this morning?" An explanation was on page 30. The idea was that your underwear-speed rating correlated to your excitement about starting the day. Zen postulated in the book that if you rated yourself each morning, you would begin to naturally make choices in your life that improved your score.

"The day will come when you will give yourself an eleven," he had written. "It would not be surprising if you scored thirty, or even three hundred."

I tasted a shot of a *daiginjo* from Nagano Prefecture while thinking back to getting dressed in the morning. The sake was sweet and smooth, and it smelled like bananas.

I gave myself a nine.

"Good," Zen said. "You're on the right track."

For dinner, we ate mackerel and smelt at a grill restaurant around the corner. I ordered a side of *shiokara*—squid fermented in, among other things, its own guts—and Zen accused me of ordering it to impress our cute waitress. Truth be told, the purplish, slimy delicacy looks like the rotting innards of a small mammal, and the first time I laid eyes on it, I nearly threw up. But I had truly come to love it, and I didn't feel the need to write anything to Momofuku Ando.

"I really love that stuff," I told Zen.

"Sure you do," he said.

After dinner, I escorted Zen to New Osaka Station, where he caught a bullet train back to Tokyo. Then I walked to my hotel, stopping off at the Internet café to print out directions to the Instant Ramen Invention Museum.

*T*hrough his businesses ventures, Ando made friends in positions of power. One was Fusanosuke Kuhara, owner of Hitachi Mine (out of which grew the electronics giant Hitachi). After the war, Kuhara counseled Ando that in times of uncertainty it was always best to buy land.

Ando followed Kuhara's advice. With the economy in shambles, landowners were so desperate to sell that buildings in downtown Osaka went for as little as forty dollars. Ando bought three stores in the Shinsaibashi district, next to the busy Sogo department store, and two parcels of land in another downtown neighborhood.

The land purchases—combined with insurance payouts covering his losses during the war—made Ando even richer than before. In just a few years, his net worth would total over forty million yen (the modern equivalent of several hundred million dollars); at least one major newspaper declared him the wealthiest man in postwar Japan. Returning with his family to Osaka, he built a new home in Izumi-Otsu, close to the shore of Osaka Bay. He describes moving day in both *Conception of a Fantastic Idea* and *Magic Noodles,* but there is a slight discrepancy between the accounts. First, the passage from *Conception of a Fantastic Idea,* published in 1983:

> In the winter of 1946, the four of us—myself, my wife, my son Hirotoshi, and a helper—left [Hyogo Prefecture] and moved to a house I had hurriedly built in Izumi-Otsu. The

158 · ANDY RASKIN

train from Kamigori was packed to more than capacity. We clambered in through a broken window and clung to the train all the way to Osaka Station. From there we walked about four kilometers and switched to the Nankai Line at Namba Station. Dressed in thick clothing, we walked calmly through the ruins. . . .

Here's the account that appears in *Magic Noodles,* published in 2002:

In the winter of 1946, my wife and I, along with a helper, left [Hyogo Prefecture] and moved to a house I had hurriedly built in Izumi-Otsu. . . .

In the second book, there is the crowded train, the broken window, and the Nankai Line.

But Ando's son Hirotoshi is missing.

I got dressed (underwear speed: 9.5) and ate salmon-filled rice balls at the park near the 7-Eleven. In New Osaka Station, I stood for a few minutes under the air-conditioning vent before following signs to the Hankyu Railway, where I boarded the Takarazuka Line for Ikeda City.

Nestled near the base of Mount Satsuki, Ikeda City boasts a zoo and the remains of a castle built in the Edo period, when the region was famous for its high-quality charcoal. In modern times, it's probably best known for Ando's invention. A year before my visit, the city had been the setting of a popular TV drama about the Iwatas, a fictional 1950s family that owned a Western-style bakery. The family received occasional visits from a Mr. Anzai, a neighbor obsessed with inventing an instant version of ramen. The family would offer Mr. Anzai (whose character was clearly based on Ando) bread from their bakery, but he always said that he preferred noodles.

The ride took twenty minutes. When I walked through the ticket-collection turnstile at Ikeda Station, a sign in front of me said INSTANT RAMEN INVENTION MUSEUM. Following a large arrow, I descended a staircase to street level. Convenience stores, supermarkets, and restaurants hugged the station, just like in any other Japanese suburb. Overlapping recordings of female voices screaming *"Irasshaimasse!"* welcomed customers into the various establishments. A large sign on the street directed me to the museum, and as I got farther from the station, the commercial district yielded to a more residential one. Homes were large by Japanese standards, with gardens and garages.

A sign on the lawn said THE MOMOFUKU ANDO INSTANT RAMEN MUSEUM, and squiggly lines ran through the words like a postage cancellation mark. (Later I learned that these squiggly lines were meant to represent both ramen noodles and "the free, unconstrained spirit of invention.") The museum's modern, glass facade might have seemed more at home on Fifth Avenue than on a quiet street in a Japanese suburb. The *Nikkei Business* article stated that the museum had been constructed opposite Ando's home, so before entering, I walked across the street. The two-story residence there was almost entirely hidden from view by a well-maintained Japanese garden, but an ANDO nameplate confirmed I was in the right place. A sturdy metal gate—with spikes on top—blocked the entrance. Through the gate, I could see a red brick driveway leading to the front door, and a basketball net perched on a pole. I tried to imagine the inventor of instant ramen playing basketball with his grandchildren, but since he was ninety-four, maybe he just watched. The *Go Forth* hosts would have rung the doorbell, but I was afraid that Yamazaki might hear about it. Instead I just snapped photos with my digital camera and walked back across the street to the museum.

Near the entrance, a black stone sculpture sat on a granite base. The sculpture was shaped like a bowl of ramen, and the base was engraved with Ando's words:

The time allotted to a man in one day is limited.
Within that time, he works, he sleeps, he eats.
If he saves time performing these activities, he can invest it in
    improving his mind, making his life more abundant and
    long lasting.
Indeed, time is life.

I thought about the words. If I was not mistaken, Ando was taking credit for accelerating the cultural progress of mankind.

Once inside the museum, I spotted Yamazaki in the gift shop. He was standing between a rack of Nissin T-shirts and a stuffed-animal version of the Chikin Ramen mascot—a Tweety Bird–like baby chicken. Nearby, a vending machine dispensed various flavors of Cup Noodles.

"Good morning, Mr. Raskin."

"Good morning!"

"Let's get started."

I followed Yamazaki up a staircase to the second floor, where around thirty Japanese second graders were busy making their own packages of Chikin Ramen. Sitting at long tables in a room that resembled a school cafeteria, the kids rolled out dough and fed it through hand-cranked noodle-cutting machines. Adult staffers steamed and fried the noodles while the kids decorated their Chikin Ramen packages with magic markers.

"Wouldn't it be great if your company's chairman were here today?" I said to Yamazaki.

He either didn't hear me, or pretended not to hear me.

One of the girls making Chikin Ramen looked older than the other children, and a photographer was hovering around her. Yamazaki told me that she was an actress, and that she had appeared in the TV drama about the fictional family in Ikeda City.

I asked the girl what she thought of Chikin Ramen.

"It's soooo good!" she said. "Why don't you make your own?"

I asked Yamazaki if I could make my own package of Chikin Ramen.

"You need a reservation," he said. "And we're booked up for the next month, so it will be very difficult."

There were only three days left in my vacation.

Yamazaki led me back downstairs to the museum's main hall, which was packed with various ramen-themed exhibits. A life-size statue of a woman shopping for instant ramen in a supermarket stood near the entrance. Behind her, a glass case displayed Cup Noodles containers from all over the world.

Along the walls, an elaborate time line traced instant ramen back to its roots. It started with the invention of boiled noodles— sometime around the birth of Jesus Christ—and continued with various international noodle developments, including hand-flattened noodles (China, 1200), udon (Japan, 1400), soba (Japan, 1600), and a beef-and-noodle stew called lagman (Central Asia, 1400). A separate, European branch presented the direct noodle ancestor of macaroni (Italy, 750), a proto-gnocchi (Italy, 1050), and spaghetti (Italy, 1400). All the branches converged at the year 1958, represented by a large bull's-eye surrounding an orange-striped package of Chikin Ramen. To the right of the bull's-eye, the time line placed instant-ramen-related developments in context with other historical events. Between 1966 and 1971, for instance, Neil Armstrong stepped on the moon, the Beatles played a concert in Japan, and Nissin introduced Cup Noodles. The 1990s saw the unification of Germany and the launch of Nissin Rao ("Ramen King"), a high-end fresh-pack line. Not a lot happened in the 1980s, ramen-wise.

Leaving the main room, Yamazaki led me to the Cup Noodles Theater, where the walls were streaked with wavy lines of various colors. Inside, we watched an animated movie that showed how Cup Noodles was partly the result of a dream that Ando had one night around 1969. In the movie, a cartoon version of Ando traveled to America in 1966 to introduce Chikin Ramen to U.S. supermarket executives. To Ando's surprise, the American businesspeople he met crumbled up his invention and put it in Styrofoam cups (not bowls!). After pouring boiling water into the cups, they ate the noodles with forks (not chopsticks!). On the plane home, a flight attendant served Ando a tin of Royal Hawaiian macadamia nuts, and Ando fixated on the container's foil lid; he realized that, fitted on a Styrofoam container, the foil could serve as the top of a revolutionary packaging design in which instant noodles could be sold, cooked, and eaten. To ensure that the contents would cook evenly (and suffer minimal breakage during shipping), Ando designed a sloped cup that would suspend the disk of dried noodles above the cup's bottom. In the factory, though, the noodle disk would often tilt to one side, allowing dehydrated shrimp, egg, and other toppings to slide off the top. That's where Ando's dream came in. In the cartoon rendering, a pajama-clad Ando is falling, headfirst, next to a Styrofoam cup that is also falling upside down. When he awakens, he designs an assembly line that holds the noodles on a platform and lowers the cup, upside down, over them.

It wasn't clear to me what made the upside-down assembly line better than a right-side-up one, but afraid of looking dumb, I didn't say anything.

"How about going inside the shack?" Yamazaki proposed.

I had thought he might never ask.

Back in the main hall, the replica of Ando's shack beckoned like a shrine. As we approached, Yamazaki told me the shack had been reconstructed from extensive interviews with Ando and careful analysis of his actual backyard. Outside it, there was a noodle-drying rack, a bicycle, and a chicken coop for the Nagoya chickens that Ando had used to make his broth. (I knew from *Ramen Discovery Legend* that Nagoya chickens were considered ideal for ramen soup stocks.) Everything inside, according to Yamazaki, was as it had been on the morning of March 5, 1958—Ando's forty-eighth birthday. (There was apparently no single day that Ando remembered inventing instant ramen, so his birthday had been chosen arbitrarily.) Yamazaki led me to the door of the shack, but he remained outside as I entered.

The interior was not unlike that of a toolshed in an American backyard except that, instead of gardening tools, it was filled with cooking equipment and food. A workbench was cluttered with a hand-cranked noodle cutter, a gas burner, a pair of cooking shears, a set of knives, a strainer, a set of dishes, cutlery, and a square-shaped wire mesh fryer. A small plaque next to a stack of newspaper advertisements explained that Ando had used the ads as scrap paper for taking notes while crafting his invention. In a large white soup pot, vegetables and chickens were being boiled for stock, and even after all the time I had lived in Japan, it took a good five minutes before I realized that the stock and the vegetables were plastic models. On the left side of the counter, (plastic) hot oil bubbled around a (plastic) piece of battered shrimp—a reference to how Ando's wife's tempura had led to his epiphany about frying. A lightbulb hung from the ceiling.

Suddenly, Ando's voice came over a loudspeaker:

"I didn't know what I was doing. No matter how many times I tried, nothing came out right. I simply couldn't produce an ideal noodle. The hardest problem was drying the noodles and infusing them with flavor. In the beginning, I was completely in the dark. I brushed the noodles with the seasonings, but when I exposed them to hot air, they fell apart."

Ando was talking about noodles, but I couldn't help thinking about Maureen and Harue and Kim and all of my failed relationships.

I walked out of the shack, but Yamazaki was gone. I found him again in the gift shop, and when he saw me, he looked down, sucking air through his teeth.

"I am filled with regret," he said, "because I just found out that it's going to be very difficult to arrange a meeting with the chairman."

I already knew the answer, but I asked why.

"I found out that it would be too difficult," Yamazaki said.

Dejected, I said good-bye and walked to the museum's front door alone. When I got there, a banner was hanging from the ceiling. The writing on it faced the museum's interior, which is why I hadn't noticed it on my way in. Four characters and one hiragana symbol were drawn several feet high in jet-black ink. The brushstrokes were bold and alive, and Ando's signature was at the bottom.

The banner said *JINRUI WA MENRUI.*

In my mind, I translated it into English.

MANKIND IS NOODLEKIND.

*D*riven by his torture-induced revelations about the importance of food, Ando supplemented his real estate activities with a venture to make salt. On a beachfront lot formerly owned by the Japanese Army, he hired young boys to pour sea water onto large iron sheets:

> We placed [the sheets] side by side on the shore as far as the eye could see. It was a grand sight to behold. The sheets were slanted to accumulate seawater, which began to evaporate when exposed to sunlight.

He launched his second food venture in 1947, founding what he called the National Nutritional Chemistry Research Institute. Two years had passed since the end of the war, but it was not yet uncommon for Japanese people, especially hospital patients, to die of malnutrition. The institute's mission, therefore, was to develop a cheap, nutritious food product. One evening, Ando lay in bed thinking about potential ingredients, when he heard a frog croaking in his backyard.

"I instantly recognized this as a potential source of nutritional food." (*Magic Noodles*)

Ando captured the frog, gutted it, and placed it in a pressure cooker.

My wife and newborn son, Koki (presently CEO of Nissin Food Products), were sleeping in the next room. About two hours later, a loud explosion shook the house. The contents of the pressure cooker flew all over the tatami room, creating a mess on the ceiling, lintel, and sliding doors. My wife scolded me.

"You didn't have to do that in here!" she said.

My experiment in using the frog as a source of nutrition had failed, but it tasted good.

Ando eventually produced a paste from cow and pig bones, which he sold to hospitals under the trade name Viseicle. It was a minor success, but more important, it put Ando in contact with officials at Japan's Ministry of Health and Welfare. Under the American Occupation, the ministry had been promoting flour-based foods because the United States had made available its large surplus of wheat. Ando had no problem with flour, but the ministry's approach irked him:

The Ministry was promoting bread and biscuits at school cafeterias. So I shared some thoughts with Kunitaro Arimoto, who was then the manager of the Ministry's Nutrition Division. . . . "With bread," I told him, "you need toppings or side dishes, so you're asking people to westernize their diets. In the East there's a long tradition of eating noodles. So why not also promote noodles, which Japanese people already enjoy, as a flour-based food?'

At the time, noodles were manufactured solely by small outfits incapable of feeding a mass market. Pointing this out, Mr. Arimoto asked, "Mr. Ando, if you are so enthusiastic about it, why don't you do some research on how to produce such noodles?"

Actually, I had virtually no knowledge about noodles so I left it at that. But over the years, that long line at the stall and my conversation with Mr. Arimoto stuck stubbornly in my mind.

I had been expecting Yamazaki's no. I was prepared for it, thanks to *Ramen Discovery Legend.*

In an episode titled "Make Those Really Thick Noodles," a burly youngster named Kano shows up at Fujimoto's ramen stall in the park. Kano, it turns out, also dreams of *dassara* and wants to open his own ramen restaurant. His plan is to apprentice at a ramen shop called Yodonaga (known for its unusually thick noodles), but when Kano asks the grumpy old Yodonaga owner to take him on, the man refuses. Undeterred, Kano returns to Yodonaga every morning, falls to his knees, and begs. On the thirtieth day, the owner relents, making Kano his apprentice.

The day after touring the museum, I woke up at seven thirty and ate salmon-filled rice balls in the park near 7-Eleven. By eight thirty, I was standing in front of the entrance to Nissin headquarters. Yamazaki reported for work a few minutes later, and when he spotted me, he seemed afraid, as if he thought I was stalking him. Well, I guess I was. Luckily, I did not have to fall to my hands and knees before he invited me inside. He ushered me past the Greek statues and the bust of Ando, and we rode the elevator, silently, to the twelfth floor. He excused himself while the same woman from two days earlier led me to the same small room near the elevator.

I sat on the same sofa again, away from the door.

This time, when Yamazaki joined me, he was accompanied by a

man who looked to be in his early forties. The older man wore black-rimmed glasses and a blue suit that looked more expensive than Yamazaki's. He took the seat nearest the door, and Yamazaki sat next to him.

"I am Matsubara," the other man said.

Matsubara handed me his business card, and from his title, his seat, his age, and his clothing, I understood that he was Yamazaki's boss.

"I am Raskin. I'm sorry that I don't have a business card."

Matsubara sucked air through his teeth and looked me straight in the eye.

"We are truly honored that you are so interested in the chairman. But—I am deeply sorry to say this—the simple truth is that he does not do many interviews."

"I see."

"He's ninety-four years old," Matsubara reiterated.

I paused to indicate that I was not taking Ando's age lightly.

"It's just that I came all the way from the United States."

The two bowed their heads and took deep breaths. I knew that it would not be easy for them to have a man travel all the way from the United States and not get what he wanted. There was a long, uncomfortable silence. In general, Japanese people can endure silence better than Americans can, but it was Matsubara who spoke first.

"You know, the chairman is going to do his annual press conference at a club for Osaka journalists in late August."

I didn't know.

"If you come back, you can attend." It was just a few weeks away.

"I would love to attend!"

"You probably won't be able to speak with the chairman directly," Yamazaki said. "But you could be in the same room."

I was filled with hope. I was so excited that I began telling Matsubara and Yamazaki about how ramen had helped me get through college, even though it was a bit of an exaggeration.

"We hear that a lot," Yamazaki said, and I realized that he probably did. "Anyway, I'll arrange a pass for you to the press conference."

Matsubara excused himself for a moment, leaving the room while Yamazaki and I sat together in another uncomfortable silence. When Matsubara returned, he presented me with two books. The first was the catalog to the Instant Ramen Invention Museum. The second was *The Story of the Invention of Instant Ramen*, Nissin's self-published English translation of *Magic Noodles*.

I accepted the books, thanking Matsubara with the most polite version of "thank you" I could muster. (There are easily over a dozen from which to choose.) While thanking Yamazaki, I backed my way onto the elevator. Walking out past the Greek sculptures and the security guard, I imagined the question I would ask Ando. Why did you suddenly commit to inventing instant ramen? I imagined myself asking it in Japanese at the press conference, even though Matsubara had said I wouldn't get to ask any questions. Out on the street, the humidity seemed bearable now. I passed gas stations and electronics shops and restaurants and it struck me that Japan was not really so different from the United States.

When I entered the hotel lobby, the front desk clerk called out my name and handed me a phone message. "Please call. From Yamazaki." It would have been expensive to call from my room, so I walked back outside and found a phone booth. Japan still had plenty.

"*Moshi moshi,*" Yamazaki said.

"This is Raskin. You left a message?"

"Mr. Raskin. Yes . . . well, I just checked with the press club, and I'm afraid I have some bad news. It turns out that you have to be a member of the club to attend the chairman's press conference."

"Can I become a member of the club?"

"Mmm. Difficult if you're not a Japanese journalist."

My jaw tightened and I felt cold, even though my shirt was soaked with sweat. I hung up the phone, and for a few minutes I just stood on the sidewalk. There were several things I could have done next.

One was that I could have gone back to Nissin the following morning. I had gone back only once so far, and the man in *Ramen Discovery Legend* went back thirty times. I hadn't even gotten on my hands and knees. Zen once told me a story about Masayoshi Son, the billionaire founder of Japan's biggest software and Internet company, Softbank, who Zen said got his start thanks to similar persistence. According to Zen's story, Son had no idea what to study in college, so without an appointment, he visited the office of Den Fujita (Zen's favorite author) to ask for advice. Fujita's secretary told Son that a meeting was out of the question, but Son returned every morning for thirty days (what was it about thirty days?), until finally Fujita noticed and asked his secretary about the kid who was always sitting on the steps outside. In the meeting, Fujita supposedly told Son, "Study computers."

Another thing I could have done was to research the curse of Colonel Sanders. I had been intrigued by the supposed curse for years, and I thought of it right then because I was standing in front of a Kentucky Fried Chicken, and a life-size Colonel Sanders mannequin was staring at me from inside the restaurant. In the rest of Japan, KFCs proudly displayed their Colonel Sanders mannequins outside. But Osaka KFCs often kept their Colonels indoors. The reason was that after the Hanshin Tigers won the 1985 Japan Series (Japan's World Series), ecstatic fans supposedly grabbed a Colonel from outside one of the restaurants and tossed him into Osaka's Dotonbori Canal. According to those who believe in the curse, as long as the Colonel remains at the bottom of the polluted waterway, the Tigers will never again reign as champion.

(The Tigers reached the Japan Series in 2003 and again in 2005, and each time, fans reportedly dredged Dotonbori Canal. They failed to raise the Colonel, and both years the Tigers lost.)

I could have done either of those things, but in order to do them, I would have needed to be in control of myself. And when I got off the phone with Yamazaki, I was not in control. I went back into the hotel and packed my clothes and ramen comics, checked out, and walked to New Osaka Station. I reserved a seat on the bullet train to Tokyo. It's amazing, looking back, that I knew exactly what to do to get what I wanted. "Wanted" is probably not the right word, though. Maybe "craved." I knew where to go, which was Tokyo. I felt more comfortable in Tokyo. I knew my way around.

On the bullet train from Osaka, I tried to write to Ando about what was happening, but something else came out entirely. It was in the second person, and in capital letters.

Momofuku: (64 days) YOU SHOULD BE ASHAMED OF YOURSELF. YOU SHOULD STOP WASTING PEO-PLE'S TIME. YOU SHOULD HAVE BEEN ABLE TO GET SOMEONE LIKE HIM TO MEET YOU. I MEAN, HE'S NOT THE EMPEROR, FOR CRYIN' OUT LOUD. YOU SHOULD HAVE BEEN A MORE IMPORTANT PERSON AND THEN MAYBE HE WOULD HAVE MET YOU. YOU SHOULD HAVE WORN A SUIT AND TIE. WELL, THINGS NEVER WORK OUT FOR YOU BE-CAUSE YOU ARE A NO-GOOD, UNGRATEFUL, DIRTY, ROTTEN IDIOT.

The words scared me, even though I was writing them with my own hand. At the same time, they seemed familiar, like an old friend.

*I*n 1948, a few days before Christmas, Ando hosted a farewell party for an American military official. The party was held at one of his downtown Osaka buildings and attended by several luminaries, including Bunzo Akama, the governor of Osaka. When the party was over, Ando walked out the back of the building. Just as he was about to get into his car, two American military police officers grabbed him, shoved him into their jeep, and drove off.

The Occupation government had filed charges against Ando for tax evasion. The problem, Ando claims in his autobiographies, was roughly fifty dollars a month that he paid the boys who made salt. Ando claimed that the money was akin to a scholarship and should not have been subject to income tax. Not persuaded by this argument, a judge gave Ando a choice. Leave Japan for good, or submit to four years' hard labor.

Aided by a team of lawyers from Kyoto University, Ando countersued. While the legal battle dragged on, he was held in Tokyo at the U.S.-run Sugamo Prison. (General Hideki Tojo, who was later executed for war crimes, and future prime minister Nobusuke Kishi were also prisoners there.) Meanwhile, the Osaka tax authority took possession of Ando's salt factory, all of his commercial real estate holdings, his home in Izumi-Otsu, the mountain in Hyogo Prefecture (where he was still making charcoal), and virtually every asset in his name, auctioning off most of them to the highest bidder.

Nevertheless, Ando insists in *Magic Noodles* that his treatment at the hands of the Americans was nothing like what he had endured in the Japanese military prison:

> It was like the difference between heaven and hell. I was given the same food as the American soldiers, and not once was I required to do any hard labor. I am sure I ate better than the general public. It was also at this time that I learned how to play mah-jongg. Wow, I thought, America really is a great, free country.

It took two years to work out a legal settlement in which Ando dropped his countersuit in return for his freedom and a clean record. After his release, he moved with his family to the house in Ikeda City, where he hoped to rebuild. But there was more hardship to come.

> I was free, and as an entrepreneur it was back to square one. Of course, it's human fate that once things go wrong, it gets harder and harder to turn them around. There must have been a deep unrest in my soul, and I guess it clouded my judgment.

I bought an iced green tea and a Korean-grilled beef bento box on the bullet train and read another episode in the comic book.

Sex—or sexual attraction, anyway—is an important theme in *Ramen Discovery Legend*. At first it's expressed subtly, through an undercurrent of romantic tension between Fujimoto and the secretary, Ms. Sakura. They visit ramen shops together on lunch breaks, and when Ms. Sakura uses vacation time to accompany Fujimoto on a ramen research trip to Fukuoka Prefecture, coworkers gossip about her intentions. The sexuality gets more explicit when the character Kyoko is introduced. If you're Ms. Sakura, Kyoko is your worst nightmare: a cute ramen freak drawn with impossibly large breasts. Kyoko has many ex-boyfriends, and she's constantly showing up with a different one. "Another ex-boyfriend?" Ms. Sakura always thinks. Ms. Sakura is afraid Fujimoto might have a crush on Kyoko, but she has nothing to worry about. He's in love with Ms. Sakura, and not tempted by Kyoko at all.

At Tokyo Station, I switched to the Yamanote Line. I got off at Ebisu Station. Why Ebisu? I know restaurants in Ebisu. I know bars in Ebisu. I feel powerful and desirable in Ebisu. Outside the station, I stood with my suitcase near a taxi stand while Japanese people jostled around me. Tokyo was not as hot as Osaka, but my clothes were already sticking to my skin. Across the street, I saw a sign running vertically along the side of a building.

The sign said HOTEL EXCELLENT.

It sounded like the setting for a Haruki Murakami short story, where behind the front desk there would be a talking goat, or something similar. I wheeled my suitcase across the street and rode an escalator to the Hotel Excellent's second-floor entrance. The walls of the lobby were a beige shade of marble, and there was something Murakami-esque about the hotel, though I don't remember any Murakami stories being set in a room with beige marble walls. Maybe the darkness of the lobby reminded me of the Gothic hallway at Princeton University where I met him, where he refused to explain the meaning of the woman who smelled her hand.

"Welcome to the Hotel Excellent," the front desk clerk said.

"I'd like a room for one night."

The clerk's uniform was brown with gold buttons. The buttons made me think of the uniforms in the comic book series *Hotel*, in which the staff take their jobs very seriously and always solve guests' problems. Like *Fantasy Island*, but indoors. I wondered if the clerk had read it.

"Certainly, sir."

I dropped my suitcase in the room and walked back to Ebisu Station, where I jumped on one of the people movers. When I was a student at International Christian University, Ebisu Station was drab and quiet, but since then a fancy department store with a high-end food court had sprouted above the tracks. People movers now conveyed pedestrians to Ebisu Garden Place, an elaborate new shopping mall anchored by a Westin Hotel and a restaurant operated by the celebrated French chef Joël Robuchon. (His restaurant is housed in a full-scale replica of a French chalet.) In a gourmet grocery store that sold foreign wines and cheeses, I asked the man behind the counter for a taste of Bleu des Causses, and I was savoring its creamy, salty goodness when I noticed a woman in the shop. I say "noticed," but I don't think that at first I even saw her. It was more like I sensed her presence.

I turned to look. She wore a blue sweater and jeans, and her body reminded me of Kyoko's in *Ramen Discovery Legend*. She was standing in front of a shelf labeled CALIFORNIA WINES. I didn't have to think about what to say. I spoke in English because it would be less threatening. Tokyo is full of Japanese-speaking foreigners who approach beautiful women, and I didn't want her to think that I was one of them, I guess because I was.

"Do you like California wines?"

She seemed surprised, but not uninterested.

"Are you Americans?" she asked.

Her English was good, not perfect.

"I'm from California."

Her eyes lit up.

"Do you recommend?"

I recognized one of the labels from a winery I had visited in Napa Valley, and when I recommended it, she smiled and I asked her name. She told me it was Masako. She also told me that she had just been divorced, and that her married name had been Ando. It's a common last name, but it was still quite a coincidence. I asked for her phone number and if she wanted to have dinner with me.

With Yamazaki everything was always difficult, but with the second Masako Ando it was not.

I didn't have to think at all. I just knew what to do. I knew that I should wait a few hours before calling her. I knew that I should wear my black shirt. I knew that I should take her out to dinner at Kitchen Five, which I feel guilty about now because it had been a special place for Harue and me. The owner was a middle-aged woman who closed the restaurant every six months and traveled somewhere in the world, usually in the Mediterranean, where she would stay with a family or cook at a restaurant. After mastering regional dishes, she would return to Tokyo and add them to her menu at Kitchen Five. Harue and I used to linger after dessert, browsing photo albums from the owner's culinary excursions.

The Kitchen Five owner always prepared all of her dishes in large serving trays, which she displayed at the counter as if she were hosting a potluck. Masako and I chose the lasagna, a lamb stew, and a stuffed artichoke. Over the course of the meal, I learned that Masako worked for a Japanese airline, but she made it clear that she was a ground-based agent, not a flight attendant. There was something in the way she said this that conveyed an image of herself as a runner-up. She was thirty-five and had grown up in Sapporo. Foreign men frequently asked her out.

"Do you think it's my breasts?" she asked, matter-of-factly.

The bill came to nearly $150. I didn't think about the money at all. Masako said she wanted to take me to her favorite bar, so after I paid the check at Kitchen Five, she hailed a taxi. She directed the driver, and when he stopped we were in an alley in a quiet residential neighborhood. I didn't see any stores, or, for that matter, bars.

The taxi door flew open on its own, which surprised me because I hadn't been in Japan for a while, and I had forgotten how taxi drivers always open the passenger's door with a mechanical remote control. Outside the cab, Masako began walking toward what looked like someone's home. When we got closer to the building, I saw a small sign above what might once have been a garage.

The sign said SOUL STATION in katakana.

I followed Masako Ando inside. Soul Station was a bar counter, a sofa, and a few chairs. The owner, a short forty-year-old with a shaved scalp, manned the bar. Behind him, three long shelves showed off his LP collection—all soul and rhythm and blues. He must have had two thousand records. We sat on stools at the counter, and Masako ordered a mojito, which she said was just becoming popular in Tokyo. I ordered one, too.

While mixing the drinks, the owner asked what kind of music I liked. I told him that I played the trombone, and he named some famous trombone players, mostly to show me that he knew them. J. J. Johnson, Kai Winding, Curtis Fuller.

"You like Fred Wesley?" he asked.

I told him that, yes, I liked Fred Wesley, and I tried not to think about the trombone striptease. The bartender served the mojitos in tall, thin glasses.

"*Kampai,*" I said, lifting my glass.

"*Kampai!*" Masako echoed. Then she asked a question. "*Ne ... nan de Ando Momofuku ni aitai no?*"

I had told Masako over dinner that I wanted to meet Ando, and now she was asking why. Zen had asked the same question. When Masako asked it, though, I felt close to her, and even without kissing her, I imagined a future in which I moved to Japan and she worked at the airport and I did translating or some other job in Tokyo and we got married and ate at lots of nice restaurants. The bar owner grabbed an album from his shelf, sliding the disk onto his turntable. The album was *Pass the Peas: Best of the J.B.'s,* and the title track started with someone (Fred Wesley?) posing a question to organist Bobby Byrd.

"Hey, Bobby, why do you like soul food?"

"Because," Bobby answered, "it makes me"—then he stretched out the last word—"haaaaaaaaaaaapy."

Why did I want to meet the inventor of instant noodles? It was a straightforward question. I shook my head at the foolishness of my reply.

"I just wanted to."

We talked about lots of other things, and then Masako asked another question.

"Where are you staying?"

I told her.

"That's a great name for a hotel," she said, and when we finished our mojitos, the owner called us another taxi.

At the Hotel Excellent, the driver flung the rear door open with his remote control, and Masako got out of the car. We rode the escalator together to the second-floor lobby.

"Do you want to hang out in my room?" I asked, even though it was not yet Day Seventy of my ninety-day commitment to Matt.

She walked into the elevator without answering, and when we got to my room, she headed straight for the bathroom, where she proceeded to take a shower. When she came out, she was wearing nothing but one of the hotel's yukata robes. The words *Hotel Excellent* were printed in katakana, hundreds of times, all over the robe. She said she hadn't been with anyone since her divorce, which meant in over a year.

For the next hour, I didn't think at all about failing to meet Momofuku Ando.

When we fell asleep, I dreamed that Yamazaki called and invited me to participate in the training on Futonjima, the deserted island. The managers and I were pitching tents on the beach when I heard a helicopter above me, and looking up, I saw the Chikin Ramen Tweety Bird–like mascot painted on the helicopter's tail. A rope ladder unfurled from the helicopter, and Nissin CEO Koki Ando, in sweatpants and a T-shirt, descended on it, then jumped onto the beach. "What do you want?" he screamed at the managers. The managers shouted answers. "I want an instant T-bone steak!"; "I want instant lobster!"; "I want instant world peace!" Staring right at me, Koki repeated his question, but I awoke before answering.

It was five o'clock in the morning, and I was alone in the twin bed. Masako lived in the neighborhood, so she must have walked home. The yukata robe lay neatly folded on the desk.

I got out of bed and jumped into the shower. The nozzle was higher than the one in the Osaka business hotel, so the water hit my chest instead of my belly. The soap smelled sweet, like apricots. I scrubbed it into my skin with a small cloth. I scrubbed hard, as if I could wash away the fact that I had broken my promise to Matt.

*A*ll of Ando's accounts are vague about how he became the chairman of the credit association, the demise of which led to his year in the backyard shack. He states only that he initially turned down the post but was eventually "sweet-talked" into it.

"Just lend us your name," someone from the association said.

Although Ando lost most of his wealth during the two years he was held in Sugamo Prison, his reputation remained intact. Making the rounds of his business contacts and friends in downtown Osaka, he gathered nearly half a million dollars in deposits in just one day.

Unfortunately, his credit association made many bad loans. Ando claims they were executed by subordinates without his knowledge. Nevertheless, when the association declared bankruptcy, depositors went after him to recoup their losses. They took almost everything he had.

"I was left with only my house in Ikeda City," he writes in *Magic Noodles*, "and a mind tormented with regret. I wondered if this was what it meant to be punished by heaven."

PART III

THE FUNDAMENTAL MISUNDERSTANDING OF HUMANITY

Let me tell you a little about Andrew. That's his real name, by the way.

When he says that he works for a "nationally published business magazine," he's trying to imply that it's a magazine you've heard of, like Fortune *or* Forbes *or* Business-Week. *Trust me, you've never heard of it. Did you know that he's disliked by many of the editors and writers he works with? It's true. One reason is that he's conceited, as evidenced by the fact that he often gets upset when his story ideas are criticized. Every Thursday morning at eleven o'clock, Josh presides over the story meeting in the large conference room, and writers and editors like Andy pitch their story ideas. While one person is pitching, others around the table chime in with their objections. Things like "Business-Week did that story last week" or "If we do that story it might not work out because" of x, y, or z. But Andrew is so sensitive that he can't handle the objections. His ego is so fragile that he gets upset hearing this kind of honest, constructive criticism. I mean, please. This is how idea meetings work at every magazine and newspaper on the planet!*

He's not so in shape anymore. There is the beginning of a paunch. A layer of flab has appeared on the insides of his thighs. I tell him YOU SHOULD BE THINNER, but he says he can't do long-distance running because he feels pain in his shins from so many marathons. I always tell him, YOU SHOULD NOT HAVE RUN SO MANY MARATHONS. I used to tell him, YOU SHOULD DO YOGA, but that was a disaster. He tried it, and aside from downward dog, he couldn't do the poses. He couldn't even do downward dog properly, and the teacher had to come around and make adjustments. Did I say anything about that? No, I didn't. I kept my mouth shut. Until one day Andrew's in yoga and it's the end of the class and the teacher is doing the shavasana *and she's saying, "Breathe in compassion for yourself, breathe out compassion for others," and before she's finished, he farts. He farts in yoga, right in the middle of this very contemplative time! Everyone hears it, and trust me, everyone knows it was him. So I tell him, DON'T GO BACK TO YOGA FOR A COUPLE OF YEARS UNTIL THE PEOPLE CHANGE OVER AND THEY WON'T REMEMBER YOU.*

Andrew's hair is falling out and it's graying. His father has all of his hair. How embarrassing is that? I always tell him, YOU SHOULD NOT BE LOSING YOUR HAIR.

He tells people he's fluent in Japanese. Well, sort of. He can read a lot of kanji characters, yes, but he's forgetting how to write them. And he spent all that time in Japan studying how to write!

Andrew plays the trombone. Is there any instrument less cool? Let's face it. No one sits around the campfire playing the trombone. In jazz ensembles, the trombones are sandwiched between the trumpets and the saxophones, so no one sees them. In orchestras, they're in the back. Talk to any trombone player, and more likely than not, that person did not choose the instrument. Usually the band director didn't have enough trumpets to go around. I remember when Andrew got put into a class to start instruments, and the band director said, "What instrument do you want to play?" And I was like, YOU SHOULD SAY NOTHING BECAUSE YOU TRIED PLAYING THE PIANO AND

THE DRUMS AND YOU WEREN'T VERY GOOD AT EITHER ONE, SO WHAT MAKES YOU THINK YOU'LL BE GOOD AT ANOTHER INSTRUMENT? So Andrew was silent, and the teacher said, "Sit down for a surprise." The surprise was a trombone. When he moved to San Francisco, he answered an ad for a funk band, and I was thinking, OK, that might get him some exposure because horn players stand in the front in funk bands. But Andrew is a bad dancer and a bad soloist. I keep telling him, YOU ARE A BAD DANCER AND A BAD SOLOIST, SO DON'T DANCE AND DON'T TAKE SOLOS BECAUSE IT'S GOING TO BE EMBARRASSING.

Andrew has very few male friends. There's Andy, who Andrew met in summer camp, but Andy has a wife and two children and has moved on to adult stages of life, while Andrew remains stunted and single. Andrew used to have three good friends from high school named Dan, Dave, and Sam, but when the four of them would get together as adults, Dan, Dave, and Sam would reminisce about how they went on a backpacking trip to Maine after high school graduation and how the three of them canoed and smoked pot and had all kinds of adventures that Andrew wasn't part of. Sometimes Dan, Dave, and Sam reminisced about a game they played in junior high school with Ritz crackers, where they would sit around and jerk off onto the crackers and the last one to do it had to eat all the crackers. Now I'm not saying those guys actually ever played the game, but Andrew was certainly never invited. So rather than watch him suffer the humiliation of being the odd man out during get-togethers, I told Andrew, YOU SHOULD BREAK OFF

ALL CONTACT WITH DAN AND DAVE AND SAM. In San Francisco, Andrew plays Ultimate Frisbee every Saturday morning with a group of thirty- and forty-something men who have known each other since college, and they all go out for beers or burgers after the games. But they never invite Andrew. Which is probably for the best, because if Andrew were going to hang out with them, he wouldn't know what to say. I guess he's still friends with Zen, but that relationship is strained. Zen is in Japan making tons of money as a management coach, so it's obvious which of the two of them has skills and value.

It's a shame, really, because Andrew was born with so much promise. He had so much of what I'll call "life potential." But I'm like, make something of that already, will you? When he didn't get to meet Ando, I said over and over, YOU SHOULD NOT HAVE TRIED BECAUSE IT WAS CLEAR THAT YOU WERE GOING TO FAIL AND ANYWAY NO ONE REALLY CARES ABOUT HIM. Then, when he broke his promise to Matt, I told him, YOU SHOULD JUST GO HOME NOW BECAUSE IT'S PRETTY CLEAR THAT YOU ARE NEVER GOING TO HAVE A REAL, COMMITTED RELATIONSHIP WITH A WOMAN, NO MATTER HOW MUCH YOU PRAY TO THE INVENTOR OF INSTANT FUCKING RAMEN FOR HELP.

*M*asako and I had planned to visit the Yokohama Ramen Museum, but I decided to change my plane reservation and fly home instead. In the morning, I called her to say I was leaving, and she walked to Ebisu Station to see me off. She let me know that she was disappointed and confused.

"What happened?" she asked. "Why did you change your flight?"

I was confused myself, so I didn't know what to tell her. We sat for a while in a coffee shop, and then I hugged her good-bye. As I passed through the Ebisu Station turnstile, I looked back. Masako was dabbing her cheek with a tissue, in the area below her sunglasses.

I had finished all of the *Ramen Discovery Legend* books I was carrying, so on the flight I had nothing to read except *The Story of the Invention of Instant Ramen*—the Nissin-published English translation of *Magic Noodles* that Matsubara had given me. The book answered questions about the invention of instant ramen that I didn't even know I had.

Q: Did Ando set goals for the instant ramen he hoped to develop?
A: Yes, he established five goals. He wanted the resulting noodles to be

1. *Tasty*
2. *Able to keep for a long time*
3. *Ready in three minutes or less*

4. Economical

5. Healthy and safe

Q: What lucky developments coincided with the 1958 launch of Chikin Ramen and helped make it successful?

A: At least three:

1. *Japanese commercial TV broadcasts began in 1953, allowing Nissin to advertise Chikin Ramen to a mass audience on shows such as* Beaver-chan (Leave It to Beaver).
2. *Japan's gross national product grew by 17.5 percent in 1959, and 14 percent in 1960.*
3. *Instant coffee was introduced to Japan in 1960, helping popularize the word* instant *(spelled "インスタント" in katakana).*

Q: What did Ando do when Nissin went public on the Tokyo Stock Exchange in 1963?

A: He recalled the year in his shack, and he was deeply moved.

Q: Why did Ando almost not make his historic journey to the United States in 1966, the one during which he got the idea for Cup Noodles?

A: There had recently been two plane crashes at Tokyo's Haneda Airport, and Masako, being superstitious, urged him to stay home. "One can die even while sitting in a room," he told her, "and it's highly unlikely another accident will occur in the wake of so many."

Q: At the offices of which supermarket did he watch American executives eat Chikin Ramen with forks out of Styrofoam cups (giving him his inspiration for Cup Noodles)?

A: Holiday Magic, in Los Angeles.

Q: How did Ando feel while watching the Holiday Magic executives eat Chikin Ramen this way?

A: "At that moment, I understood what it meant to be awakened by the truth."

The book provided practically every detail about Ando's life and his invention of instant ramen except for the one that I had wondered about in the first place. Why did he suddenly devote himself to developing an instant noodle? He said he was inspired by the line at the ramen stand behind Umeda Station and by the health ministry official who challenged him to research noodles. But why did he commit himself ten years later? I still didn't see it. It struck me, however, that aside from taking only three minutes to prepare, the goals Ando set for his noodles also described the kind of healthy romantic relationship that had eluded me.

When I got home, I slept for sixteen hours. Then I called Matt. We met at a Vietnamese restaurant in the Mission District, just a few blocks from Dolores Park. He hugged me when I got there.

"Welcome back! I want to hear all about it."

We ordered bowls of pho—Vietnamese noodle soup topped with thin slices of raw beef—and I related everything that had happened. I told Matt that I felt like a failure for breaking my commitment, and that I would understand if he quit as my mentor.

"Don't beat yourself up about it, buddy," he said.

I felt better hearing Matt call me "buddy."

"It was Ando's will."

I felt worse when he talked like Ando was really God. He grabbed a stem of fresh basil from a side plate and tore the leaves off, sprinkling them over his soup.

"Did you write in your notebook before you went to Tokyo?"

I remembered that I did, and I told Matt about the second-person capitalized voice that came out on the page.

"So you've started hearing your voice," he said.

He made it sound like everyone had one.

"You have a voice, Matt?"

"Mine sounds like my father."

"Really? What does your father say to you?"

"Well, it sounds like my father, but it's not my father. And that's an important distinction. Anyway, I just started dating someone, and she's great. But my voice is always telling me that she's out of my league."

"So you ignore it?"

Matt slurped his noodles.

"Ignoring it will get you into trouble. You have to listen to it."

"Then what?"

Instead of answering the question, Matt made another demand.

"I want you to commit to another ninety days of no dating and no sex."

I was sure that I would be single for the rest of my life, but I still didn't know what else to do.

"OK."

"I also want you to write a few pages as if you are that voice. Be it."

"OK."

"Then I want you to think back to your childhood and try to recall when you heard the voice. Write to Ando about what you remember."

"But I just started hearing it last week, when I was in Japan."

"Yeah, well, it's probably been with you for a long time. It might help if you write as if the past is happening now."

"You mean, in present tense?"

"Right."

"OK." It was all I could do not to roll my eyes. "Anything else?"

"Uh, one more thing. This time, jot down in your notebook whenever you want something that is *not* related to dating or sex. Then listen to what this voice has to say about what you wrote."

"OK."

"Repeat after me."

Before I could stop him, Matt put his hands together in what looked like the *gassho* pose. He closed his eyes.

"O Momofuku."

"Matt, I'm sorry. This praying to Ando thing is a joke. It didn't work."

"What are you talking about?" Matt said. "It worked perfectly."

"No it didn't. I broke my commitment."

"Listen, by not meeting you, Ando put you in touch with your voice. This was the luckiest thing that could have happened. Don't you get it? Ando made this happen."

The waiter brought the check, and when he saw both of us with our hands in front of our chests in the *gassho* pose, he gave us a look.

"O Momofuku," I repeated.

"Please show me how not meeting you was lucky, how not meeting you was the way to better do your will."

I repeated it, and then I went home to write about the voice. As usual, Matt was right. It had been there for a very long time.

Dear Momofuku,

I am seven years old, and I am walking in front of a toy store with my mother. In the window, I see Trouble, the Milton Bradley board game, and I am overcome with the desire to own it.

Trouble comes with two dice encased in a plastic dome—the trademarked Pop-O-Matic. When you push down on the dome, a taut metal strip underneath buckles, rolling the dice. I am the only kid on our block in Brooklyn without Trouble, the only kid without a Pop-O-Matic.

"Can you buy me Trouble?" I ask my mother.

"No," she answers. "You'll play it once and you'll get tired of it. Then it'll sit in the closet, and you'll feel like an idiot for wanting it in the first place."

I start to cry.

"Stop your crying," my mother says.

I don't stop crying. "I want Trouble!"

"I told you to stop your crying!" she yells.

I can't stop.

"Stop your crying this instant!"

I don't stop, so she raises her hand. She clenches her teeth and shuts her eyes, and there is so much anger coursing through her body that she starts to tremble. As she spanks me, she punctuates each attack with a word.

"You"—whack—"better"—whack—"stop"—whack—"crying"—whack—"this"—whack—"minute"—whack—"you"—whack—"no"—whack—"good"—whack—"dirty"—whack—"rotten"—whack—"idiot!"

She pauses to catch her breath, then continues.

"What"—whack—"is"—whack—"wrong"—whack—
"with"—whack—"you?"

There is a rhythm to her hitting, the pain and the volume of her insults rising then falling, like waves crashing on a beach.

I am still crying when my father comes home from work.

"Stop your crying!" my father says.

He doesn't say anything while spanking me. He is six feet tall and built like a linebacker.

When he leaves the room, Momofuku, I hear the voice for the first time.

YOU SHOULD NOT TRUST YOUR DESIRES, BECAUSE THEY WILL MAKE YOU FEEL LIKE AN IDIOT AND BRING YOU SO MUCH PAIN.

Sincerely,
Andy

I didn't suddenly remember the spankings and the insults when I started writing the second set of letters to the inventor of instant ramen. Long before I learned about Momofuku Ando, I had discussed them with my parents. We would sit together—in a park when they visited me in San Francisco, or at their house on Long Island when I visited them—and I would ask what I had done that made them so angry. My mother would rub her forehead and cry, and through her tears she would say that if there were one thing she could go back and do differently in her life, it was that. She would tell me that as a young child I was always crying and that my crying touched off a rage that she could not control. My father would apologize, too, though he defended the spankings as standard practice for the times. "People spanked their kids back then," he would say, and he was certainly right. These discussions always ended with my parents feeling blamed for something they regretted but couldn't change, and they would urge me to take an antidepressant. I would refuse, and sometimes we would stop speaking for months.

After writing this last letter to Ando, I made a list five pages long of all the wonderful things my parents did for me, and while I thought about reproducing the list here, suffice it to say that I have been very lucky to have them. Nevertheless, when I tried to remember the first time I heard the voice, it was after one of the spankings.

Meanwhile, my second abstinence period went more smoothly than the first. I still had the occasional thought about placing online dating ads, but I didn't count the days. Whenever I wanted to do something—anything at all that was unrelated to dating or sex—I would record it as a memo to Ando in my notebook, per Matt's instructions. Then I would listen to what the voice had to say about it.

Momofuku: *I want to watch* Seven Samurai.
ANOTHER SAMURAI MOVIE? WHY DON'T YOU TAKE UP ORIGAMI WHILE YOU'RE AT IT?

Until renting *Samurai Trilogy I: Musashi Miyamoto,* I had never watched a samurai movie in my life. I had been proud of the fact that I had never watched any, the way I was proud that I didn't know anything about karate or tea ceremony or flower arranging. I was not *that* kind of *gaijin.* But because I had rented that first samurai movie, *Seven Samurai* showed up one day in my online video store's "Movies You'll ♥" list.

Seven Samurai turned out to be a tale of isolated men trying to find connection and meaning in their lives. My favorite part was when the head samurai, Kambei, recruits his old deputy, Shichiroji, to defend the farming village from bandits. As his recruiting pitch, Kambei says, "It will bring us neither money nor fame. Want to join?" To which Shichiroji immediately replies, "Yes." What Shichiroji values above all else is the connection to his former master.

I rated *Seven Samurai* five stars out of five, so the online video store recommended more samurai movies, including *Yojimbo* and what would become my favorite samurai movie of all, *Hara-kiri.* (The latter is about a castle where samurai show up—without appointments—asking if it's OK to kill themselves in the courtyard). Next I rented *Tale of Zatoichi,* the first film in the long-running Zatoichi series. The synopsis label on the DVD sleeve said "(1962) Blind masseur and swordsman Zatoichi (Shintaro Katsu) is living and working in a province that's under siege by rival warlords. . . . Unwilling to sit idle while his province is ruthlessly destroyed, Zatoichi must take matters into his own hands, regardless of the consequences."

Unable to go on dates, I had plenty of time to sit idle in my living room. I rented eighteen more movies in the Zatoichi series, watching one Zatoichi movie after the next. The online video store shipped the exact same synopsis label on all of them, but because the plot in every Zatoichi film was more or less the same, the description was never far off. If anything changed from movie to movie, it was Zatoichi's approach to women. In the early Zatoichi installments, when young girls fell for the main character, he tended to reject them, putting himself down as a good-for-nothing wandering samurai. But around 1970, Shintaro Katsu, the actor who played Zatoichi, started his own production company to make Zatoichi and other films. In these he played swaggering studs who conquered women and swordsmen alike. In *Hanzo the Razor: Sword of Justice* (1972), Katsu's character is a detective who pounds his penis with a stone (to keep it in shape) and drags secrets out of courtesans by suspending them naked from the ceiling, bound in a net, and lowering them over his erect member until they orgasm.

I watched *Incident at Blood Pass, The Twilight Samurai, Kagemusha, Chushingura, The Sword of Doom, Sanshiro Sugata, Sanshiro Sugata 2, Hidden Fortress,* and *Lone Wolf and Cub: Baby Cart in the Land of Demons.* I watched *Samurai Rebellion.* I watched the disappointing *Yojimbo Meets Zatoichi.* For months it seemed like all I did was watch samurai movies. I watched them mostly at night and on weekends, but sometimes I watched them on the DVD player in my office computer. If there was one thing, above all, that surprised me about samurai movies, it was that, in general, the heroes don't do very much. A lot of the time, they just sit around. For instance, in *Samurai Trilogy II: Duel at Ichioji Temple,* Takezo spends a good part of each day in his room, whittling. Sometimes he peruses ancient texts. Zatoichi can frequently be found sharpening his sword, gambling, or giving massages.

Of course, this is how they prepare for battle. A silly thought crossed my mind. Was it Ando's will that I watch samurai movies in preparation for some kind of battle?

Dear Momofuku,

I am eleven years old, and I'm at sleepaway camp for the summer. I live in an A-frame cabin with nine other boys. My best friend is Adam. Adam and I have a lot in common. We both have curly brown hair, we like to play baseball, and we're the only boys in the bunk with pubes.

One night, just after the sun sets, Adam walks outside the cabin and howls. Like a wolf.

"Aooooooooooooooooo!"

A few days later, we have what's called a boy-girl social. That's where we get together with girls and have a campfire in the woods. The counselors build the fire and play their guitars, while we kids roast hot dogs and marshmallows on sticks. Adam and I are chewing on burned marshmallows and singing folk songs like "Circle Game" and "Leaving on a Jet Plane," but I'm not singing very loud.

YOU SHOULD JUST KIND OF MOUTH THE WORDS BECAUSE IF PEOPLE HEAR YOUR SINGING VOICE THEY'LL MAKE FUN OF YOU.

In the middle of "Puff the Magic Dragon," a girl our age approaches us.

"Who did the howl?"

She must have heard Adam all the way over where the girls' cabins were.

"It was me," Adam says.

The girl walks away. Later she returns, but this time she's joined by three of her friends. The four girls crowd around Adam.

"Do the howl," they cry. "Come on, do the howl!"

Adam acts embarrassed, but then he stands up. He plants his right foot on the large rocks that surround the campfire. He tilts his head back, cupping his hands around his mouth. Even before he makes a sound, as he's doing this preparation, the girls' eyes track his every movement.

Their lips tighten.

Adam howls at the stars, undulating the pitch and dragging it out for what feels like forever.

"Aooo, aoooo, aoooo . . . !"

The girls applaud and laugh and jump up and down.

"Do it again," they scream. "Do the howl again!"

Adam is bathed in female attention. Watching this, I come to the conclusion that any reasonable person would come to, which is that what girls want, what makes them want you, is howling.

I am about to howl myself.

YOU SHOULDN'T TRY IT BECAUSE, WELL, YOU'RE NOT A HOWLER. YOU'RE JUST NOT. I MEAN, IT'S GOING TO BE EMBARRASSING IF YOU TRY AND FAIL. BESIDES, HOWLING IS ADAM'S THING, SO EVEN IF YOU CAN DO IT, YOU'LL LOOK LIKE A COPYCAT. YOU SHOULD FIND SOMETHING THAT IS HOWLING-LIKE, BUT NOT HOWLING.

I try to think of something else. One idea is to memorize the names of all of the episodes of Star Trek. *But of course that is being a copycat, too, because Adam has memorized not only the names of all the episodes, but also the order in which they were originally broadcast. Another idea is model rockets. I love model rockets. At home, I buy kits with my allowance money and after I build them, my father takes me* to a park near our house to shoot them off. Sometimes they fly so high I can't see them until the parachute pops out.

It takes time and effort to make my knowledge of model rockets a selling point to the girls at camp. The rockets are manufactured by the Estes Aerospace Corporation, so during rest periods I memorize the names of all the models in the Estes Aerospace catalog, including Big Bertha, Apogee II, and the Mars Lander. I memorize their weights and lengths, and details about which ones fly highest on C6-5 engines and which ones can handle D engines. I memorize how high each one is expected to fly with a given engine, and so on.

At the next boy-girl social, I am flipping through the Estes Aerospace catalog next to a blond-haired girl, hoping she will notice.

"What's that?" she asks.

"It's a catalog of model rockets."

"Do they really fly?"

"Yeah. I'm going to shoot off the Shark on the baseball fields tomorrow. My parents brought it on Visiting Day, and last week I cut the fins from balsa wood and applied the decals. I'm thinking of using a C6-3 engine on it."

"I'm thirsty," the girl says, and she walks away.

WHAT KIND OF IDIOT THINKS THAT GIRLS ARE GOING TO BE IMPRESSED BY YOUR KNOWLEDGE OF MODEL ROCKETS?

When I get back to the cabin, I lift the Shark off the Estes Aerospace launchpad, and rip it to shreds.

Sincerely,
Andy

*M*omofuku: *I want to learn how to paint.*
    CAN YOU EVER MATCH "THE DRIP-UP"?

The last time I painted something, I was in the first grade. I tried to paint a man standing outside on a sunny day, but I mixed too much water into the watercolor paint, and the blue in the sky dripped down, obscuring the scene. I turned the painting upside down and titled it the "The Drip-Up." It's still hanging in my parents' living room.

As for where the desire to draw came from, I'm not sure. It's possible that watching Takezo whittle in *Samurai Trilogy II* had something to do with it, because there was something attractive about that, though I didn't feel like whittling. My friend Carla, who is a painter, suggested that I start out with a drawing class, so I enrolled in one at City College of San Francisco. On the first day, the teacher placed a plastic duck on a pedestal in the middle of the classroom.

"Your assignment," the teacher said, "is to sketch the duck with a stick of charcoal." But there was a catch. "You may not look at your hand or your paper."

"Just look at the duck," the teacher urged, over and over. "Really *see* the duck."

When I was done with the sketch, I looked at my paper.
THIS LOOKS LIKE A SHOE, NOT A DUCK.

And then I understood that the purpose of the exercise was to hear that voice, and that there were many ways to begin hearing it, not only trying (and failing) to meet the inventor of instant ramen without an appointment.

A woman in the class said, "My drawing so does not look like a duck!" She must have found the voice in her head unbearable, because soon she was in tears, hitting herself over the head with a pencil sharpener. She left the classroom and never came back.

Momofuku: I want to try yoga again.
NOT WISE. I THINK THERE WILL STILL BE PEO-
PLE WHO REMEMBER.

Momofuku: I want to buy a new trombone.
WHAT'S WRONG WITH THE YAMAHA?

The trombone I had played for twenty-five years, the one my parents bought me when I was in high school, had been stolen from my car in a San Francisco parking lot. For several years I had played a spare Yamaha model, but I didn't like it very much. It just didn't feel like me.

I tracked down a used instrument shop in the phone book, and drove over. I blew into nine used trombones, but they were all either too wispy- or fat-sounding. On my way out, I spotted a tenth trombone, a 1959 Conn 78H, and when I blew into it, I heard a tone that was not too wispy and not too fat. It sounded regal, but kind of dirty. Like a king standing in a swamp.

I traded in my Yamaha for the 78H, and on the way home from the instrument shop, I stopped at a Starbucks, where I sat down at one of the tables to read the essay at the end of *Ramen Discovery Legend* Book 13, the one about hard versus soft water in ramen broths. (An essay by real-life ramen critic Hideyuki Ishigami—under titles such as "Toppings," "Scallions," and "Roast Pork"—appears at the end of every *Ramen Discovery Legend* paperback.) Halfway through, I noticed a woman standing in front of me.

"You play bone?" the woman asked.

I looked up. She had gray hair and she was pointing to the instrument case at my feet.

"Yes."

"You like jazz?"

"Yes."

She asked a barista for a napkin and a pen. Then she wrote an address on the napkin and handed it to me.

"Go there on Monday night," she said.

"What's there?"

"Just go. And bring the horn."

The following Monday night, I found the address on a gray warehouse in a narrow alley. As I approached the building, I began hearing the sounds of wind and percussion instruments. I knocked on the heavy front door, but no one answered. I gently pushed the door, but it wouldn't budge.

I pushed harder, and the door flew open. The band was coming to the end of a modern, up-tempo arrangement of "Take the A Train."

The musicians were all men. Most looked past retirement age, and they sat surrounded by lathes, drills, and computer-controlled saws. I noticed the cereal-box man staring down from the open loft above the saxophones, and the golf-cart-cum-spaceship parked near the piano.

"Come on in," the bass player said. "We were hoping you'd show up."

A big band usually has eighteen members. This one had only seventeen, because nobody occupied the third trombone chair. I set my case on one of the lathe tables, assembled my horn, and took that seat. The first trombonist reached out a well-worn hand.

"Name's Gary."

"Andy."

After shaking my hand, Gary examined my trombone.

"That's a fine instrument you've got there, son."

"Thanks. Just bought it the other day."

The bass player called out "one hundred thirty-five," which was the number of a tune called "Blues Machine." My 78H sounded warm and full on it, and when we got to the last note, I wanted to hold it out forever.

"You know, my old friend Archie used to play that horn," Gary said.

The 78H had once been a popular model.

"Is that right? I heard that a lot of people played this horn back in the day."

Gary shook his head.

"No. I mean, he used to play your 78H."

The C. G. Conn company must have sold thousands of 78Hs. I had never met anyone who could identify an individual trombone just by looking at it.

"You don't believe me?" Gary asked.

"I don't think so."

Gary pointed to the tuning slide atop the bell section of the horn. "Archie loved tuning that horn extra-sharp for ballroom gigs—he wanted room for slide vibrato in first position—so one time he cut the inside of your tuning slide with a hacksaw. Take a look, you'll see."

I had never looked closely at the inside of my tuning slide. But when I pulled it all the way out, I saw that the ends of the metal tubes were slightly jagged. It wasn't a factory cut.

The next tune the bass player called out was the Thad Jones arrangement "Low Down." Gary played the first trombone part on it. In spite of his age, he was a powerful player. His high-note range was far better than mine.

THAT'S NOT SAYING MUCH.

At nine o'clock, the band took a fifteen-minute break. I put my trombone back in the case and explored the warehouse. A pistol catalog from 1968 lay next to a belt sander, and hanging on one of the brick walls was a framed newspaper article about the band and how it had been together for more than fifty years. (The article had been published in the early 1990s.) Atop a tool case, I found a plastic alarm clock shaped like a samurai warrior. I pressed the topknot on the samurai's head, and a voice came out in Japanese.

"Wake up! Wake up!" it said. "The sun is rising over Japan!"

Gary heard the alarm clock.

"Son, when I was a teenager, I played on a cruise ship to Japan, and oh, boy, that was fun."

The way Gary said *fun* suggested that his fun had involved Japanese girls.

"I've spent some time in Japan," I told him. "I was in Osaka a few months ago."

"You don't say. Gig?"

"Not a gig."

"What, then?"

I wasn't sure if I should get into it.

"You know what instant ramen is?"

"The noodles?"

"I tried to meet the inventor of that."

"Why?"

I definitely didn't want to get *that* into it.

"I was researching a story for a business magazine where I'm on staff."

"How'd it go?"

"Not so well. I didn't get to meet him."

"Sorry about that," Gary said, and I could tell that he really was.

I asked Gary when the band's next gig would be, and one of the trumpet players, a thin man with a mustache, overheard. He and Gary chuckled as they explained that the band had been rehearsing,

208 · ANDY RASKIN

more or less consistently, since 1939, but that the last gig had happened sometime in the 1970s. Then the two of them debated whether what happened in the 1970s actually qualified as a gig.

The following Monday night, Gary brought me a CD of his friend Archie playing my trombone in a 1960 session with the Woody Herman Orchestra. There was no mistaking the lush yet gritty sound of the horn.

"You like prime rib?" Gary asked, the Monday night after that.

The woman at Starbucks turned out to be the girlfriend of the second tenor saxophonist. I think they broke up, though, because I never saw her again.

Dear Momofuku,

Only one kid in the class gets a perfect score on the electricity test.

"It's Andrew!" my sixth-grade teacher announces.

I am so proud of myself that I beam as I walk past my classmates to pick up my test. Later, in the hallway, a girl named Debra approaches.

"You are so conceited," she says.

I don't know what the word means, but from Debra's tone I know that it must be something bad. Maybe it's dirty. At night, I look it up in my dictionary.

YOU SHOULD NOT THINK YOU ARE A SMART PERSON.

"Oh, right," I start saying in algebra class, "you have to divide by x." As if I've just realized the mistake. I used to get straight As, but by giving wrong answers on purpose, I've turned myself into a solid B student. That isn't winning me friends either, though. Other kids begin dating and going to parties where everyone plays spin the bottle. I don't get invited.

LISTEN, NO ONE WANTS TO DATE OR KISS A KID WHO'S CONCEITED.

To not face that fact, I go to bed after school and sleep until dinnertime. I wake up to eat and do my homework, but then I go right back to sleep. I do this every day for three months.

"Why are you sleeping all the time?" my mother asks. "And why do you destroy your model rockets when you get mad?"

I don't know how to explain it. My mother is concerned, so she takes me to see a psychologist named Dr. G.

We're sitting in Dr. G's waiting room, which is on the second floor of his home. A bust of someone I assume to be Sigmund Freud (I'll learn later that it's Dr. G's idol, Carl Jung) rests on a pedestal.

CRAZY PEOPLE GO TO PSYCHOLOGISTS.

The door to Dr. G's office opens, and he invites me in. He's a middle-aged man with greasy gray hair. On the first visit, he runs me through a battery of diagnostic tests that include sentence completion, short-term recall, Rorschach inkblots, scene drawings, storytelling, and pattern recognition. The tests take several hours.

A week later, my parents accompany me to Dr. G's office to hear the results. Dr. G first meets with them alone, while I wait in the waiting room and stare at Freud (Jung). When Dr. G opens his door, I take a seat between my parents on the sofa in his office.

Dr. G starts with the sentence completions.

"Let's look at the first one. The sentence says, 'My father ___.' And Andrew filled it in with 'is Frankenstein.' "

YOU SHOULD NOT BE A FATHER-HATING BOY.

I try to deny it.

"Just before taking the test, I was watching The Munsters.*"*

The Munsters *is a TV show about a family of monsters in which the father looks like Frankenstein. Dr. G goes right to the next sentence completion.*

"This one says, 'I want to go ___.' You wrote 'to Paris.' Hmm."

Dr. G's "hmm" makes my mother anxious.

"What does that mean, Dr. G?"

"It indicates," Dr. G says, straightening his glasses, "a certain desire to escape."

YOU SHOULD NOT BE A FATHER-HATING BOY WHO WANTS TO ESCAPE.

I protest. "It says 'go.' So you have to go somewhere, right? How would you fill in that blank without sounding like you want to escape?"

Dr. G smiles. "You could have said you wanted to go swimming. Or fishing."

YOU HAVE TO ADMIT THAT DR. G HAS A POINT ON THAT ONE.

The next piece of evidence on Dr. G's docket is my drawing of an adult woman. He holds it up for my parents and me to see, directing our attention to the woman's chest.

"Notice," Dr. G says, "that this woman has no breasts."

My drawing is little more than a stick figure with a wavy line meant to indicate long hair.

"Is that unusual at his age?" my father inquires.

"He's twelve," Dr. G says. "Well, a little."

YOU SHOULD NOT BE A FATHER-HATING BOY WHO WANTS TO ESCAPE AND WHO HAS AN UN-USUAL SEXUAL ISSUE.

By the time Dr. G tells us how high I scored on the memory portion of the test, I am no longer paying attention. That's because my entire consciousness is focused on a single thought.

YOU ARE CRAZY.

For the next two years, my mother takes me, two

afternoons a week, to see Dr. G. Usually I just sit on his sofa and talk about what's going on at school.

IT DOESN'T MATTER WHAT YOU TALK ABOUT, AS LONG AS IT ISN'T ABOUT BEING ANGRY WITH YOUR PARENTS, WANTING TO ESCAPE, OR BEING UNCOMFORTABLE ABOUT SEX. BECAUSE IT'S PRETTY CLEAR FROM DR. G'S TESTS THAT THOSE ARE NOT FEELINGS THAT A NORMAL, SANE PERSON IS SUPPOSED TO HAVE.

Dr. G often stares at me from his big, black leather chair. There are many uncomfortable silences during our sessions. The two of us just stare each other down for minutes on end.

YOU SHOULD MAINTAIN EYE CONTACT WITH HIM. BECAUSE IF YOU BREAK IT, IT WILL BE EVIDENCE THAT YOU ARE HIDING SOMETHING, LIKE THE FACT THAT YOU HATE YOUR PARENTS AND THAT YOU WANT TO ESCAPE AND THAT YOU HAVE AN UNUSUAL SEXUAL ISSUE.

I often have the urge to look away, but I always resist it.

Sincerely,
Andy

*J*osh twirled spaghetti on a fork.

"Are you happy?" he asked.

After I returned from Japan, he promoted me from senior writer to senior editor, and then again to assistant managing editor. But he was putting pressure on me to develop stories about famous technology companies. "I want you to do stories about Apple, Microsoft," he was always saying. "You know, companies people care about." I knew that he needed those stories to sell his magazine, but big companies like those have big public relations departments that are very good at controlling what's written about them. Where was the fun in that? He had taken me out to lunch because he knew something was wrong.

"I don't know," I said, biting into a slice of pizza.

"Well, you don't look happy. These last few months, you seem like you're somewhere else. You don't talk much at the idea meetings. You don't seem like you want to be here."

I thought about telling Josh that, after failing to meet the inventor of instant ramen, I had been paying attention to things that I wanted to do (aside from dating and sex), and that they included making art and watching samurai movies and playing the trombone in a 1940s-style big band that had not had a gig in thirty years. I thought about telling him that I watched samurai movies on company time, and that I suspected I might be preparing for a battle, the nature of which I did not yet understand.

"I've just been going through some things," I said instead.

Josh slurped his spaghetti.

"Anything I can do to help?"

"I don't know."

"Maybe you need a vacation?"

I had another two weeks saved, so I took Josh up on his offer.

> *Momofuku: I want to get back in shape.*
> YOU SHOULD JUST CUT PROCESSED SUGARS
> FROM YOUR DIET THE WAY YOUR MOTHER HAS.
> IT'S THAT SIMPLE.

I spent the first week of my vacation at a spa resort in Mexico, near the U.S. border. It was the type of place that attracts women of a certain age who also want to get back in shape. I went on hikes in the surrounding mountains, and did Pilates. Every week, the spa hosted a guest lecturer, and the week I was there, the guest lecturer was an elderly woman with a Ph.D. who had coauthored a seminal book about the G-spot. One evening, she led a sexuality workshop in which she discussed, among other things, a surefire method for giving men multiple orgasms. "Can anyone lend me a water bottle so I can demonstrate?" she asked the audience. The technique involved squeezing, and as she acted it out on the water bottle, I glanced at her husband, who was running the slide projector. Amazingly, he wasn't smiling. While at the spa, I felt that it would be good to get Ando off my mind for a while, so I tried not to think or talk about him. I wasn't entirely successful. As I boarded the bus to return home, a graying lesbian announced that she was changing her cat's name to Momofuku.

> *Momofuku: I want to study creative writing with Katy*
> *Butler at Tassajara.*
> WHAT, BUDDHISM?

For the second week of my vacation, I enrolled in a creative writing workshop at Tassajara, a wooded retreat area affiliated with the San Francisco Zen Center. I wasn't drawn by the Buddhism part of it, but rather by Katy Butler, a creative writing teacher who had been recommended by a friend. I found out when I arrived, though, that Katy would be co-teaching with a monk. I enjoyed the class, though it was often difficult to reconcile Katy's insights about narrative structure with the monk's koanlike directives, such as "Start anywhere" and "You don't need more knowledge." Every morning at five thirty, members of the monastery would run around ringing chimes to summon guests for a Zen sitting mediation. I usually slept through it, but one morning I dragged myself out of bed and walked to the Zen-do, a temple in the middle of the grounds. The ritual wasn't unlike the sitting training I had been forced to do as a student in Kyoto, except that everybody was American (and no one, as far as I could tell, worked at a gas station). I had been sitting silently on a cushion for half an hour when the head monk began chanting in English:

> *Beings are numberless, I vow to save them*
> *Desires are inexhaustible, I vow to end them*
> *Dharma gates are boundless, I vow to enter them*
> *Buddha's way is unsurpassable, I vow to become it*

Later the head monk identified what he had chanted as the four great vows of the bodhisattva. I didn't know what that was about, but number two made me think of the hosts on *Go Forth*.

I came home thoroughly rested, and before reporting back to work, I wrote something else in my notebook.

Momofuku: *I want to quit my job.*
YOU SHOULD JUST HUNKER DOWN AND WRITE
SOME STORIES ABOUT BIG COMPANIES. YOU

*SHOULD NEVER QUIT A JOB BEFORE YOU HAVE A
NEW JOB.*

When I told Josh I was going to leave, he seemed to understand. He threw a good-bye party in the large conference room, where he made a speech about my contributions. Everyone ate Vietnamese sandwiches, which was what Josh always served at resignation parties. I left the office in the afternoon and rode home on the Muni streetcar.

The next morning, I got dressed and walked out to the Muni stop. When I remembered that I no longer had a job to commute to, I just stood at the stop and watched the trains come and go. Matt had asked me to pay attention to my desires, and now I was not only single, but also unemployed. I didn't know whether to move my right foot or my left foot, so for a long time I didn't move either one.

Eventually I went home and watched a samurai movie.

Dear Momofuku,

I wake up and my nipples are burning. I tell my mother about it, and she makes an appointment with Dr. D, our pediatrician.

Dr. D examines me, then directs me to wait in the waiting room. This is unusual, because Dr. D always invites kids back to his office to hear the diagnosis with their mothers. In the car on the way home, my mother doesn't say anything about what Dr. D has told her. I wonder if it's something serious.

I'm doing homework at night, when there's a knock at my door.

"Hey, And. It's Dad. Can I come in?"

"Yes."

My father enters my room and sits down on the floor, cross-legged, next to the blue-and-red bookcase that he built for me. I have decorated the bookcase with Planet of the Apes stickers.

"So your mother tells me your body is going through certain changes," he says, "and I thought I would come in and talk to you about that."

Now it's all clear. Dr. D saw my pubes, the nipple burning is a symptom of puberty, and my mother has ordered my father into my room to give me a talk about the birds and the bees.

My father's version is more like a vocabulary lesson.

"There are certain words and phrases you're probably hearing from your friends," he begins, "and I just want to make sure you know what they mean."

THIS IS EMBARRASSING. YOU SHOULD TRY TO GET HIM TO LEAVE.

"*I'm really busy, Dad.*"

"*For instance,* bag." *Do you know what* bag *means?*"

"*Dad, I have a lot of homework to do!*"

"*It means 'scrotum.'*"

My entire life, I will never hear anyone use the word bag *in this manner.*

"*You also might hear your friends throw around the phrase* jerk off. *Do you know what that means?*"

OH GOD, JUST SAY YOU KNOW.

"*Yesssss, Dad.*"

I have no idea what jerk off *means.*

My father gets through necking, intercourse, *and* balls *before he finally leaves. A year later, our family moves from Brooklyn to the suburbs on Long Island because my mother wants better schools for my sister and me. Our new house is not far from Dr. G, so I still see him twice a week. The kid next door, Stuart, asks what my name is, and I tell him it's Andy, not Andrew. Andy sounds less conceited, friendlier.*

My parents join a yacht club in Manhasset Bay, which is not far from our new house. They belonged to a yacht club in Brooklyn, too, but it wasn't very fancy—just some docks and a locker room. This one has a pool.

I'm swimming in the yacht club pool when a girl named Sharon jumps in next to me. She's wearing a lime green bikini, and she has long blond hair. She's treading water. That night, before going to bed, I think about Sharon treading water in her lime green bikini, and after about an hour, a jet of milky liquid shoots into the air and lands on the clock radio behind me.

It's the kind of clock radio where white digits are printed on black plastic tabs, and the display is illuminated by an orange LED.

Every night I think about Sharon and her bikini before bed, and every night, after about an hour, my clock radio suffers a hit. The reason it takes so long is that I don't yet know how I can speed the process along.

I'm hanging out at Dan's house, listening to Monty Python Live at the Hollywood Bowl, *when I notice a crusty tube sock on the floor near his bed.*

"What's that?"

"My spooge sock," Dan says, and because he's cupping his hand and shaking it in the air, I get the idea that you're supposed to touch yourself.

"What do you use?" Dan asks.

"Spooge sock," I say, even though I've never heard of one. I've been using plain old Kleenex to wipe down the clock radio, but from the way Dan talks, it sounds like all our friends have spooge socks.

My family takes a vacation at the Nevele, a resort hotel in the Catskill Mountains. We go ice-skating and enjoy all-you-can-eat buffets. Every evening, there's a celebrity guest speaker, and on the night before we leave, the celebrity guest is Tommy Lasorda, the manager of the Los Angeles Dodgers. The New York Yankees, my favorite baseball team, have just defeated Lasorda's Dodgers in the World Series, and he's recapping the games. The TV announcers made a big deal about how Lasorda dedicated the World Series to the memory of his friend, a baseball player who recently passed away. I am such a huge Yankee fan that I want to rub it in.

"Yes, the girl in the back," Lasorda says during the question-and-answer session. My hair is puffed out in what will become known as a "Jewfro." I think it looks great, but Lasorda thinks I'm a girl.

"You dedicated the World Series to the memory of that friend of yours. Now that you lost, how do you feel?"

The Nevele audience buzzes. I've said something I shouldn't have.

ARE YOU SO INSENSITIVE, SO UNCARING, THAT YOU COULD EQUATE WINNING A BASEBALL GAME WITH THE DEATH OF A MAN?

"You know, young lady," Lasorda says, "that's just base-ball. And you're talking about a good man's life. Shame on you."

My mother is sitting next to me, and she's clearly embarrassed.

"I wish you had told me you were going to ask that question."

My family checks out of the Nevele the next morning, and I am silent in the car.

WHAT IS WRONG WITH YOU?

When we get home, I go to my room and think about Sharon in her green bikini. For a little while, at least, nothing is wrong with me.

Sincerely,
Andy

*B*etween watching samurai movies and writing the letters, I searched the Internet for books written by Ando. I found the two autobiographies, *Conception of a Fantastic Idea* and *Magic Noodles*, and I learned that he had penned several essay collections, including *Peace Follows from a Full Stomach, Noodle Road,* and *Food Changes with the Times: Field Notes of Momofuku Ando.* I ordered them all.

In his essay collections, Ando documents a series of culinary research excursions—in Japan and abroad—during which he studied noodles and other foods. Some of these have oddly beautiful titles, such as "Noodles Are Ambassadors of Peace" and "The Sadness of Tea." More interesting, however, is the way in which the autobiographies seem to hide details of his life. There's his murky decision to reside permanently in Japan, the paucity of details around his marriage to Masako, and of course, the mysterious disappearance of his eldest son, Hirotoshi. I knew from Nissin annual reports that Hirotoshi served as Nissin's CEO in the early 1980s, shortly before his younger brother Koki took over, but in the books published after that, there was no mention of him.

One night, just as I was about to go to bed, an instant message popped up on my computer screen.

"Did you hear about the summit?"

The message was from Zen.

"The what?" I instant-messaged back.

Zen e-mailed me the URL of a Japanese newspaper article describing the fifth biennial World Ramen Summit, a conference sponsored by an organization called the World Instant Noodles

Association. Under the official slogan "Happy World with Ramen," the summit had brought together representatives of the world's largest instant noodle manufacturers. Previous summits had taken place in Tokyo, Bali, Bangkok, and Shanghai; Seoul had hosted this fifth one. On the summit's official Web site, I found a photograph of Ando presiding over a dais, and another in which he was enjoying a performance by South Korean schoolchildren. The summit had ended with participants signing the Seoul Declaration, in which they pledged to uphold common manufacturing standards and to donate more instant ramen to disaster relief efforts around the world.

"When did this happen?" I typed to Zen.

"Last week."

I probably could have gotten a press pass, even though I had quit my job. I could have met Ando.

I typed back an expletive.

"Andy, do you still want to meet him?"

> **Momofuku:** *I (still) want to meet you.*
> *ENOUGH ALREADY. YOU SHOULD WANT SOME-*
> *THING ELSE.*

"OK," Zen typed. "In the next five seconds, tell me how you're going to do it."

"Five seconds?"

Zen sent another link. This one led to the page on Amazon Japan for Zen's newest book, *Wow Meetings*. A line of marketing copy under the title said, "Based on the management coaching philosophy of Jew Howard Goldman!" Howard was the management coach we had hired at our start-up, and Zen considered him a mentor.

"You make it sound like Jew is his title," I typed.

"Andy, it's a term of respect."

Zen explained that quickly coming up with ideas was a tenet of *Wow Meetings*, though a similar concept also appears in *Wow Method* under the heading "Answer Your Big Question in Five Seconds." Adopting speed chess as a metaphor, Zen asserts that 86 percent of all moves are just as good as moves the same players would make without time limits. Of course, it's virtually impossible to know what a player would do in the exact same situation without a time limit, so Zen had obviously made up the figure. I decided to go along anyway.

"I could write him a letter."

"You've never written him a letter?"

"I e-mailed his PR people a bunch of times, but I guess I've never written directly to him."

"I find that when I write a letter directly to the person I'm trying to meet, my success rate in hearing back from that person jumps thirty-six percent."

Another made-up number, to be sure, but I was grateful for Zen's support.

"By when will you write the letter?" Zen asked.

Wow Meetings, I learned later, was all about making clear commitments with firm deadlines.

"How about in the next hour?"

"Wow," Zen typed back.

I could have written it faster in English, but I felt that I would make more of an impact by sending the letter in Japanese.

I typed out a draft.

Dear Mr. Ando,

Japan must be in the rainy season now. Are the hydrangeas in bloom?

I'm an American writer, currently living in San Francisco, on the west coast of the United States. I can write in Japanese because of a study-abroad program I did almost twenty years ago in Tokyo. In those days, the automated teller machines were only open on weekdays from nine to five, and I often forgot to withdraw cash before the weekends. I survived many weekends with only a few hundred yen in my pocket thanks to your instant ramen.

I have been moved by many of your famous sayings, such as "Mankind is noodlekind" and "Peace follows from a full stomach." Recently I have been reading your books, and I find myself wanting to hear your thoughts directly. In particular, I'm still unsure why you set out to invent instant ramen after losing all of your money.

I would very much like to meet you, and I'm wondering if it would be possible to arrange an interview. I can visit Japan this summer, and would be grateful for any time you can spare.

Sincerely,

Andy Raskin

I e-mailed the letter to Zen so he could check my Japanese, and he made several edits. He struck the part about the ATMs because he felt it would be better if I sounded like a man who always walked around with only a few hundred yen in my pocket. He also changed the closing salutation from "Sincerely" to "Praying that these sentiments have reached your heart, I am . . ."

"Do you have his mailing address?" Zen typed.

I didn't, but then I remembered a *Brady Bunch* episode where Bobby takes a photograph of Greg's football game and blows it up to find out if one of the players stepped out of bounds. It might have been a real *Brady Bunch* episode, or it might have been a dream. (As a child, I often dreamed that I was a friend of the Brady kids, and that they would invite me over for lunch.) I connected my digital camera to my computer and downloaded the photos of Ando's front gate. I zoomed in on the ANDO nameplate.

The address was right under the kanji characters for Ando's name!

I sent the letter by Federal Express, and after two days, checked the tracking number. The letter had been delivered and signed for by "M. Ando."

I e-mailed Zen: "That's either Momofuku or Masako!"

Three days later, I received another express mail envelope. It came so quickly that I never imagined it could be a response. Unfortunately, Ando hadn't written it.

> Mr. Raskin:
>
> Greetings. I apologize for taking so much time to write back.
>
> Unlike America, Japan is now in the middle of the rainy season. It's one rainy day after the next.
>
> It is wonderful that you read Mr. Ando's books, that you identified with his thoughts, and that you desire a meeting with him.
>
> Unfortunately, Mr. Ando is very busy with his daily duties. In addition, he is ninety-six years old. So I am going to have to deny your request to set up an appointment with him. I wish that I could have been more helpful in realizing your desire, but I hope you will understand that it is very difficult.
>
> However, if you like, you are welcome to visit Ikeda City's Instant Ramen Invention Museum, where you can learn more about Ando's philosophy and the history of instant ramen. I am sure that one of our Public Relations staff members would be happy to be your guide.
>
> I hope you will consider it.
>
> Praying for your continued success,
>
> Kazuhiro Fujioka
>
> Manager, Secretary Division
>
> Nissin Food Products Co., Ltd.

There was obviously poor interdepartmental communication at Nissin, because this Fujioka seemed unaware of my previous attempt to meet Ando and my visit to the museum. I was about to throw out the envelope, when I felt something inside. I reached in and pulled it out. It was a small green book.

The book was titled *Praise the Appetite* and it was a newly published collection of Ando's short, food-themed essays. Most were about his invention of instant ramen, but not all. In "I Am a Salad Bar Man," he proclaimed a preference for simple foods (like salad) over lavish meals when traveling abroad. An essay about fish began with the line, "Striped bass brings up certain memories." In "Instant Ramen Finally Reaches Outer Space," he summarized Nissin's successful effort to develop a version of instant ramen that could be prepared and consumed in zero gravity. First enjoyed by Japanese astronaut Soichi Noguchi aboard Space Shuttle *Discovery* (on July 26, 2005), Space Ram came in a basic soy sauce flavor and—in response to Noguchi's requests—also in curry, miso, and *tonkotsu* varieties.

Many of the stories in the book had been recycled from previous collections, but Ando had written a new introduction. It began,

> My life has been one of ups and downs. I experienced difficulties in my work, and I faced hardships. Many times I tasted despair. At my lowest point, I lost all of my wealth, but I put all of my trust in what seemed like a tiny desire.... I made the decision that food would be my life's work, and then I was saved.

Ando continued by talking about the importance of food in society, but then there was this:

> Human beings have all kinds of desires. Some we must hide. Some, as we get older, we must learn to control. Perhaps it is only the desire for food that we can continue to indulge without shame.

What kind of desires, I wondered, was Ando talking about that he had to control?

In the back of the book, a bibliography listed Ando's previously published work, including *Noodle Road, Peace Follows from a Full Stomach,* and the autobiographies. There was one title, though, that I had never seen before:

Kukyo kara no Dasshutsu.

Dasshutsu means "to escape." The first character of that word, 脱, is the same as the first one in *dassara*. As for *kukyo*, I knew the meanings of the two characters, but not the combined word. Looking it up in my Kenkyusha Japanese-English dictionary, I discovered that *kukyo* is a fancy word for "difficulty."

In 1992, Momofuku Ando authored a book called *How to Escape from Difficulty*.

The book was out of print, but I found it in the online catalog of a Kyoto bookseller. The company wouldn't ship to the United States, so I had it mailed to Zen, who forwarded it to me. The jacket showed a shimmering white sphere with a long rainbow tail. I had read enough about Ando to know that the image was a reference to Halley's Comet.

How to Escape from Difficulty was yet another telling of Ando's life story. Based largely on his previous autobiographies, it included the episode about being tortured during World War II, and the two years he spent in Sugamo Prison fighting charges of tax evasion. This book, however, started at a different point, and it was organized in a different way. Namely, it began with Ando losing everything in the credit association debacle. Then it described a transformation that took place in his soul, and how that transformation enabled him to invent instant ramen. The key to the transformation, he wrote, was his realization that, his entire life, he had suffered under a delusion. He called this delusion the Fundamental Misunderstanding of Humanity.

Dear Momofuku,

Is there any better way to prove to Dr. G that I am not a father-hating boy than to take up sailing?

I enroll in sailing camp, and on the first day, I look around at my classmates. Sharon is one of them.

In the pool, she barely noticed me. But now when I look at her, she meets my gaze. We practice sailing in small boats called Blue Jays, and Sharon goes out of her way to get assigned to my Blue Jay. She calls me on the phone one night, and we talk about the Blue Jays and the other kids and about the sailing instructors. She calls the next night, too.

"Is she your girlfriend?" my father asks at the dinner table.

YOU SHOULD NOT ADMIT THIS, BECAUSE IF YOU DO, THEN IT WILL MEAN THAT YOU ARE A SEXUAL PERSON, AND HOW CONCEITED WOULD THAT BE?

"No."

My father doesn't believe me. "Love is blind," he says, "but the neighbors ain't!"

I never kiss Sharon, because I'm too shy. Somehow, though, just knowing that a girl is interested in me, I feel better about myself.

"I'm feeling better about myself," I tell Dr. G.

"Let's run some tests," he says.

Dr. G runs the exact same tests—the same sentence completions, the same inkblots, the same drawing exercises. Perhaps he has forgotten how well I scored last time on the memory portion.

In the next session, he shows my parents the evidence for how much I have changed.

"My father helps me with my homework."

"I want to go fishing."

My drawing of an adult female includes two prominent semicircles on her chest.

Dr. G says I can stop seeing him, so I do.

I consider Sharon to be my girlfriend, even though we have never kissed. But one afternoon, I see her out on a Blue Jay with another boy. He's the son of a famous sailmaker.

YOU SHOULD FORGET ABOUT HER BECAUSE OBVIOUSLY SHE'S GOING TO BE MORE INTERESTED IN HIM. HE'S TALL AND HE HAS BLOND HAIR, AND HE'S THE SON OF A SAILMAKER. YOU SHOULD NOT TELL HER YOU'RE JEALOUS BECAUSE THAT WOULD MAKE YOU LOOK WEAK AND LIKE AN IDIOT. WHAT YOU SHOULD DO IS PRETEND THAT YOU DON'T CARE ABOUT HER ANYMORE SO THAT SHE CAN'T HURT YOU FIRST.

The next night, I call another girl from the camp.

Sincerely,
Andy

"*A*re you hungry?" my mother asked.

It was Thanksgiving, and she had just met me at the baggage claim in Kennedy Airport. I thought about making a crack about Woody Allen, but instead I just hugged her.

By transcribing the voice in my head, I had learned to recognize it in others. When my mother asked me about being hungry, I felt its presence. It was telling her that she needed to keep me well fed in order to be a good mother. Had it told her that she was a bad mother when I cried as a child? Had it somehow been responsible for her lashing out at me? I wondered, too, if she had inherited the voice from her mother, and I realized that she probably had. Grandma Millie died in a car accident caused by a teenager who ran a stop sign, and after we all cried for a month, Grandma Millie's friends told us that she had been stockpiling sleeping pills in case her body deteriorated to where she couldn't take care of herself. The voice in Grandma Millie's head told her that she shouldn't be a burden on her children or her grandchildren. She must have inherited the voice from her parents, who must have inherited it from their parents.

"What's new?" I asked my mother.

We were in the Denali now, exiting the short-term parking lot.

"Not too much. Oh! Your father's walking across Long Island."

"What do you mean, he's walking across it?"

"He joined a club. They print maps, you know, trails that connect up across the Island. Some go east-west, some go up and down."

"How long does it take to walk across?"

"Depends if you're going east-west or up and down. He does a little section one day, and then another section the next. He's going tomorrow to do one of the sections. You should go with him before all the relatives arrive for dinner. It'll be nice. A father-and-son walk."

Momofuku: *I want to walk across Long Island with my father.*
HE DOESN'T REALLY WANT TO WALK WITH YOU. IT'S JUST YOUR MOTHER FORCING HIM INTO IT.

I slept in my old room, and in the morning my father pulled the Denali out of the garage. He was sixty-four years old, and he still looked like a linebacker, probably because of all the time he spent on his sailboat. His hair was graying, but he still had all of it, which the voice never let me forget. Before we left, he told me he had been traversing an east-west trail. Actually, he had started on the western border of Nassau County and was making his way to Montauk, so technically it was a west-east trail. His last segment had ended in Oyster Bay. I got into the passenger seat, and he drove toward the expressway.

"So what are you going to do for money?" he asked in the car.

"I don't know yet."

"If you need it, we can help."

YOU SHOULD NOT BE DEPENDENT ON YOUR PARENTS, GIVEN THAT YOU'RE ALMOST FORTY.

"Thanks, Dad. I wanna try and figure this out."

"You know, I always say that you should never leave a job before you have a new job."

At least I knew where that one came from.

"Ever think about writing a book?" he asked.

"What would I write a book about?"

"The stories of your life. Like that time you climbed to the top of the bridge with the Japanese people."

Back when I lived with Maureen, I worked for the Manhattan office of a Japanese television company. I would scout locations, rent lighting equipment, and translate for the directors. Once we were hired to produce a profile about the city's bridge inspector, a former Czech acrobat who loved to walk on suspension cables without safety equipment. A cameraman and I climbed a rickety staircase to the top of the Williamsburg Bridge, where we filmed the inspector making his way up the cable.

"I don't think anyone wants to read a book about that, Dad."

"I don't know, I thought it was exciting stuff."

In high school, I used to wonder why my friend Dan could talk about girls and sex with his father, yet I couldn't with mine. At some point, I came to the conclusion that it was my fault. If I hadn't been so impatient and embarrassed during his birds-and-bees talk, he wouldn't have given up on building a closer relationship. I once asked Dan how he and his father became so open with each other, and he remembered the exact day it happened. He was sixteen years old, and his father came into his room with comic books from the 1930s that showed famous characters like Betty Boop engaging in kinky sex acts. Dan and his father bonded over the comics. For a long time, I thought that if I could just bring up a sexually explicit topic with my father, the same thing would happen. I tried it once, but it was a complete disaster. I was in my early thirties, and I was eating dinner with both my parents at an Italian restaurant in Tribeca. Before the main course, I said, "I just want to put it out there that I have had sex." My mother said, "Yeah, we figured." My father said, "There are certain topics that just aren't appropriate to talk about with your parents." Maybe I should have waited until I was alone with my father, but I was so embarrassed that I never tried again.

My father exited the expressway near Oyster Bay, continuing a short distance along the service road. He stopped in front of a chain-link fence, checking his club map.

"This is the spot," he said.

We got out of the Denali and walked to the gate, which had been secured with a rusty chain and a combination lock. Behind the fence, a dirt path led into some woods. I had probably driven past the spot dozens of times in high school, but I had never noticed the woods.

My father grabbed the lock, spun the numbered dials, and popped open the latch.

"How did you know the combination?" I asked.

"It's a public trail, so you can call the park service and they'll tell it to you. But the club also prints it on the map."

He unraveled the chain, swinging the gate open, and we both passed through. Then he relocked the gate, and together we continued his walk across Long Island.

The sun cast sharp shadows over the trail's carpet of brown leaves, though it was cold enough that we both wore thick coats. Sloping downward at first, the trail leveled out and we came upon a large pond. A family of ducks floated past clumps of reeds near the edge. I scanned for other wildlife, but didn't see any.

We had walked halfway around the pond's perimeter when the trail veered back into the woods.

"You smell the maple sap?" my father asked.

I didn't. "I do."

We were silent the rest of the way. One reason was that my father had begun walking a few paces ahead of me.

It was only a few paces, so I didn't think much of it at first. Soon, though, he was a good three yards in front. When the distance was five yards, I heard the voice in my head.

YOU SHOULD REALLY WALK FASTER.

In *How to Escape from Difficulty*, Ando defines the Fundamental Misunderstanding of Humanity as "believing that we can achieve all of our desires, without limitations." The implied double negative is a less awkward construction in Japanese, but I still had to reread it several times before I parsed it correctly.

HE'S EASILY TEN YARDS AHEAD OF YOU. WILL YOU WALK FASTER ALREADY?

Ando tells his reader, "I am about to reveal some very shameful things. And it is my hope that together we will uncover hints about how one can escape from a difficult situation." The shameful things are the many failures he chronicles in his other books—the loss of his businesses and real estate holdings, the wartime torture, his arrests and imprisonments.

HE MUST BE TWENTY-FIVE YARDS AHEAD OF YOU. LET'S GET A MOVE ON.

Ando attributes many of these failures to circumstance, but not the credit association collapse. For that he takes responsibility, if simply for allowing himself to be "sweet-talked" into getting involved. He recounts the shame he felt. "It was the most difficult period of my life. I went from being a success to being penniless, and I experienced the harshness of this world." This time he couldn't run from his shame. He didn't have the money to start a new company or to buy land.

THIRTY-FIVE YARDS. THIS IS YOUR IDEA OF A FATHER-AND-SON WALK?

"Be it the desire for food, sex, or power," Ando writes, ". . . desire always breeds more desire. Eventually, it becomes difficult to control." Ando saw how shame powered so many of his desires, and that, unless he made peace with his shame, it would continue to rule him. (I assumed he was talking about his quest for wealth, though the mention of sex hardly passed unnoticed.) Walking thirty-five yards (and counting) behind my father, I recognized the voice in my head as the shame Ando was talking about.

HE'S ABOUT TO DISAPPEAR AROUND THAT BEND IN FRONT OF YOU. THERE ARE THREE POSSIBLE EXPLANATIONS FOR THIS: (1) HE'S THINKING, "MY SON IS A SLOW

WALKER, SO FUCK HIM." (2) HE CARES SO LITTLE ABOUT
YOU THAT HE HASN'T NOTICED YOU'RE THIS FAR BE-
HIND HIM. (3) HE DOESN'T LIKE YOU VERY MUCH, AND
HE PREFERS TO KEEP HIS DISTANCE.

So this was the battle I had been preparing for. Not with my father, but with the voice in my head, a collection of thoughts that had
long been unconscious yet controlled my behavior in ways I was just
beginning to comprehend. Whenever I was on the verge of admitting
things I was ashamed of—as Matt liked to put it, whenever I was
about to become intimate with myself or another person—this voice
would stop me. Now, feeling the urge to walk faster, I understood that
if I gave in I would again be running from the truth. So I followed
Matt's advice and focused on what the voice was saying. I gave it all
of my attention.

OH, MY GOD, HE'S NO LONGER VISIBLE. ARE YOU RE-
ALLY THIS PATHETIC?

Only when Ando accepted his failure—his limitations—did he
become aware of another kind of desire, one rooted not in shame but,
as he puts it, "the innate human urge to connect with the world." His
wife's friends began asking about her husband's activities in the backyard, and when she told them, they said, "Oh," because they felt
sorry for her that she was married to a man who had devoted his life
to ramen, the lowest of all foods. Of course, once he committed to his
true desire, the opinions of others no longer held sway over Ando. "I
realized that all of my failures were like muscles and blood added to
my bones," he writes. "I had no choice but to keep on moving in the
direction of the dim light ahead."

What were my limitations? One, obviously, was that I wanted to
walk with my father, but our walking speeds were such that I could
no longer see him. Another was that I couldn't talk to him about
sex. I was nearly forty years old and not married. I had a critical voice
in my head, no job, and no prospects. I had dated many women,
but when I got close to them I often felt an uncomfortable physical

sensation. I always cheated. I couldn't say "Beeyotch!" I had tried and failed to meet the inventor of instant ramen. The list of limitations was much longer, but these were the ones that came to mind while walking across Long Island.

Could I accept these limitations?

NO, YOU SHOULD DEFINITELY NOT ACCEPT THEM. THEY'RE NOT GOOD THINGS TO ACCEPT IN YOUR LIFE. WEAK PEOPLE ACCEPT LIMITATIONS. ARE YOU WEAK? WHAT YOU SHOULD DO IS, YOU SHOULD GET ON CRAIGSLIST OR THE MEMBER DIRECTORY OR JUST CALL ONE OF THE WOMEN IN YOUR PHONEBOOK AND FORGET ABOUT THESE LIMITATIONS. YOU SHOULD HAVE FUN.

And there it was, the Fundamental Misunderstanding of Humanity.

I understood now that the voice's beating heart was a question: "WHAT IS WRONG WITH YOU?" It gathered strength from virtually any limitation I encountered, be it my inability to participate in a conversation at a Lake Tahoe ski house, my failure to meet the inventor of instant ramen, or the distance between my father and me on a walk across Long Island. I had learned to use women to shout back, "Look! Nothing is wrong with me!" But like a security alarm, if a woman got too close, the voice would grow louder and louder. Then I would look for someone new to appease it, and the cycle would start all over.

Did I create this voice to shield myself from some pain I suffered as a child? Was I born with it? The answer didn't really matter. What mattered was that I had more resources now. I had Matt, for one, and I had my faith in Ando, even if I communicated with him only through letters I never sent and books he wrote long ago. I had a drawing of a duck that looked like a shoe, and I had samurai heroes too numerous to name. I had the horror of how I behaved in relationships, and every Monday night I sat next to an aging trombone player who offered me restaurant tips and the detailed history of my Conn 78H.

So I kept walking at the same pace, which felt like jumping off a cliff. I asked Ando to catch me.

O Momofuku. Show me how to live so that I may better do your will.

The trail made a wide circle, eventually looping back to the pond, up the hill, and to the gate, where my father stood waiting. I wiped the tears from my eyes before he saw them. I thought about asking why he had walked so fast, but I was so filled with sadness that I didn't have the strength. He didn't mention it either. We passed through the gate and he locked it again. We climbed back into the Denali.

On the way home, my father talked about his new home-building projects in Suffolk County. In the past when he talked about his projects, I would get angry and change the subject, and even now I heard the voice telling me that he cared more about his construction business than he did about me. This time, though, I was also aware that I was proud of him—proud that he was a man who loved building houses and sailing and smelling maple sap in the woods, even if I was bad at all those things. And I wondered: Had my father walked so fast, leaving me to confront the voice, because Ando had willed it?

One thing puzzled me.

"Since the trail was a circle," I asked while we were still in the car, "how does it connect to the next segment of your walk across Long Island?"

My father's eyes remained fixed on the road.

"The club will tell you the trails link up all the way across," he said. "Truth is, there are rough connections. There are gaps."

PART IV

MANKIND IS NOODLEKIND

*T*he bassist signaled the cutoff at the end of "Four Brothers," and Gary returned his silver King Liberty to its place on his knee. He awaited an answer.

Why did I go to meet the inventor of instant ramen?

A lot had happened since the walk across Long Island. Upon returning to San Francisco, I ran into Matt on a street corner. When I told him about the walk with my father, he hugged me. Then he filled me in on why he had asked me to place stars next to the names of the women in my letters to Ando. These were the people to whom I had to make amends. Where possible, I did it in person or with a phone call. If I had no way to make contact, or if I judged contact to be ill advised, I simply wrote a letter to that person in my notebook. In cases where I did get in touch, it was difficult to balance honesty with the pain it might cause. I asked Matt how to do that, and predictably he told me to ask Ando for guidance. In general, I apologized for dishonesty, betraying trust, and my inability to be present for the relationships. One woman told me that she had been cheating, too, a possibility that had never occurred to me. Another ex-girlfriend questioned my sincerity. Matt said it wasn't my job to manage the reactions; all I could do was to tell the truth.

With Matt's blessing, I had begun dating again. Together we came up with some ground rules. I was not to have sex until the fifth date (the number was relatively arbitrary; Matt said I could pick anything higher than three), and if I chose to do so, then I was not to date or have sex with anyone else. After a breakup, I was to wait at least thirty days before dating someone new (to ensure I wasn't using a new person to squelch the voice in my head). If I ever felt like breaking these rules—these limitations—I was to pray to Ando. If that didn't work, I was to call Matt. I had a couple of short-term relationships, and once I broke the five-date rule. But for the first time in my life, I didn't cheat.

I had yet to find a job, but I was having success selling personal essays. Instead of writing about climbing the Williamsburg Bridge, I mined the transcriptions of the voice in my head for themes. I sold a story based on "YOU SHOULD BE MARRIED LIKE THE PEOPLE IN THE *NEW YORK TIMES* WEDDING ANNOUNCEMENTS" to National Public Radio, and I performed one about "YOU SHOULD BE ABLE TO FINISH THE LARGE AT RAMEN JIRO" for a San Francisco reading series. I wrote a piece on "YOU SHOULD BE ABLE TO FIND GREAT PARKING SPOTS, THE WAY YOUR FATHER ALWAYS DOES," though I had yet to find an outlet for publication. The voice, I came to realize, was like a pointer to things that I cared about. Interestingly, the more I wrote about it, the more it came out in the first person, and in lowercase. It hardly disappeared, but its power over me seemed to wane. Sometimes it even made me laugh.

I had been on a date with a woman in a movie theater—we were watching Alfonso Cuarón's *Children of Men*—when my cell phone vibrated in my pocket. I pulled out the phone and saw a series of square symbols, which was how my phone displayed Japanese Google Alerts. I had programmed my Google Japan account to send alerts to my phone whenever Ando's name appeared in the news, but I received them so frequently that I rarely paid attention. Usually they were triggered by nothing more than a Nissin press release about some new Cup Noodles brand extension or a limited-time Chikin Ramen promotion. I once received one after a speech by the conservative politician Shinzo Abe, later elected prime minister, who during a campaign stop in front of the Instant Ramen Invention Museum likened his political fortitude to Ando's persistence in the shack. (Abe would eventually resign as prime minister, citing among other insurmountable obstacles, a chronic case of diarrhea.) After the movie, I said good night to my date in front of her apartment building, and when I got home, I logged into my Google account. The alert I had received in the theater contained a link to a newspaper article from the *Tokyo Shimbun*. I clicked on it, reading the headline:

"Momofuku Ando, the Father of Instant Ramen, Is Dead."

Why did I go to meet Ando?

"I think I went, Gary, because he wanted me to not meet him."

Gary looked confused and was about to ask more questions, but then the bassist called out another song and then another, and soon it was time for our fifteen-minute break. I put my trombone back in its case, grabbed a root beer from the warehouse's makeshift kitchen, and walked out to the alley in the back. Gary was already outside smoking a cigarette, his trombone hanging from his elbow, and he was reminiscing with John, the second trombonist, about the days when they supported their families by playing dance halls and musical theater. Gary described how his friend Archie—the man who owned my Conn 78H before I did—made a good living in Las Vegas until producers won concessions from the musicians' union. "First they moved the orchestra to a back room and piped the sound in through speakers," Gary said. "It wasn't long before they plugged a computer into the speakers and sent the musicians home."

I wanted to know more about Archie, but just then my cell phone vibrated in my pocket again. I had just purchased a new one, with special software that displayed Japanese characters. After Ando's death, I had been receiving Google Alerts on his name almost every hour—mostly obituaries and blog posts about him. Like Lawrence

Downes, the *Times* editor who wrote "Appreciations: Mr. Noodle," the rest of the world seemed as amused as I had been to learn that there was an inventor of instant ramen.

I flipped open the phone, and sure enough, it was a Japanese Google Alert. This one was a tiny item from a regional newspaper called the *Tokushima Shimbun*:

Funeral for Momofuku Ando,
Chairman of Nissin Food Products, Is Announced

The funeral for the late Momofuku Ando (the chairman of Nissin Food Products, who died January 5) will commence February 27 at one o'clock at Kyocera Dome Osaka. The funeral committee chairman will be former Prime Minister Yasuhiro Nakasone. Chief mourner will be Nissin President Koki Ando, the deceased's second-eldest son.

Gary saw the Japanese characters on my cell phone.

"What does it say?"

I told him.

"Are you going?"

"I don't think so."

"Why not?"

I had learned that I was suffering from the Fundamental Misunderstanding of Humanity. I was dating women while honoring my limitations. I had learned to accept and love my parents in ways I previously could not.

"Gary, I don't even know if it's open to the public. Anyway, I just don't think I need to go."

Gary flicked his cigarette onto the pavement, extinguishing it with his foot.

"Yeah," he said. "But what if Ando wants you to?"

*T*here were no cheap flights from San Francisco to Osaka, but I found a good deal into Tokyo. Even adding in the cost of a Japan Rail Pass to ride the bullet train, I was coming out ahead. As the plane descended toward the Narita Airport runway, I remembered how on my last visit to Japan the waves reminded me of drops of lard atop a bowl of ramen. This time the Pacific Ocean seemed calmer. Tiny ripples were visible on its surface, like scales on the body of a big black fish.

At Narita, I exchanged dollars for yen and bought a ticket for the Narita Express, the train line that connects to downtown Tokyo. Boarding my assigned car, I stowed my suitcase in the luggage compartment and took my reserved seat. Next to me, a young Japanese man was staring out the window. His suitcase lay at his feet, not in the luggage compartment, and I could make out the initials "YVR" on the tag wrapped around the handle. It had been nearly three years since my last trip to Japan—the one when I failed to meet Ando—and I wanted to practice my Japanese.

"Excuse me," I said, "but I noticed the tag on your suitcase. Were you skiing at Whistler?"

I knew that YVR was the airport code for Vancouver, which is only a two-hour drive from Whistler Mountain. A lot of Japanese people ski there.

"No."

I waited for the man to tell me why he had gone to Vancouver, but he didn't say anything.

"So why did you go there?" I finally asked.

"Did you know," he said, "that there are seventeen casinos in British Columbia?"

I did not know that. "So you went to Vancouver to gamble?"

"No. I went to hike in the mountains."

"How was the hiking?"

He raised his left arm, extending it straight out. It was covered in the sleeve of a blue jacket.

"I'm sorry," I said. "I don't understand."

The man sighed, as if his meaning should have been obvious.

"Look how thin this jacket is," he said, pinching the material. "What I'm saying is, it was snowing in the mountains, and I couldn't go hiking because I didn't have a warm coat."

"So you gambled instead?"

"A little. And I stared longingly at the mountains."

My conversation partner got off the train at Shinagawa Station, and I got off a few stops later. I wheeled my suitcase through the food court and rode the escalator down to the street. Spotting my destination, I crossed the busy intersection at Komazawa-dori, ascended on the escalator, and walked into the lobby. The marble walls looked lighter than I remembered.

"Welcome to the Hotel Excellent," said the man at the front desk.

This time, I had made a reservation before leaving San Francisco. After checking in, I went up to my room, which looked exactly the same, except that the yukata robe on the bed was plain white. It didn't say "Hotel Excellent" in katakana. I wondered if it was a cost-cutting measure.

I had e-mailed the second (ground agent) Masako Ando that I

would be arriving in the early afternoon, and she had offered to meet me after work. Greeting me in the Hotel Excellent lobby, she led me on a short walk to her favorite restaurant, a trattoria called Uncle Tom. The restaurant's name was derived from the last name of the owner, Mr. Saotome, who happened to be a fan of the Beatles. He played only Beatles music in the restaurant, and he had decorated the walls with the art of John Lennon. He kept a diorama on his bar counter in which miniature Beatles dolls were arranged on a miniature concert stage. I ordered spaghetti and meatballs. Masako chose the penne with eggplant and asparagus.

"So I quit," she said.

"You quit the airline?"

"Yes. I'm no longer a ground-based agent!"

"I thought you said that you were coming from work today."

"I work at a publishing house now. We translate new-age books from America and issue them in Japan."

"Isn't that like opening a car dealership in Tokyo to import Chevrolets?"

"Funny. Anyway, I love my job," she said. "I'm also studying *fura*."

"Fura?"

"You know, *fura* dancing."

I still sometimes get tripped up by the katakana words. "Hula dancing?"

"Yes, *fura*."

The owner's wife, Mrs. Saotome, brought our dishes.

"Masako, one of the reasons I wanted to see you was to apologize for what I did last time."

She nodded, as if she was remembering, and for a while she didn't say anything. Then she did.

"You left so suddenly. I thought that maybe I did something to make you mad. I kept asking myself what I did wrong."

Japanese people, I realized, had voices in their heads, too.

"This is hard to explain," I said, "especially in Japanese, but you didn't do anything wrong. I think that I used you to escape my shame about not meeting Ando, and my shame about some other things, too."

"Yes. That was how I felt. Used."

"I am really sorry. I know it doesn't change anything, but I've spent the last three years trying to understand why I behave like that."

Masako chuckled. "Andy, a lot of men behave like that."

"I don't know if that's true."

"Well, none of them ever apologized before. So thank you."

"You're welcome."

We went back to our pasta, but then Masako looked up.

"You know," she said, "you really missed out that day. After the Ramen Museum in Yokohama, I was going to take you to see the fireworks with two of my hot flight attendant friends. It was going to be *yori-dori midori.*"

The expression literally translates as "green all over the place," but as an idiom it means to be surrounded by beautiful women.

I offered to walk Masako home, but she said that her apartment was so small she didn't want me to see it. I told her that I had lived in some very small Tokyo apartments, but she still refused. I was exhausted from traveling, so I didn't argue. I hugged her good-bye, and she walked home by herself.

By the time I got back to the hotel, I was so jet-lagged that I had passed the point where I could sleep. So I opened my laptop computer and connected to the Hotel Excellent Wi-Fi network. The hotel may have skimped on the yukata robe, but now it had Internet access. I found the Web site of Kyocera Dome Osaka, the venue for Ando's funeral, and learned that it was a baseball stadium. It had been called Osaka Dome until 2006, when electronics maker Kyocera bought the naming rights. The stadium held more than 35,000 people, and was home to the Orix Buffaloes, a team formed by the 2004 merger of the Orix Blue Wave (Ichiro Suzuki's team when he played in Japan) and the Osaka Kintetsu Buffaloes. Madonna had performed there, as had Bon Jovi, Aerosmith, and the Rolling Stones.

I wondered if Japanese newspapers had published information about getting tickets, so I checked the Japanese search engines. There were several mentions of the funeral, but nothing more detailed than the time and place. I was about to give up and try again to sleep when, in the results of one of my search queries, I noticed an intriguing title: "Momofuku Ando's Three Wives and Last Will and Testament."

Clicking the title led me to an article in *Shukan Bunshun*, a gossipy weekly magazine. The article turned out to be an interview with Hirotoshi Ando, the son that Momofuku had deleted from his second autobiography. It began with a quote from Hirotoshi:

> I have maintained silence since resigning as president in August of 1983. I recognize the achievements of my father. However, he died after destroying the bonds between the family he left behind. He practically disowned me, but I harbor no ill will toward him. Nevertheless, I have decided to tell the truth.

Now seventy-six years old, Hirotoshi went on to accuse his father of polygamy.

According to Hirotoshi's account in the article, he was born in Taiwan in 1930, when his father, Momofuku, was only twenty years old. His mother was a Taiwanese woman whom Momofuku had married. When Momofuku emigrated to Japan, he left Hirotoshi and this first wife behind, but when Hirotoshi was still young, his mother sent him to Japan to live with his father:

"I believe that I came to Japan just before entering elementary school," Hirotoshi said in the article. "My mother stayed back in Taiwan. My father had brought with him another lady from Taiwan, a so-called 'other woman.' This other woman became my father's second wife, and she bore a child, though she (the mother) has since passed away. His current wife (Masako) is number three."

Hirotoshi asserted that his mother was still alive in Taiwan, and that she received no financial support from Momofuku, to whom her marriage was still on the books. In 1981, Momofuku arranged for Hirotoshi to succeed him as Nissin's CEO, but two years later Momofuku forced Hirotoshi to resign. Hirotoshi attributed his father's change of heart to "a difference in management philosophy." He didn't offer details, but charged that his father wanted to "obliterate me from society." Nevertheless, Hirotoshi expressed compassion for Masako, his stepmother. "Regarding my resignation, I was told that she later remarked, 'I should have warned [Momofuku] that if he made [Hirotoshi] resign in a painful way, the bad feelings would persist for generations.' When I heard that, I felt that [Masako] was trying to help me. She devoted her life to supporting that selfish man, and she gave everything she had until the end."

Hirotoshi said that when his father died, his stepsister (Momofuku's daughter with Masako) called him in tears, begging him to attend a mourning service for close relatives. Hirotoshi agreed, bringing along his two sons. "At my age, family bonds are important," he said, "and I don't want my sons to experience what I had to go through."

After reading Hirotoshi's story, I found more evidence online to support it. The previous day, an English-language newspaper in Taiwan had run a piece about Mei-ho Wu, a Taiwanese woman identified as Momofuku's daughter from his second wife. According to the article, Wu and her mother had lived with Momofuku in Japan, but he had left them behind in Taiwan during a visit when she was three years old. In the 1970s, she arranged a meeting with Momofuku during which he admitted paternity, but he refused to do so publicly. Wu visited Nissin again several times trying to see her father, but her requests were always denied. Once, she claimed, Nissin CEO (and, if her account is true, her half brother) Koki Ando reported her to the police, and she was jailed for half a day. In the wake of Momofuku's death, she petitioned Nissin for a sizable portion of his reported $3 billion estate, but according to the article, the company offered her only around $100,000. She was reportedly planning to sue Masako for more.

I never fell asleep that night.

I had long wondered what Ando meant when, explaining his decision to leave Taiwan, he wrote "something was cutting into my heart." I had wondered why he spoke of desires "one must learn to control," and why I was always reading messages between the lines when he talked about ramen.

Now I had some idea.

*A*fter taking my last shower at the Hotel Excellent, I put on my underwear. On a scale of one to ten, I rated my speed one million seven hundred seventy-one thousand five hundred sixty-one.

I checked out at five thirty in the morning and walked back to Ebisu Station, where I waited for the Yamanote Line train—the one that circles Tokyo proper. On the platform, a billboard advertisement for a brand of intimate apparel said LINGERIE IS LOVE JEWELRY. During the train ride, I noticed advertisements for iced coffee drinks, iced tea drinks, and adult education programs. A new service allowed consumers to pay bills using their cell phones. A men's magazine called *Straight*,—the trailing comma was part of the name—touted its latest cover story, "How to Have Fun with Your Wife and Family."

I got off at Tokyo Station, where I had to wait forty-five minutes for the bullet train. I was tempted by a "morning curry" set in the food court but chose instead to eat breakfast at the soba shop next door. I ordered a bowl of buckwheat noodles topped with shungiku tempura, a batter-fried leafy green. My Japan Rail Pass prohibited me from riding the express Nozomi ("desire") bullet trains, so I got a ticket for a Hikari ("light") bullet train to Osaka. The ride would take three hours. Before boarding, I stood in front of a bento-box lunch stand on the platform and considered my options. There was a "Tokyo bento," a "salmon bento," a "Japanese Flag bento," a "beef-over-rice bento," and a "veggie bento," plus many more. The fanciest one cost thirty dollars. Bewildered by the choices, I dragged myself away from the bento stand only to be drawn in by an array of unfamiliar Kit Kat flavors at a newspaper kiosk. There was a strawberry Kit Kat, a green tea Kit Kat, a custard Kit Kat, a mandarin orange Kit Kat, and an Exotic Tokyo Kit Kat (an assortment sold in a package designed by renowned pastry chef Yasumasa Takagi to evoke Tokyo nightlife). On the wrappers, Nestlé's Japanese subsidiary was promoting the bars as good-luck charms for college entrance exams, playing up how the candy's name sounds like *"Kitto katsu!"* ("You'll surely win!"). I bought a cherry Kit Kat and a Kit Kat flavored with sweet adzuki beans, and both were amazingly great.

I should have bought the salmon bento at Tokyo station because on the bullet train, I ordered a fried oyster bento from a girl speaking in a high-pitched voice, and the oysters were cold and soggy. As always, the day's news headlines scrolled across the display at the end of the car. "Toyota Market Cap Tops 39 Trillion Yen." "Red Sox Attendance Up Due to Matsuzaka." "Cabbies to Get Coached on Courtesy."

Arriving at New Osaka Station, I rode the escalator down to the underground mall, where I found a room of coin-operated lockers. I retrieved a printout of directions to Kyocera Dome Osaka from my suitcase, shoving it into my backpack. Then I squeezed my suitcase into a locker so I wouldn't have to drag it to the stadium. I was early, so for old times' sake I walked around searching for the air-conditioning vent I had stood under on my previous visit. I was disappointed not to find it, but it was late February, so New Osaka Station was comfortably cool.

The directions said to take the Kanjo ("loop") Line to Taisho Station, which was a seven-minute walk from the stadium. I bought a ticket and ascended the escalator to the platform. I didn't notice right away that everyone around me was dressed in black. I didn't notice it until the train pulled up and the doors opened, and everyone inside the train was wearing black, too. The men wore black suits and black ties, the women black dresses. Everyone wore black shoes.

My outfit: jeans, blue sweater, brown suede coat, brown work boots. A green Timbuk2 backpack hung from my shoulders.

YOU ARE SUCH AN IDIOT.

I should not have assumed that just because the funeral was being held in a baseball stadium it would be a casual affair.

On the train, I struck up a conversation with a middle-aged man from Yamaguchi Prefecture. He worked for a Nissin supplier, and he said that most of the funeral attendees would likely be businesspeople whose companies had ties to Nissin. I realized that, aside from a few movies with scenes of Japanese funerals (most notably Juzo Itami's *The Funeral*), I had never witnessed one, and knew very little about them. "The body was already cremated, right?" I asked the man from Yamaguchi. He said that it probably had been, and that the family had most likely conducted a private ceremony shortly after Ando's passing. That must have been the one that Hirotoshi attended with his sons.

When the train arrived at Taisho Station, black outfits poured from the car doors, through the turnstiles, and into a river of black clothing that was already flowing down the street. The black current carried me first along a four-lane road, then across the street and over Iwamatsu Bridge. I let myself be swept along like a piece of inappropriately dressed driftwood. At every intersection, men wearing NISSIN FOOD PRODUCTS armbands held signs displaying large arrows that merged my black flow with other black flows. After exactly seven minutes, I was deposited into a pool of black clothing that had formed outside the massive silver blob that was Kyocera Dome Osaka. Signs above me advertised Orix Buffaloes home games.

Just then, a gray-haired man to my left reached into the pocket of his black suit jacket and pulled out a bright white envelope.

I looked around. Lots of people were opening bright white envelopes.

"Excuse me," I said to the gray-haired man. "What's inside the envelope?"

Unsealing it, he removed a bright white card. "It's the invitation."

Two lines had formed in front of Kyocera Dome Osaka's entrance number six, so I positioned myself at the end of one of them. It took fifteen minutes to get close enough to see that several young women— sporting NISSIN FOOD PRODUCTS armbands—were handing each black-clad invitee a funeral program and a white shopping bag. They were also collecting the invitation cards. When I reached the front of the line, the woman who greeted me seemed wary. Her caution was un-derstandable. I was the only person within a one-kilometer radius not dressed in formal funeral attire.

"May I see your invitation card?" she asked.

"I don't have an invitation card."

"Mmm."

I thought that maybe I could guilt her into letting me through.

"I came all the way from America to pay my respects."

"Just a moment."

The woman disappeared into the tunnel behind entrance num-ber six. She was gone more than a minute. When she came back, she was sucking air through her teeth.

"I'm sorry, but it will be difficult for you to enter this gate without an invitation."

I should have checked if I needed an invitation before I trav-eled halfway around the world to attend a funeral. I should have inquired about proper attire. I should not have wasted so much time and money.

"Can I at least take a program?"

"Of course," she said, smiling.

She handed me an English version. It had been printed on a single sheet of heavy white paper and folded in thirds. The front cover said, "Company-Sponsored Funeral Service for Dr. Momofuku Ando, Founder." The "Dr." was a reference, no doubt, to the honorary Ph.D. from Ritsumeikan University. The inside of the program listed the order of events:

1. Opening Remarks
2. Reading of Sutras
3. Memorial Address
4. Reading of Condolence Telegrams
5. Address of Thanks
—Mr. Yasuhiro Nakasone, Funeral Committee Chairman
—Mr. Koki Ando, Chief Mourner
6. Thurification
7. Closing Remarks

I had never heard the word *thurification*.

The back of the program carried excerpts from the *New York Times* article, the one by Lawrence Downes. "The title of the article itself was extraordinary," the program stated. "It was called 'Appreciations: Mr. Noodle.'" The Nissin public relations department was clearly citing the *Times* article as proof of Ando's global importance.

I stood near entrance number six for some time unsure what to do.

O Momofuku. Please show me how to live so that I may better do your will.

I had begun walking against the black current back to Taisho Station when, passing entrance number five, I saw a sign.

The sign said PRESS ENTRANCE.

Only two times in my life have I pretended not to speak Japanese. The first was during spring break at International Christian University, when the ticket collector on the bullet train asked for my special express ticket. To ride the bullet train you need a regular ticket and a special express ticket, but I had forgotten to purchase the latter. The conductor decided that finding the English words to make me pay would have been more difficult than forgetting about it, so he forgot about it.

The second time was at entrance number five to Kyocera Dome Osaka. Still, I didn't really have a plan.

"Are you on our registered press list?" the woman at the gate asked.

"I'm a writer," I said in English.

She made a small rectangle with her hands, miming that she wanted to see my business card.

"I don't have any cards," I said, slapping the pockets of my jeans.

The woman had no choice but to switch to English.

"Newspaper name?"

I didn't work for a newspaper. But then I remembered the story I had written about "YOU SHOULD BE ABLE TO FIND GREAT PARKING SPOTS, THE WAY YOUR FATHER ALWAYS DOES." It had been published in *The New York Times* the day I left San Francisco. I had purchased the newspaper just before boarding my flight, and it was still in my backpack.

"New York Times!" the woman at entrance number five said when I showed her the article.

"Yes," I said, pointing to my byline. I also showed her my California driver's license to prove it was me.

"You wrote . . . 'Appreciations: Mr. Noodle?'"

Luckily, the funeral program didn't print Downes's name, just the excerpts from his story.

"I'm not on staff at the *Times*," I said. "I just sold this piece to them as a freelancer. I'm really hoping to write more for them. It is so hard to sell them stories, though. And the pay isn't the greatest, but I guess the exposure makes it worth it—"

The woman was so excited to meet the man she believed to be the author of "Appreciations: Mr. Noodle" that she handed me a program and one of the white shopping bags. She also wrote out an official name tag.

The name tag read ANDY RASKIN, *NEW YORK TIMES*.

"Hurry up," she said, waving me inside the stadium. "The ceremony is about to begin."

I walked past the woman at entrance number five and entered a long, dark tunnel. When I came out the other end, I could barely see anything in front of me. That was because nearly all the lights in the domed stadium had been turned off. It took a few seconds for my eyes to adjust to the darkness, and when they did, the difficult part was believing them.

The inside of Kyocera Dome Osaka had been designed to look like outer space.

Huge video screens hanging from the upper deck displayed images of slowly rotating galaxies, and thousands of bluish-white LEDs twinkled in the bleachers. A black tarp covered the playing field. Futuristic synthesized music blared from giant speakers near the foul poles. Occasionally, the galaxies would fade from the screens, only to be replaced by satellite video of Earth or the moon. It felt like I had walked onto the set of *Star Wars*.

Of course, the decor was not a tribute to *Star Wars*, and I shook my head as I figured it out. The funeral was going to be one final homage to Ando's special relationship with Halley's Comet.

Thousands of people were already seated in folding chairs that filled the playing field. (The official attendance was nearly seven thousand.) The audience faced out toward the home run wall, where a magnificent stage had been constructed. Long and white, the stage was fringed on both sides by white orchids and rows of Buddhist monks sitting *seiza* style. The monks sported shaved heads and formal robes—some yellow, some purple. Above them, another large video screen displayed a head shot of Ando wearing a turquoise suit, a blue diamond-patterned tie, and clear, wire-rimmed glasses. I judged that the photo had been taken when Ando was in his eighties. He seemed happy.

I had emerged from the tunnel in foul territory, somewhere in the vicinity of third base. In front of me, a long line of armbanded Nissin employees wielding flashlights greeted guests and helped them find their way in the dark. A female Nissin employee bowed in front of me, and I followed her to an empty seat in shallow center field.

"Would you like a blanket?" she asked.

With the synthesized music and the spinning galaxies and the offer of a blanket, I felt as if I had boarded a spaceship in which the Nissin staff members were flight attendants and we were bound for another galaxy. It was chilly.

"I would love a blanket."

Wrapping my legs in the thin blue wool, I squinted to examine the contents of the white shopping bag in the dark. There were three items:

- *A five-serving package of Chikin Ramen*
- *An ECO Cup—Nissin's new, environmentally friendly version of Cup Noodles (consisting of a reusable plastic cup and one separately sold noodle-and-topping insert)*
- *A book titled* Thus Spake Momofuku

The book was a 235-page collection of Ando's famous sayings, and it had been published the day before the ceremony. (The Japanese title employed an archaic construction meant to evoke Friedrich Nietzsche's *Thus Spake Zarathustra*.) Thumbing through, I recognized many of the sayings from Ando's autobiographies. Some, however, were unfamiliar:

*"Inside every human being there are two minds. One wants to
do good things. The other wants to do what it wants to do."*
"Flavors taste best to those who appreciate them."
*"Viewed from outer space, the Earth is nothing more than a
limited, tiny sphere. Unlimited desires in a limited world
give rise to all sorts of contradictions."*

Guests were still filing in when the deep voice of a male announcer
boomed through the sound system:

"He was the inventor of instant ramen. It was easy to eat, and
economical. He also invented Cup Noodles. He came from outer
space, and now we send him back to outer space. That is our theme
today."

The spinning galaxies faded out again, and a video tribute to
Ando filled the monitors. It began with images of the first Chikin
Ramen package, above which was printed another of Ando's famous
sayings: "In life, there is no such thing as too late!" A folksy pop song
by the Japanese band Mr. Children played while the video cut quickly
between scenes from Ando's life: the first Nissin assembly lines;
Ando standing next to the Golden Gate Bridge (during his legendary
trip to America in 1966); a container of Cup Noodles (and Ando saying, "Let's put it in a cup so they can eat it with a fork!"). Over a
montage in which people of all colors and sizes were enjoying instant
ramen, a narrator declared, "It was an invention that changed the
world!" Here was Ando fishing with Masako during the days when
he ran the salt operation in Izumi-Otsu; Ando receiving the honorary
doctorate from Ritsumeikan University; his noodle-study trips
throughout Asia; astronaut Soichi Noguchi eating Space Ram aboard
the space shuttle; Ando sinking a particularly difficult putt in 1987.
"He was a man who lived life on a planetary scale," the narrator said.
The video ended with computer-generated images of Halley's
Comet.

Next, a procession of more monks emerged, slowly and in single file, from an area near the bull pen. As they made their way up to the stage via a long white ramp, their faces filled the stadium displays. The only thing behind them was the dark, star-filled bleacher section, so on the monitors the monks appeared to be ascending a path to heaven. Once all the bull pen monks had joined the monks who were already onstage, the head monk—distinguished by robes more elaborate than those of his colleagues—began waving what looked like a white-haired doll. The stadium cameras zoomed in, and I saw that it was not a doll but a ceremonial wand from which hair dangled at one end. The head monk waved the hairy wand in circles over his head, and then in circles to his left and to his right.

"Please assume the *gassho* pose," the announcer said.

Everyone in the stadium stood up and brought their hands together. Meanwhile, the monks chanted a single sound.

"Oooooooh . . ."

Absolute silence.

The monks beat drums now, which was the cue for the audience to sit back down. One monk played what sounded like a shakuhachi, the traditional Japanese flute. There was more chanting, but this time it came from only the head monk. His back to the audience, he bobbed back and forth, still seated *seiza*-style in front of the large photo of Ando's face. The first words of his chant were the mantra said to guarantee all who utter it automatic entrance to the Land of Happiness.

"Na-Mu-A-Mi-Da-Bu-Tsu . . ."

The monk chanted the syllables in the growling drone of an outboard motor. He went on and on for minutes, allowing my mind to drift. Specifically, I recalled how Zen once told me that the cost of a funeral was directly proportional to the number of monks in attendance. I counted more than thirty monks at Kyocera Dome Osaka. When Zen's father died, his mother initially tried to save money by hiring only one monk, but the monks at his family's temple had a clever up-selling technique. They explained to Zen's mother that each monk would carry a different percussion instrument, and that at a key point in the ceremony, they would play a melody that sounded like "cheen-tone-shan." One monk's instrument would make the "cheen" sound, another the "tone," and a third the "shan." If Zen's mother hired just one monk, they told her, her husband would hear only "cheen," which was not ideal for his happiness in the next world. She gave in and hired three monks. Later, the monks explained how Zen's father would benefit from a longer *kaimyo*—afterlife name—and charged his mother for every kanji character they added to it.

When my mind returned to the head monk chanting in front of me, I realized that he was no longer chanting Buddhist syllables. His chant had morphed into modern Japanese words spoken in the same monotonous drone. This is what they would have sounded like in English:

"...In-Vent-Ed-In-Stant-Ra-Men-Found-Ed-Com-Pa-Ny-Gave-To-The-World-Not-Just-Ja-Pan..."

Drums and flutes accented every syllable.

"...Born-Nine-Teen-Ten-A-Long-With-HaL-Ley's-Co-Met-Two-Thou-Sand-Five-In-Vent-Ed-Space-Ram..."

The monk concluded with another "Na-Mu-A-Mi-Da-Bu-Tsu" and some other typically Buddhist chants. The announcer said, "Former Prime Minister Yasuhiro Nakasone will now deliver the main address."

If you're looking for a prestigious keynote speaker at your Japanese funeral, it would be hard to do better than Nakasone, who, despite being implicated in the notorious Recruit stock scandal, presided over Japan's economic boom of the mid-1980s. A thin, spry-looking eighty-eight-year-old, Nakasone got up from his seat on the field and ascended the ramp to the main podium. A white ribbon, like a prize ribbon at a county fair, hung from his black suit jacket, and he was bathed in a heart-shaped spotlight. His speech had been printed on a white scroll, which he unfurled to read. He spoke in highly formal Japanese, so I didn't understand everything.

"He made a huge contribution to the everyday life of people around the world. . . ."

"A man who invented a great food product . . ."

"I respected and loved him. . . ."

"He failed time after time . . . Chikin Ramen . . . Cup Noodles . . . I learned so much from him."

Following Nakasone were the chairmen of Itochu and Mitsubishi, Nissin's big distributors.

"He was like a father to me," the Itochu chairman said. "I always called him Momofuku, so I think I'll call him that now. I talked to Momofuku about anything and everything. I often spoke to him on the phone early in the morning. Someone told me that Momofuku kept my telephone number written on a piece of paper in his house so he could always reach me. I was happy to hear that."

The chairman of Mitsubishi was more poetic.

"In heaven," he said, "play a round of golf for me. Then, make yourself some ramen."

After the announcer read a condolence message sent by Shinzo Abe, the current prime minister, a condolence video recorded by Soichi Noguchi, the space shuttle astronaut, played on the stadium screens.

"Mr. Ando was really great for us astronauts," Noguchi said, holding up what looked like shrink-wrapped dried noodles. "I took this Space Ram with me on the Shuttle *Discovery* and ate it in space. I'll never forget how delicious it tasted. When I went to the Instant Ramen Invention Museum, Mr. Ando showed me around himself, and together we enjoyed Chikin Ramen."

I should have been an astronaut, because then Ando would have shown me around the museum and made Chikin Ramen with me.

"Mr. Ando," Noguchi concluded, "now that you're traveling among the distant stars, please look over us and protect us."

The last person to speak was the man designated in the program as Chief Mourner: Nissin CEO Koki Ando. In person, Ando's second-eldest son looked more like his father than in photos I had seen. Like everyone else I had met at Nissin, he referred to his father as "the chairman."

"The chairman was really into outer space," Koki said after reaching the podium. "And his life was connected to Halley's Comet, so we decided to make outer space the theme of today's ceremony." Koki paused for a moment. He looked as if he were about to cry. "The chairman once told me something that I have never forgotten. He said, 'Son, nothing in this world is real, except for love.'" Now Koki *was* crying. "And he told me, 'If I'm strict with you, it's because I love you so much.'" He paused again, but he was still crying when he continued. "Why couldn't I ever say 'thank you' to the chairman while he was still alive? I guess I'll never know the answer to that. But at least I can say it now. Chairman, wherever you are, go ahead and eat Chikin Ramen. Play golf. And please accept the deepest, deepest thanks—from me, and from all of the people you have touched on this Earth."

I almost cried, too.

The last part of the service was the thurification, which turned out to be a ritual burning of incense, known in Japanese as *shoko*. The announcer invited Nakasone to thurify first. The former prime minister rose from his seat again, stopping at a long table that stretched nearly the width of the stage. Twenty or so ceramic pots had been set out on the table, and Nakasone, standing in front of one of the pots, clasped his hands together in the *gassho* pose. A video close-up on the monitors showed him reaching with his right hand into the pot and pulling out a pinch of black incense between his thumb and forefinger. He brought the incense to his forehead, held it there for a moment, then tossed it into another pot, where a piece of red-hot coal incinerated it. As the incense burned, Nakasone brought his hands together again and bowed deeply in front of Ando's image on the central video screen.

Next the announcer called Ando's wife, Masako. She emerged

from the crowd in a wheelchair, pushed by a helper toward the incense table. After reading Hirotoshi's tale of Ando's former wives and Masako's struggles, I wondered if she was happy with the way her life had turned out. Still seated in the wheelchair, she reached into one of the pots, pinched some incense, and brought it to her forehead. She looked up at Ando's picture, and for a while she just sat there. Then she tossed the incense into the coal jar in front of her, bowing her head. The man pushing her wheelchair returned her to the audience.

The announcer invited various business leaders, relatives, and politicians (including popular ex–prime minister Junichiro Koizumi), one by one, to thurify next, and a long line formed in front of the table. Forty-five minutes later, the announcer was still calling up VIPs. People around me began looking at their watches. I figured it was time to leave, so I threw my backpack over my shoulders and picked up the white shopping bag.

I should have been a more important person, because then I would have gotten to thurify.

"Now," the announcer said, "everyone seated on the field is invited to perform the thurification."

So many hundreds of people wanted to thurify that eight lines formed in front of the table. Nissin employees at the head of each line directed thurifiers to open jars. I waited in line for nearly an hour, carefully studying those ahead of me as they performed the ritual. Everyone seemed to have a personal thurification style. Some touched their hand to their forehead three times. Some did it just once. Some didn't touch their foreheads at all. Some bowed deeply, others less so. The monks chanted mantras throughout, while more images flashed on the stadium screens: Ando enjoying a strawberry shortcake for his ninety-sixth birthday; Ando with his grandson; the Earth again, big and blue.

When it was finally my turn, I walked toward the table. I stood in front of the jar with my feet together as I had seen others stand. I reached my hand in as I had watched others reach. The incense between my thumb and index finger was coarse, like rock salt. Up close, it was mottled, gray and black. I lifted it to my forehead three times—why not go all out?—and tossed it into the jar with the hot coal. I smelled the incense turn to ash and clasped my hands together, bowing to the portrait of Ando on the video screen. I closed my eyes.

O Momofuku. Thank you for helping me get into your funeral, even though I was dressed inappropriately and I did not have an invitation. Thank you for bringing me closer to my parents, my friends, and myself. Thank you for writing about how you thought and thought and thought until you thought so much you began to piss blood. Thank you for giving me the strength to understand, if just a little bit, the truth of my life. Thank you for showing me how to escape from difficulty. O Momofuku. Please continue to show me how to live so that I may better do your will.

When I opened my eyes, Ando's face seemed to be staring at me, though I'm sure that every thurifier thought the same thing.

Turning around to pick up my white shopping bag, I noticed that Masako Ando was sitting only a few yards away in her wheelchair. Our eyes met, and she nodded in my direction. I wasn't sure if she sensed a deep connection between me and her husband or if she was just surprised to see a foreigner. Perhaps she was simply aghast at my improper attire.

I nodded back, and made my way, across the field, toward the exit behind first base.

After the funeral, I rode the Kanjo Line back to New Osaka Station, where I retrieved my suitcase from the coin locker and boarded another Hikari bullet train, bound not for Tokyo but for Hakata Station, in Fukuoka Prefecture. The reason was that I wanted to taste a thick, milky bowl of the *tonkotsu* ramen that I remembered from when I worked in Fukuoka as a management consultant (and which appears in many episodes of *Ramen Discovery Legend*). Six hours later, I was slurping such a bowl in Nakasu, a thin strip of land between the Hakata and Naka rivers that's famous for its waterfront food stalls. One of the Japanese cooks had been an exchange student in Oakland, California. "Oaktown!" he called it, and for a while we talked about the Raiders. On my way back to the station, I spotted a stall where, ten years earlier, the owner had served me a delicacy known as *gyu sagari*, which I remembered looking like sausage on a stick. The owner had described it as "the down thing of a steer," and for several years I had believed I ingested the grilled penis of a bull. I found out later that it was probably only the diaphragm.

I slept at a hotel near Hakata Station, and in the morning rode the bullet train back to Osaka, where I made a final visit to the Instant Ramen Invention Museum. *Thus Spake Momofuku* was already on sale in the gift shop under a marketing poster that said MR. NOODLE: A MAN WHO CHANGED THE WORLD! The museum had undergone a major renovation since my previous visit. The biggest addition was My Cup Noodle Factory, a cafeteria shaped like a Cup Noodles container in which visitors can assemble their own servings from a variety of dried toppings. On the main floor, a curved wall had been constructed around Ando's shack, marginalizing (in my opinion) the shack's prominence. I stepped inside hoping to hear Ando's voice one last time, but I waited and waited and it never came on. I inquired in the gift shop, where a woman told me that the tape of Ando's voice had been removed during the renovation. She wasn't sure why.

I rode the bullet train back to Tokyo, switched to the Yamanote Line at Shinagawa Station, and returned to the Hotel Excellent, where I reserved a room for the final night of my stay. Then I walked back to Ebisu Station, rode the Hibiya Line subway to Kayabacho, changed to the Tozai Line, and got off at Nishi-Kasai, where I met Harue in a pasta restaurant.

She was as beautiful as I remembered. She ordered spaghetti and I ordered a pizza, and she showed me pictures of her lovely daughter, who was now five years old. She told me that I was looking more and more like my father. We didn't call each other Pumpkin or Dark Cherry. Mostly we talked about people we knew in common, and what they were doing now. It took me a while to find a way to say it, but I apologized. I didn't discuss specifics, though I think she knew. I saw that she still carried some sadness. "Maybe everything happens for a reason," I said, and I was thinking about her daughter, who would not have been born if I had been able to love Harue the way I wished that I could have. Harue didn't respond, maybe because she thought I was trying to let myself off the hook. Well, maybe I was.

We said good-bye after lunch, and as soon as I turned around to leave, I felt a hole in my stomach. I felt it as I boarded the Tozai Line, and it was still there when I switched to the Hibiya Line. I felt it while passing a pachinko parlor broadcasting the prerecorded sounds of cascading coins as a marketing ploy, and I felt it while reading a billboard advertisement for a new cell phone model. I prayed to Ando to make it go away, but I still felt it. Perhaps I always will.

I should be happy for Matt because he married his girlfriend, the one who the voice in his head said was out of his league. Of course, I am happy for him, but I'm also sad because he moved to Oakland and I don't see him so much anymore. We talk on the phone every so often, but it's not like it used to be.

I should be sad because Gary died of lung cancer, and I am sad, but sometimes I'm at rehearsal on Monday nights and I feel like he's there. I went to the memorial service, which was held at his son's house, in the backyard. Per Gary's instructions, four of his oldest friends performed Beethoven's Drei Equale for Four Trombones under a tent, and everyone reminisced about Gary's kindness and his trombone playing and his restaurant tips. Archie flew in to attend, and at first he didn't remember the 78H, but then he did, and he ran his hand over his thick white hair and opened his eyes wide and said it was a magic horn, a horn that let you sing through it. He couldn't recall why he had parted with it. The reason, he figured, was probably money. I offered to return it to him, but he said that, no, he was happy for me to have it.

I should explain why I didn't call Zen while I was in Japan for Ando's funeral. It's because he was out of the country on business. He had tipped me off, though, to his favorite sushi bar in the Tsukiji fish market, and on the morning of my flight home, I woke up at six o'clock and rode the Hibiya Line to Tsukiji. I walked up and down the market's narrow, bustling alleys for a good half hour until I found it. I ordered ten types of *nigiri*—plus a take-out portion of home-made *shiokara* (the fermented squid). Before the chef presented the bill, I got nervous because all I had in my pocket was a 10,000-yen note (around ninety dollars). The bill came to 9,800 yen, leaving me with barely enough change for the subway ride back to the Hotel Excellent. When I e-mailed Zen about it, he assured me that my experience was proof of the sushi chef's talent. "He knew exactly how much he could extract from you just by looking at your face!" Zen e-mailed back.

I should say whether Fujimoto achieves *dassara* in *Ramen Discovery Legend*, but the story is still unfolding. Frankly, it's getting bogged down. Fujimoto won nearly a hundred thousand dollars in *Ramen Mania Quiz*, a ramen-based reality TV show, and even though that's enough money to quit his job and open a ramen shop, the author is making him have more adventures to determine what kind of ramen he'll serve in the shop. There's a fundamental difference, I guess, between *Ramen Discovery Legend* and *Shota's Sushi*, which is that the main character in the latter is driven by love for his father, leading to a natural resolution when he returns home to fight the evil sushi chain. I can't remember an appearance by Fujimoto's father— or any of his family members, for that matter—in *Ramen Discovery Legend*. Fujimoto is more of a loner. In Book 21, the most recently published collection of episodes, Fujimoto's employer has invested in a ramen theme park called Ramen Time Tunnel, and Fujimoto is busy settling fights between the cantankerous shop owners.

I should be married at the end of this story, but I'm still single. I have a girlfriend, though. Her name is Emily, and we've been together for six months. She has beautiful green eyes, and when she smiles, a dimple forms at the top of her right cheek. We met at a Yom Kippur breakfast, after a guy named Ben, who I know from Ultimate Frisbee, invited me to come along. I made gefilte fish from one of Grandma Sylvia's recipes, but it didn't come out too well, so as an experiment,

I spread the ground fish into a casserole, added fresh crab, and baked it. At the party, I placed the casserole on a buffet table next to a noodle kugel. I saw Emily try it, and I overheard her telling a friend, "This tastes weird." She wore jeans and a blue top with what I later learned was an Empire waist. I told Emily that the casserole was an experimental dish, and she assured me that it needed more testing. She also said, "Anyway, it's hard to compete with a kugel." Ben saw us talking and asked me later, "Are you interested in her?" I was embarrassed, so I said no. The next day I e-mailed Ben admitting that I really was interested, and that I had been feeling embarrassed. Ben e-mailed back that he totally understood, and he attached Emily's phone number.

For our first date we shared a whole snapper at a Mediterranean restaurant. Over dinner, Emily told me that she used to be an artist, but that now she was a management consultant. She was about to enroll in an executive MBA program, and she was nervous about whether she could handle both the course load and her full-time job. Just after our desserts arrived, my cell phone vibrated in my pocket.

I pulled it out just to check the caller ID, and when I saw the number, I recognized it immediately. I could hardly believe it.

"This is going to sound rude," I told Emily, "but would you mind if I went outside and took this call?"

Emily said she didn't mind. But in her green eyes I saw that she did mind, and I wondered if there was a voice in her head that told her to say she didn't. Just in case, I let the call go to voice mail, and I related the story of how I had been banned from a sushi bar.

"You should really go outside out and call them back," she said, laughing.

So that's what I did.

"Hai, Hamako desu."

"Junko?"

"Hakata Andy!"

"Did you just call me?"

"Wasn't it a beautiful day today?"

So much time had passed, yet she was asking me about the weather.

"Yes, it was," I agreed.

"So sunny lately. Anyway, I'm sorry to bother you. I know you must be busy."

"It's OK. What's up?"

"It's our credit card terminal."

"Your what?"

"It keeps flashing the word *error*. I think it's broken. Can you come fix it?"

I had never touched a credit card terminal in my life, let alone repaired one. In the background, I heard Tetsuo's voice.

"Tell him the calls were disrupting my sushi making."

"I told him before!" Junko whispered.

Now it all made sense. I imagined the conversation that led to the phone call:

"Hakata Andy posted that thing about us on the Internet."

"The Internet runs on computers."

"Our credit card terminal is a computer."

"Maybe Hakata Andy can fix it."

I showed up at eight thirty the next morning. The same green sake bottles were lined up along the windowsill, and Tetsuo had yet to invest in a sign. Junko was waiting for me inside the restaurant. It was strange, even after all that time, to see her in regular clothes, without an apron. She hadn't aged a day. She greeted me with another "Hakata Andy!" and led me to the credit card terminal, which was next to the refrigerator. I dialed a customer service telephone number printed on the machine, and an operator led me through a series of diagnostics. The problem, it turned out, was a single transaction that had failed to clear the night before, probably because of a disruption in the phone line. The terminal was fine, and the operator showed me how to resend the transaction. As a thank-you, Junko sent me home with a ripe yellow peach. She also made a request.

"Would you come for dinner on Saturday night? Tetsuo will want to thank you himself."

Emily was excited, but also nervous because I had told her about the rules regarding the soy sauce and the wasabi and the counter. She was afraid of messing up.

"Don't worry," I said. "It's going to be OK."

When I said that, she really appeared to stop worrying. She trusted me.

"Hakata Andy!" Junko cried.

I introduced Emily.

"Nice to meet you," Junko said.

"Nice to meet you, too," Emily replied. "I've heard so much about you!"

Junko directed us to the counter, where Tetsuo stood waiting. He was holding his knife.

"It's been a long time," he said.

"Yes. It's been a long time."

I introduced Emily to Tetsuo, and ordered *omakase*. Up close, I saw that, unlike Junko, he had aged a bit. There was more gray in his hair, and his eyes looked heavy. His hands were still thick and muscular, though. I thought about asking why he never closed the restaurant, but decided against it. Instead, in the middle of preparing our sushi, Tetsuo had a question for me.

"Hakata Andy, why do people call me the Sushi Nazi?"

I had heard him called that more than once, but I didn't want to hurt his feelings.

"Who calls you that?"

"A customer came in the other day and told me that people in San

Francisco call me the Sushi Nazi. Is it because Japan fought with the Germans?"

I translated for Emily, who began giggling. Then I told Tetsuo that the Soup Nazi was a character from an American television show, and that he was based on a real soup chef in New York City who sometimes withholds soup from people who don't follow his rules.

"How is his soup?" Tetsuo asked.

"I went there once and had the mushroom barley. It was excellent."

"Well, this Soup Nazi sounds like a fine gentleman," Tetsuo said, "and I'd very much like to meet him. Maybe you can take us to his restaurant one day."

I need not have worried about Tetsuo's feelings being hurt. He considered the Sushi Nazi nickname a compliment.

I was imagining a visit to the Soup Nazi with Tetsuo and Junko when Tetsuo placed a tray of sushi on the counter in front of Emily and me. Junko came over and explained the origin of every piece. "This is *hamachi*, from Spain. *Unagi* from Japan." Emily and I had barely begun eating when Tetsuo screamed at us.

"Hakata Andy, look at that!"

He was pointing at Emily's lips, and I could tell that she was afraid.

"This woman," Tetsuo continued, "is an excellent sushi chewer!"

Tetsuo explained while I did my best to simultaneously translate for Emily. Most Americans, Tetsuo said, chewed in the fronts of their mouths, and to illustrate this, he began chomping like a squirrel. Emily, on the other hand, chewed in the middle of her mouth, which was closer to what Tetsuo called "European or Japanese chewing."

"Where are you from?" he asked her.

"Miami."

"Of course," Tetsuo said, as if Miami were somehow culturally closer to Europe and Japan than the rest of the United States.

"You know, Hakata Andy, Americans sometimes come in and tell me, 'Your sushi is so delicious.' Then I watch them chew, and I know I can't trust them. They're not even tasting my sushi! But Emily's middle-of-the-mouth chewing—that is what lets you really taste food. She is world-class, Hakata Andy. Better than you."

I translated this last part for Emily, and she laughed out loud. Junko was laughing, too.

"Don't say such things around Hakata Andy," Junko scolded Tetsuo. "He might write them on Chowhound!"

Tetsuo glared at me, and I knew what I was supposed to say next.

"I promise I will never write anything else about you on Chowhound as long as I live."

He seemed satisfied with that. Then his expression turned somber.

"Hakata Andy, sometimes when we're not very busy, I walk over to that window and look out at the tapas restaurant across the street. I watch all those Americans chewing in the fronts of their mouths, completely oblivious to all the flavor they're missing. I just shake my head and think, 'How did the world come to this?' "

Emily and I shot each other a look, and it was hard not to burst out laughing again. Tetsuo returned to his sushi making, plying us with *hamachi* belly cuts, *kohada,* and freshly shucked oysters. Emily especially enjoyed a piece of amberjack with a *shiso* leaf underneath.

I was about to ask for the check when Tetsuo said, "Do you have room for one more?"

I looked at Emily, and she nodded. Several minutes later, Tetsuo placed two pieces of *nigiri* onto the wood tray in front of us. The fish was a whitish shade of pink, marbled throughout with a fine grain of fat.

I lifted one of the pieces between my thumb and forefinger, dipped the fish side in soy sauce, and brought it to my lips. I placed it, fish side down, over my tongue, and the buttery flesh began melting on impact. I rolled it around in my mouth, tasting the fish as it melded with the rice. I tasted the relationship between the fish and the rice, and then I tasted something else—the relationship between me and Tetsuo. I tasted the relationship between me and Junko, and then I tasted the relationship between me and Emily. I tasted the relationship between me and my parents, between me and my sister, between me and my brother-in-law, and between me and Grandma Sylvia and Grandpa Walter and Grandma Millie and Grandpa Herman. I tasted the relationship between me and Matt and Gary and Josh and Momofuku Ando and Yamazaki. . . .

"What is that?" Emily asked.

"This," I said, "is the first-best piece of fatty tuna I will eat in my life."

Emily seemed confused, so I offered her the other piece.

She made a face. "Nah."

"Nah?"

"I don't like fatty tuna," Emily said.

I should not be upset, because being upset at a woman for not liking fatty tuna is ludicrous. I should not be mad, because who gets mad at someone for something like that? I should tell her it's no problem, that it's no big deal. I should tell her, "To each his own." I should—

"What's wrong?" Emily asked. "Wait, are you mad at me because I don't want to eat the fatty tuna?"

It was such a small thing that I could have easily lied about it. But I knew where that would lead. I would have lied about bigger things, and then even bigger things. There would have been no limitations.

"This is going to sound strange," I said, "and I'm really ashamed to admit it. But, yes, part of me thinks things will never work out between us because you don't like fatty tuna."

Emily stared at me for a moment. Then she smiled. The dimple formed on the top of her right cheek, and soon we were both laughing at how ridiculous I sounded.

In the following weeks, Emily told me about some things that she was ashamed of, and I told her about more things that I was ashamed of. One night, not too long ago, we were in bed when I told her about an uncomfortable sensation I experienced as she touched my arm. Her initial reaction was anger. "I make you uncomfortable when I touch you?" she said. "Great." Without describing the voice in my head, I told her that I thought the feeling might be related to my fear of getting close. That didn't make Emily any happier.

"How is this ever going to work?" she asked.

I didn't know what to say, so we lay in bed, silently, holding hands. Then, after only a few minutes, something totally unexpected happened: The uncomfortable sensation disappeared. Just like that, after telling Emily about it and lying next to her, it vanished.

When she saw for herself that it was really gone, her dimple appeared, and I was overwhelmed with desire. Was this Ando's so-called true desire—a manifestation of "the innate human urge to connect with the world" that led him to invent instant ramen?

Yes, and it was hot.

EPILOGUE

*D*ear Koki,
          These days, we are gradually being warmed by more and more
rays of the sun.

I hope that you don't mind my writing in English. I read in *Nikkei
Business* magazine that you were once a student at Columbia University in
Manhattan, so I figured it would be OK.

It has been many months since the passing of your father, and I
wanted to begin by expressing my condolences. I was in the audience at
Kyocera Dome Osaka for the funeral, and I could tell from your speech
that your father meant a great deal to you. I had hoped to say hello, but I
was the only one in attendance not wearing a black suit. I guess I was
embarrassed about that.

By the way, I also read about the recent passing of your half brother,
Hirotoshi. I don't believe that you were close to him, but I offer
condolences nonetheless.

Like the other attendees at your father's funeral, I was grateful to
receive, along with the complimentary packages of instant ramen, *Thus
Spake Momofuku*. Although I had already read nearly all of your father's
books, many of the sayings were new to me, including "Flavor knows no

borders"; "Live to the fullest, die to the fullest"; and "Don't promise anything too far in the future because tomorrow is the only thing you can never really understand." In your afterword to the book, you invited readers to contact you directly regarding any of the sayings, and that is the purpose of my correspondence.

In particular, I am writing about the parenthetic note on page 183 that says, "Momofuku Ando often asked about how to translate this saying into English, but not a single person could tell him."

I would like to offer a proposal. How about "Mankind Is Noodlekind"?

True, you won't find *noodlekind* in an English dictionary, but I think most English speakers will understand it. As for what the saying means, I've been pondering that for a long time. I read your father's essay "Mankind Is Noodlekind" (if you will permit this translation), in which he points out that noodles are enjoyed by nearly all people on Earth. Still, I can't help wondering if he also intended a deeper meaning.

Recently, I rented an old episode of *Go Forth! Air Wave Youth* from a Japanese video store in San Francisco. Did you ever watch the show? The episode I rented was the one where the female host screams, "I wanna sing a duet with Yasir Arafat!" (You can also find the segment on YouTube). She flies to Gaza and, amazingly, gains entrance to the late Palestine Liberation Organization leader's compound. She's led into what looks like a conference room, where Arafat, clad in his trademark black-and-white kaffiyeh headdress, greets her in a warm embrace. Then she pulls out a portable karaoke machine and holds up a giant cue card with the lyrics to "Ladybug Samba"—the 1973 hit by the Japanese husband-and-wife duo Cherish—transliterated into Arabic. As you may know, the song is a favorite at Japanese weddings, and begins, "You and I, together in the land of dreams." The female host has rewritten it on the cue card as "Arafat and I, together in the land of dreams." Arafat stares at the cue card, but when the female host presses "play" on her karaoke machine, he doesn't sing along. A caption at the top of the screen says, "Take Two." The female host tries again, but still nothing from Arafat. The words "DUET FAILURE" flash across the screen, and the female host is ushered out of the building. Tears stream down her face.

Remarkably, they are tears of joy. "I'm so happy," she says, pressing a portrait of Arafat to her cheek. Then she hugs members of her crew. "Thank you," she tells them. "Thank you."

Your father's noodles were the product, as he said so often, of failure upon failure. But when he accepted his limitations, concepts like success and failure slipped away, and all that remained were steps on a sacred path. Is it possible that your father was trying to equate mankind to noodles in this way?

I would be interested to hear your thoughts about what I have written, and if you're available, I would even to travel to Japan to meet you.

I imagine, though, that it might be difficult.

Praying that these sentiments have reached your heart, I am

Andy Raskin

*W*riting this book required the translation of many Japanese-language sources into English. With one exception, I performed the translations myself. The exception is material from *Magic Noodles: The Story of the Invention of Instant Ramen* (*Maho no Ramen: Hatsumei Monogatari*). Because Nissin published its own English translation (*The Story of the Invention of Instant Ramen*), I adopted the Nissin translation wherever possible. Occasionally, I made modifications for readability and accuracy.

In granting me permission to reprint the lyrics to his song "Ramen in the Morning" (*"Asa kara Ramen no Uta"*), Haruki Murakami allowed me to use my own translation. It is not an official translation of the song.

The comic book series with titles I translated as *Embassy Chef, Natsuko's Sake,* and *Train Station Bento-Box Single Traveler* were not yet published as paperback collections at the time I described a clerk showing them to me in a Japanese bookstore. I enjoy their titles and plot lines so much that I added them to that scene.

In one of the letters to Ando about my childhood, I described former Los Angeles Dodgers manager Tommy Lasorda dedicating World Series games to the memory of a friend. I searched for references that he did so, but I was unable to find any. Since the letter is a record of my memory, I left it as is.

I e-mailed Koki Ando an edited version of my letter to him, but I have yet to receive a response.

The names and identifying characteristics of some people and places appearing in this book (but not Zen's!) have been changed.

*H*ave a problem with relationships, career, or life in general? Perhaps the inventor of instant ramen can help.

If you think he can, submit a "Dear Momofuku" letter about your problem at www.RamenAdvice.com. I will do my best to answer it based on the life and famous sayings of Momofuku Ando.

ACKNOWLEDGMENTS

*T*his book would not have been possible without support and encouragement I received from T. D. Allman, Don Bennett, George Birimisa, the Blurt Group, Carla Borelli, Katy Butler, Sean Chou, Jane Churchon, Emily Cohen, Jim D., Gary Drumn, Kelly Drumn, Helena Echlin, Daniel Fisher, Bill Herr, Judy Hisamatsu, Cindy Kano, Junko Kashiyama, Tetsuo Kashiyama, Gillian Kendall, Mikiko Kitajima, Yoko Kondo, Matt Kowalski, Yuriko Kuchiki, Archie LaCoque, Thais Lange, Mike Lenhart, Ellen Luttrell, Charlotte Melleno, Mariko Mikami, Gregg Miller, Michele Miller, Harris Moore Jr., Makobelle Niinuma, Zen Ohashi, Yoshimi Oiwa, Masa Okawa, Miho Okawa, Katherine Ozment, Pat Parker, Dan Pecoraro, Josh Quittner, Andrea Raskin, Thorina Rose, Rick Rutherford, San Francisco Writers' Grotto, Chiharu Shaver, Nancy Spector, Robert Stark, Danielle Svetcov, Manami Tamaoki, Robert Thomas, Jo Ann Thrailkill, Dale Walker, Meghan Ward, Tara Austen Weaver, Andy Weisskoff, and the Witch.

Thanks to my parents, Richard and Judy Raskin, who gave me everything, not least of all their blessing to tell this story.

Thanks to Cecile Moochnek, who listened every other Thursday. To call her a writing coach would be to fail miserably at communicating the value of what she does, which cannot be expressed in any language.

Thanks to Bill Shinker and everyone at Gotham Books—

especially my editors, Erin Moore and Jessica Sindler, who among many other things, helped me figure out what this book was about.

Thanks to my agent, Stuart Krichevsky, who served as proposal editor, permissions go-between, morale booster, and all-around consigliere. This book began as a 250-word submission to Stuart's agency, and it came to life only after he requested more.

The publications below were helpful to me as source and background material. Unofficial translations of Japanese-language titles appear in parentheses.

BOOKS AUTHORED OR EDITED BY MOMOFUKU ANDO

Ando, Momofuku. *Kiso Tengai no Hasso (Conception of a Fantastic Idea)*. Kodansha, 1983.

Ando, Momofuku (editor). *Shoku Tarite Yo Wa Tairaka (Peace Follows from a Full Stomach)*. Kodansha, 1985.

Ando, Momofuku (editor). *Men Rodo wo Iku (Noodle Road)*. Kodansha, 1988.

Ando, Momofuku (editor). *Nihon Men Fukei (Japan's Noodle Scene)*. Foodeum Communication, 1991.

Ando, Momofuku. *Kukyo kara no Dasshutsu (How to Escape from Difficulty)*. Foodeum Communication, 1992.

Ando, Momofuku. *Shoku wa Jidai to Tomo ni: Ando Momofuku Firudo Noto (Food Changes with the Times: Field Notes of Momofuku Ando)*. Asahiya Shuppan, 1999.

Ando, Momofuku. *Maho no Ramen: Hatsumei Monogatari (Magic Noodles: The Story of the Invention of Instant Ramen)*. Nikkei Publishing, 2002.

Ando, Momofuku. *The Story of the Invention of Instant Ramen*. Nissin Food Products, 2002.

Ando, Momofuku. *Hyaku-sai wo Genki ni Ikiru (How to Live Happily to One Hundred)*. Chuo Koron Shinsha, 2005.

Ando, Momofuku. *Shokuyoku Reisan (Praise the Appetite)*. PHP Kenkyujo, 2006.

Ando, Momofuku. *Ando Momofuku Kaku Katariki (Thus Spake Momofuku)*. Chuo Koron Shinsha, 2007.

JAPANESE COMIC BOOKS (MANGA)
Many of the following originally appeared as serial episodes in comic books and were later released as paperback collections. Citations refer to the first paperback collection in each series.

Hashimoto, Mitsuo. *Tsukiji Uogashi Sandaime (Third-Generation Tsukiji Fish Market Man)*. Shogakukan, 2001.

Ishinomori, Shotaro. *Hoteru (Hotel)*. Shogakukan, 1985.

Kariya, Tetsu, and Hanasaki, Akira. *Oishinbo*. Shogakukan, 1985.

Kenna, Mai, and Kato, Tadashi. *Za Shefu (The Chef)*. Nihon Bungei-sha, 1985.

Kube, Rokuro, and Kawai, Tan. *Ramen Hakkenden (Ramen Discovery Legend)*. Shogakukan, 2000.

Nishimura, Mitsuru, and Kawasumi, Hiroshi. *Taishi Kakka no Ryorinin (Embassy Chef)*. Kodansha, 2004.

Ogawa, Etsushi. *Chuka Ichiban (Best Chinese)*. Kodansha, 2003.

Oze, Akira. *Natsu no Kura (Natsu's Brewery)*. Kodansha, 2003.

Oze, Akira. *Natsuko no Sake (Natsuko's Sake)*. Kodansha, 2004.

Sakurai, Kan, and Hayase, Jun. *Ekiben Hitori Tabi (Train Station Bento-Box Single Traveler)*. Futabasha, 2005.

Takahashi, Miyuki, and Taiga, Toshiyuki. *Nissin Shokuhin no Chosen (The Challenges of Nissin Food Products)*. Bijinesusha, 1995.

Terasawa, Daisuke. *Shota no Sushi (Shota's Sushi)*. Kodansha, 2002.

Ueyama, Tochi. *Kukkingu Papa (Cooking Papa)*. Kodansha, 1986.

OTHER BOOKS AND PUBLICATIONS

Chang, Ling-yin. "Daughter of Noodle Mogul Plans to Wage Legal Battle," *Taiwan News*. February 25, 2007.

Downes, Lawrence. "Appreciations: Mr. Noodle," *The New York Times*. January 9, 2007.

Hall, Kenji. "Remembering the Ramen King," *BusinessWeek*. January 7, 2007.

Haney, Robert E. *Caged Dragons: An American P.O.W. in WWII Japan*. Momentum Books, 1991.

Hevesi, Dennis. "Momofuku Ando, 96, Dies; Invented Instant Ramen," *The New York Times*. January 9, 2007.

Kunishida, Takuji. *"Dokuso ni Ueru Osha"* ("The King Who Hungers for Creativity"), *Nikkei Business*. February 23, 2004.

Momofuku Ando Instant Ramen Invention Museum, The (editor). *Insutanto Ramen Hatsumei Monogatari (Instant Ramen Invention Story, Catalog to the Instant Ramen Invention Museum)*. Asahiya Shuppan/Nissin Food Products, 2000.

Moro-oka, Yukio. *Kanda Tsuruhachi Sushi Banashi (Kanda Tsuruhachi Sushi Stories)*. Soshisha, 1986.

Murakami, Haruki. *Yoru no Kumozaru—Murakami Haruki Asahido Cho Tampen Shosetsu (Spider Monkey in the Night—Haruki Murakami Asashido Ultra-Short Fiction)*. Heibonsha, 1995.

Ohashi, Zentaro. *Sugoi Yarikata (Wow Method)*. Fuso Publishing, 2004.

Ohashi, Zentaro. *Sugoi Kaigi (Wow Meetings)*. Daiwa Shobo, 2005.

Smith, Patrick. "Ask the Pilot," *Salon.com*. January 19, 2007.

Unattributed writer. "Obituary: Momofuku Ando," *The Economist*. January 20, 2007.

Unattributed writer. *"Ando Momofuku San-nin no Tsuma to Igonsho"* ("Momofuku Ando's Three Wives and Last Will and Testament"), *Shukan Bunshun*. February 1, 2007.

*A*ndy Raskin is a longtime NPR commentator whose essays have been heard on *All Things Considered* and *This American Life*. He has written for *The New York Times, Gourmet, Wired, Women's Health,* and *Playboy* (the Japanese edition). Andy holds an MBA from the Wharton School and a BS in computer science from Yale. Fluent in Japanese, he currently lives in San Francisco, where he is a member of the San Francisco Writers' Grotto.